A Cultural History of Fashion in the 20th and 21st Centuries

Figure 0.1 Filming *Portraits in Fashion* for Prestige Ltd (Textiles), Australia, early 1950s, with models Elly Lukas and Max Wyman in foreground. Photo: Gerard Herbst. Collection: Powerhouse Museum, Sydney. The magic of haute couture was captured in this photograph, which highlights the careful construction of an image that exudes glamour, elegance and wealth.

A Cultural History of Fashion in the 20th and 21st Centuries

From Catwalk to Sidewalk

SECOND EDITION

Bonnie English

BLOOMSBURY

LONDON • NEW DELHI • NEW YORK • SYDNEY

Bloomsbury Academic

An imprint of Bloomsbury Publishing Plc

50 Bedford Square	175 Fifth Avenue
London	New York
WC1B 3DP	NY 10010
UK	USA

www.bloomsbury.com

First published 2013

British Library Cataloguing-in-Publication Data

A catalogue record for this book is available from the British Library.

ISBN: HB: 978-0-8578-5134-5
PB: 978-0-8578-5135-2

Library of Congress Cataloging-in-Publication Data

A catalog record for this book is available from the Library of Congress.

Typeset by Apex CoVantage, LLC, Madison, WI
Printed and bound in Great Britain

Dedicated with love to

**my beloved daughters, Sarah and Katie,
and to my parents, Edna and Bruce,
to whom I owe everything.**

Contents

List of Illustrations

FIGURES

COLOUR PLATES

1 Changing room at the Zwieback department store, Vienna,
Austria, c. 1910.

2 Victorian balloon-sleeved dress, red russet silk from the
David Jones department store in Sydney, Australia, 1890s.

3 Paul Poiret, oriental-inspired clothing displayed
at Richelieu-Drouot auction house, Paris, May 2005.

4 Madeleine Vionnet, satin hand-draped wedding dress, 1939,
Les Arts Decoratifs museum exhibition Paris, 2009–10.

5 Cristóbal Balenciaga, flamenco-inspired evening dress, 1951.

6 Martin Margiela, *The World According to Its Creators* installation,
Museum of Costume and Fashion, Paris, 6 June 1991.

7 Hussein Chalayan, garment made of crystals and over 15,000
flickering LED lights entitled *Readings*, 'From Fashion and
Back' exhibition, Design Museum, London, 21 January 2009.

8 Ralph Lauren, Autumn/Winter collection, February 2012, New York.

9 Billboard on Broadway, New York, featuring Kate Moss modelling
Calvin Klein (CK) jeans.

10 Pierre Cardin, silver and black outfits, Cosmocorps line, 1963–4.

11 Zandra Rhodes reclines on bed with model wearing wedding dress, 1985.

12 Vivienne Westwood, blue super-elevated gillies, alligator leather/cork/silk,
London, Autumn/Winter 1993/1994.

13 John Galliano, black deconstructed and beaded evening dress
for Dior Haute Couture, Spring/Summer, Paris, 2000.

14 Rebecca Patterson/Megan Salmon for SpppsssP label,
fabricated dissolve wool dress, deconstructivist/reconstructivist,
Rubens series, Perth, Australia, 1999.

15 Issey Miyake label, fashion collection showing, ready-to-wear collection,
Autumn/Winter, Paris, 1997–1998.

Preface

Yes, it is bigger and better! This book now encompasses a broad overview of 150 years of fashion and provides an excellent foundation for students of all ages. Being adopted as a textbook by the world's leading fashion schools and institutions, this version adds a detailed and up-to-date look at fashion over the past ten years. The four new chapters and additions of *A Cultural History of Fashion in the 20th and 21st Centuries: From the Catwalk to the Sidewalk* look closely at the key issues facing fashion designers and the fashion industry globally since the turn of the second millennium. It provides a comprehensive overview of changes that have resulted from sociopolitical upheavals, economic downturns and a growing social consciousness of the role that industry plays in the world around us. It considers the impact of eco-fashion, e-commerce, social networking and the emerging Asian markets upon business sustainability and enterprise. It reinforces the words of Coco Chanel: 'A fashion that does not reach the streets is not a fashion.' I hope you will enjoy this updated version.

Acknowledgements

It is with the greatest pleasure that I acknowledge the support of my students over the years at the Queensland College of Art, Griffith University, who have not only inspired my teaching but have touched my soul with their enthusiastic commitment to the study of the interrelationship of fashion and art. Years later, these gifted artists, designers, photographers and filmmakers recounted to me how the knowledge of fashion history has impacted upon them, opening new directions in their work. For a visual arts educator, this is the greatest reward of all.

The successful completion of this book was manifest in the love and support of my family, who all read drafts of the book manuscript and offered helpful suggestions and comments at various stages of writing. Thank you for putting up with long absences and lack of attention as I buried myself for months in my study.

The research for this book has been generously supported by a fellowship from the Creative Public and Cultural Ideas Research Centre, Griffith University, which has allowed time away from teaching to prepare and write the text. I wish to thank the Research Centre director, Fiona Foley, as well as Susan Jarvis for laboriously copyediting the manuscript and offering beneficial suggestions. I am indebted to the curatorial staff of the International Decorative Arts and Design Department and the photo library of the Powerhouse Museum in Sydney, which have been extraordinary in their efforts to support this project. The prestigious Powerhouse Museum in Sydney, which houses the largest collection of fashion and textiles in Australia, has been a remarkable source of fashion ideas and images. Special thanks are due to Louise Mitchell, curator of fashion and textiles, and to Kathy Hackett, photo librarian, for their expertise, professionalism and goodwill. The visual wealth and diversity of the collection is clearly evident in the photographs used to illustrate the text in this publication.

Without the collegial support of QCA's Deputy Director Research, Pat Hoffie, and teaching staff of the Art Theory Department at the Queensland College of Art, who have taken on extra duties in my absence, this fashion book would have remained a vision of my imagination. I am grateful to have worked with Keith Bradbury, Marilyn Carney, Rosemary Hawker, Robert Jadin, Paul Jolly, George Petelin and Charles Zuber at the time of the first printing, individuals who have consistently encouraged my efforts, shared knowledge, insights and resources with me and rightfully deserve acknowledgement for their help and loyalty over the years. In particular, I share any success that I have with my valued friend and colleague Craig Douglas, who co-curated the 'Tokyo Vogue: Japanese and Australian Fashion' exhibition with me—the first major contemporary Japanese fashion exhibition held in Australia. His patient and invaluable assistance has been a cornerstone in all of my research efforts.

I thank my University of Toronto roommate and cherished long-term friend of forty years, Lynda Shearer, for her enthusiasm and research assistance in finding interesting international fashion reviews for the book; my dear friend and retired colleague, David Seibert, for the motivation he provided with his unwavering support from the onset of the project; my esteemed RMIT colleague, Lilliana Pomazan, for her encouragement and offers of assistance; and to Dr Jess Berry for her collegiality and help covering my classes in my absence.

I am also indebted to numerous reference librarians from the National Gallery in Canberra, the State Libraries of New South Wales and Queensland, the Victoria and Albert Museum in London and the Bibliothèque Fornay in Paris, with special gratitude to librarian Cheryl Stevens, Queensland College of Art, Griffith University, for her dedication to encouraging visual arts research. Research material has also been gathered over the years from interviews that have been graciously granted with Valerie Mendes of the Victoria and Albert Museum, London; Akiko Fukai of the Kyoto Costume Institute, Japan; and Laurence Delamare of Yohji Yamamoto Studios, Paris. I am thankful for the assistance of my master's student, Linglin Zhu, who travelled to Beijing, China, with me to attend the Beijing Fashion Week to photograph and arrange interviews with leading academics, designers and organizers of the collection showings.

Most of all, I wish to thank Tristan Palmer, editor (first edition), and Anna Wright, editor (second edition), at Berg Publishers (now Bloomsbury) for providing the opportunity to share my interest with others who are also impassioned by a love for fashion history.

QUEENSLAND COLLEGE OF ART, BRISBANE

The Research and Postgraduate Studies Department of the Queensland College of Art, Griffith University, Brisbane, Australia, has generously supported the production of this publication. The heritage-listed Queensland College of Art (QCA) is a specialist arts and design college located in South Bank, Brisbane, and Southport, Gold Coast, Queensland, Australia. It was founded in 1881 and is the oldest arts institution in Australia. The College offers courses including Fine Arts, Design Animation, Digital Media, Film and Screen Media, Multimedia Photography, Contemporary Indigenous Australian Art and Visual Art and Design History. The College amalgamated with Griffith University in 1992.

THE POWERHOUSE MUSEUM, SYDNEY

The Powerhouse Museum has kindly allowed permission to use images from its photo library collection in both the first and second editions of this book. The Powerhouse

Museum is Australia's largest museum. Established in 1880 as the Museum of Applied Arts and Sciences, it has a reputation for excellence in collecting, preserving and presenting aspects of world cultures to present and future generations. The Powerhouse has one of Australia's most extensive textile and fashion collections. The collection ranges from samplers, embroideries and fine dressmaking to textiles from around the world, and historical and contemporary costume and fashions by significant international and Australian designers.

NOTES

Every effort has been made to acknowledge the source of each picture correctly and to contact copyright holders. The author apologizes for any unintentional errors or omissions, which will be corrected in future editions of this book.

Portions of the book, in somewhat different form, have appeared in the following publications: Chapter 7, 'Japanese Conceptual Fashion', first published (in part) as 'Fashion and Art' in Mitchell, L. (ed.) (2005), *The Cutting Edge: Fashion From Japan*, Sydney: Powerhouse Publishing; and Curtin University (2004), *The Space In-Between: textiles_art_design_fashion*, CD Conference Proceedings, Perth, Australia.

Introduction

OVERVIEW

The history of fashion has a thousand stories to tell—stories built on myths and fairy tales; descriptive portraits of heroic men and gracious ladies; social histories locked in time. Fanciful images abound with glass slippers, cloaks shot through with threads of gold and silver, gossamer veils and pussycat bows. While fashion trends can be amusing, and seemingly light-hearted, throughout history fashion has also been forced to bow to imposing political, social and economic change. Stylistic change in both fashion and art multiplied at an ever-increasing pace, especially in the twentieth century, and the observer must seriously consider how fashion has been, and continues to be, embedded in the cultural fabric of society.

A *Cultural History of Fashion in the 20th and 21st Centuries* discusses how fashion reflects the essence of its society, how it can be moulded by many forces, such as art, music, politics, or advertising media. We can step back in history or step forward into the future by merely changing what we wear. We broadcast our views about our society, its politics, its environmental concerns or its social issues through dress. The more we learn about the history of fashion, the more we realize the nature of its complexity. 'Fashion makes the world go round'—a hackneyed cliché but, perhaps, quite true in both commercial and cultural terms. The intercontextual relationships that exist among designer fashions, popular culture, big business, high-tech production and the multimedia world of television promotion, Web site sales and electronic journalistic publications will be discussed and analysed in this study of twentieth-century fashion. While this book can only touch upon fashion's interdisciplinary character, it will highlight similarities that it has shared with other visual arts practice over the last 150 years. This book will attempt to unravel the com-plications and contradictions behind stylistic changes in order to chart the cultural history of modern fashion. The recognition of fashion design as a justifiable part of culture has been illustrated in recent years by the rise of the celebrity designer, the increased number of blockbuster fashion exhibitions held in key international museums and the proliferation of academic fashion texts published which underline the interdisciplinary connections between the applied arts, design, fine art, film and the fashion industry. By providing a sociohistorical review of major trends that have emerged since the late nineteenth century, *A Cultural History of Fashion in the 20th and 21st Centuries: From the Catwalk to the Sidewalk* will consider the significant role that both haute couture and prêt-à-porter designers have played in the interpretation of the fashions of their day.

A central argument of the book is based on the premise that, while haute couture reigned supreme at the turn of the twentieth century, ironically, it predicated its own demise. This process first began with the Parisian couturier, Englishman Charles Frederick Worth—known for his exquisite creations which he sold to all the royal heads of Europe. Scandalously, Worth also reproduced similar, but less expensive, lines for the middle-class American market. When other designers, such as Paquin, Poiret and Vionnet, followed suit in the early 1900s, this trend paved the way for the subsequent rise of prêt-à-porter—or ready-made clothing. Yet it wasn't until 1929 that Chanel, Lelong and Patou officially began to sell prêt-à-porter from their haute couture salons. Over the next three decades, with the rapid escalation of ready-to-wear designer garments and the decline of haute couture, mainly due to a shrinking market, the balance finally shifted. With designer fashion in the 1960s catering for the growing younger middle-class market, it is not surprising that Yves Saint Laurent—highly regarded as one of the most fastidious couturiers of the century—looked to street styles for his main inspiration. Both fashion and art became driven by society's obsession with popular culture. The revolutionary spirit (and buying power) of youth played a significant role in the triumph of street fashion, a form of stylistic pastiche which has dominated fashion for more than fifty years.

By challenging nineteenth-century conventions, fashion—like art—evolved in new directions not hindered by tradition, rules or moral standards. In the early years of the twentieth century, the 'democratization in fashion' was realized: corsets were abandoned, hair was cut short, and machine-made clothing was increasingly widely distributed. In sociological terms, the rise of the middle class signalled the gradual decline of elitist fashion codes. This revolutionary change evolved as each key designer dared to challenge the established status quo. History has repeatedly shown that radical thinking threatens established hierarchies, synthesizes into new ideas which challenge complacent traditions, and ultimately is accepted into mainstream ideology. As Cathy Horyn, Fashion Editor of the *New York Times*, concluded: 'What once looked unwearable now seems ordinary, and what once seemed banal now looks right' (Horyn, 2000b).

Fundamental to a designer's success was the ability to critically analyse communal and cultural trends and to know intuitively when to respond to social change. For example, in the post-war years, Chanel's working-class background allowed her to respond pragmatically to the shortage of fine textiles by replacing them with pedestrian fabrics. More importantly, the material symbolically represented a revolutionary—and at the same time bourgeois—response to the previous use of expensive haute couture fabrics. In fashion history, timing has been crucial. Many famous designers have tried to introduce new design standards at the wrong time, only to see the same innovation become central to the success of another designer a few years later. When Balenciaga brought out his rendition of the 'New Look' in 1939, just before the Second World War started, it was overlooked. Yet when Dior reintroduced the same ultrafeminine hourglass silhouette in 1947, it changed the fashion world. Understanding the reasons *why* changes have taken place and being able to contextualize these changes within a sociohistorical setting is paramount for the fashion student, the emerging designer, the fashion historian and the avid follower of fashion history. Considering fashion from a cultural studies perspective helps to frame fashion within a broader context, to engage with multicultural and multidisciplinary issues, and to forecast future developments. This provokes an obvious question: if one does not know the past, how can one possibly read the future?

Since the 1960s, many fashion designers have emerged from art schools as well as fashion institutions, and conceptualization in the design, as well as the art, process has become an essential part of the work. In simple terms, both fashion and art have become ideas rather than objects or products. In fact, the question of whether fashion is art is no longer relevant. Since the 1980s, fashion displays are akin to art installations, and fashion parades became a type of performance art. This book argues that fashion has now bridged the gap between a commercial and a cultural product. Contemporary fashion garments can be viewed in exhibition spaces and have been purchased by galleries and museums for their permanent collections. International fashion exhibitions have become a huge draw card for museums as the public is able to identify with both the functional and aesthetic appeal of the work.

A Cultural History of Fashion in the 20th and 21st Centuries will outline how fashion was adopted as a communicative political tool and served as a beacon for sociopolitical statements in dress. It will show how fashion visually promoted the dissention of youth groups, like the hippies and punks, in protest against mainstream ideals and beliefs. It will consider the ways in which it appropriated visual tropes from non-Western ethnic cultures to become a form of sartorial pastiche which heralded the development of street-style fashion. In a postmodernist context, the latter chapters will illustrate how fashion became a vehicle to express meaning and memory, as it became more closely allied with individualism and the search for greater intellectual depth. Arguably, over the past few decades, Eastern as well as Western cultures have contributed to this growing democratization of fashion as multiculturalism has enriched and infused Western dress with more divergent symbolic references, codes and conventions. This cultural history will define how the Japanese designers, between the 1980s and 1990s, helped to change the face of fashion through the concept of deconstruction and reconstruction. A growing interest in vintage or secondhand clothing in the 2000s further consolidated the move towards a conglomeration of styles underlined by a DIY (do-it-yourself) philosophy.

Over the last ten years, fashion styling has mirrored political unrest and instability, economic downturn and the effect of industrial globalization, and this new edition will explain how these world events have substantially impacted upon individual designers, corporations, retailers and associated fashion businesses. During the first decade of the new millennium, Belgian designers, in particular, took a strong lead in determining the new image of the twenty-first-century woman, and a rejuvenated image of the sartorial man also emerged as a lucrative niche market. Photographer Nick Knight created the leading fashion Web site *Showstudio* in 2000, which championed film and moving image as the ideal medium for fashion in the digital age. By turning fashion into a multimedia production, he changed the way that fashion was perceived, presented and marketed.

The last chapters of the book highlight major international changes that have occurred in sustainable business practices, including reference to the luxury market boom with the new niche markets of Southeast Asia. New fashion publicity and promotional strategies will be discussed in relation to the revolutionary developments associated with the proliferation of designer Web sites, sartorial blogs and social networking, all of which have become an important factor in the promotion, sale and distribution of fashion goods and accessories. A current overview is provided of the emerging fashion industries in both China and India, countries that are attempting to establish infrastructures concurrent with the Western nations which will enable them to join the competitive international luxury market. Finally, the book concludes with an insight into the ethical issues associated with eco-fashion and its sustainable practices that will ensure the future of the fashion industry.

I hope that *A Cultural History of Fashion in the 20th and 21st Centuries: From the Catwalk to the Sidewalk* will provide you with a cultural and historical insight into some of the many developments which have changed the world of fashion over the past century and a half. The book is not meant to cover all periods of the twentieth and twenty-first centuries, nor all leading designers, nor fashion trends. It is meant, instead, to be informative, outlining the major factors that turned the tide away from exclusivity and regulation in fashion towards a more streetwise, casual and individual way of dressing. This study is only a beginning. I welcome you to the wonderful world of fashion!

The Interplay of Commerce and Culture before the First World War

Fashion has always been an immediate barometer of culture and of the preoccupations and interests that mark an epoch or period.

David Rivère McFadden

THE RISE OF HAUTE COUTURE

Notions of Taste

Elitism in fashion has always been linked closely with status and social class, with success, and with what was perceived to be impeccable taste made publicly visible through dress. For centuries, royal courts used fashion as a means of publicizing their superiority, strength and influence across Europe. Louis XIV, for example, demanded that his courtiers pay scrupulous attention to their grooming, and insisted on the conspicuous display of finery at all palace events. He maintained a mental inventory of the garments worn by the female members of his entourage to ensure that his reputation was not tarnished if one was seen wearing the same garment too frequently. He believed that this form of dress code upheld the exclusivity of his court.

Prior to the twentieth century, the established canons of taste in the arts—including fashion—were once considered to be the exclusive priority of aristocrats. While cultural debate questioned the extent to which other groups, notably the haute bourgeoisie and the *demi-monde*, played a part in establishing these canons, in his essay 'The Aristocracy of Culture' Bourdieu refers to 'an object like taste' as one of the most vital stakes in the struggles fought in the field of the dominant class and the field of cultural production. Bourdieu explains that: 'The upper class propriety treats taste as one of the surest signs of true nobility and cannot conceive of referring taste to anything other than itself' (1984: 11).

By linking cultural practice to social origin, Bourdieu emphasizes the discrete nature of 'the games of culture' between the upper-class intellectuals and the bourgeois, in which their 'self-interested representations of culture' provoke 'mutual lucidity and reflexive blindness' (1984: 12). Bourdieu's observation could equally be applied to

Britain in the late nineteenth century, when the artist/craftsmen and the industrial manufacturers rarely compromised their opposing ideologies. This schism not only widened with the growth of mechanical reproduction and the mass production of artistic goods, including fashion, but was also further accentuated by the emergence of a commercially minded middle class, encouraging the emergence of a new, non-elitist direction in the decorative arts. However, for Ruskin—the influential mentor of the Arts and Crafts movement—art was inextricably linked with morals rather than with trade, and ironically he purportedly passed on to generations of Englishmen the dogma that quality could not be separated from rarity. Bayley's seminal essay, 'Commerce and Culture', argues that the social and technical upheavals brought about by mass production were the 'stigmatization of commerce' (1989: 5).

Thornstein Veblen, a notable late Victorian writer, underlines this notion of the 'pecuniary canons of taste' as the dominant male economic factor impacting upon the evolution of dress in the late 1880s. In *The Theory of the Leisure Class*, originally published in 1899, he maintains—making reference to Victorian female trappings—that 'the hindrances of women's dress . . is evidence of her economic dependence on a man, and is reflective of male pecuniary strength in society' (Veblen 1965). Veblen's argument suggests that individual or family status was the motivating factor for the uniformity of dress within Victorian society. Quentin Bell, who relies heavily on Veblen's work to provide a framework for his own study, argues that this theory is limited because it is time- (or period-) specific—in this case, to a nineteenth-century sociological determinant.

Bell's classic text *On Human Finery* refers to this as 'class solidarity', and concludes that 'the usual desire of the great majority of those who follow fashion is not so much to achieve personal distinction, as to emerge discreetly into a "distinguished class"' (1992: 181). He maintains that the most important overall determinant in the history of dress is the condition of the class struggle. Bell argues that fashion was a European product which was never to be viewed as a 'universal' condition of dress (1992: 115). However, he adds: 'Within any stratified society, you are almost certain to have a classification of dress', maintaining that this 'challenges the lower strata to compete with the higher strata'. Bell further explains:

> Emulation occurs where status can be challenged, where social groups become strong enough to challenge the traditional pattern of society, in fact, in those places where a strong middle class emerges to compete with the aristocracy and, at a later stage, a strong proletariat emerges to compete with the middle class. (1992: 115)

In Bell's terms, if the middle class has the financial and the political power—which seems to have been the case in the late nineteenth century—this 'distribution of wealth allows more than one class to afford the luxury of sumptuous dress' (1992: 113). In other words, a society that is changing will produce fashions that are also changing, and this in turn stimulates greater production of consumer goods.

Figure 1.1 Henri Gervex, *5 o'clock chez Paquin*, 1906. Haute couture clients inspect fabric samples and view a garment being modelled by a young woman in the background.

Complementing and refining Bell's theory, other cultural studies researchers have underlined the notion that while lower social class groups attempt to emulate the tastes of higher groups, this causes the latter to respond by adopting new tastes that will re-establish and maintain the original distance. Again, this was particularly evident in the nineteenth century, when the simulated attempts of the bourgeois class to imitate *le bon monde* of an elitist society found working-class women packing dusters or newspapers under the backs of their skirts to replicate the modish bustle backs of high fashion. Once there was no longer a code arising from social distinctions, fashion soon ceased to be a prerogative; rather, it became a question of means. In summary, these trends signalled the relatively fluid social structure and cultural consumption that would prevail in contemporary Western societies.

Charles Frederick Worth

At the same time, a new dictatorial hierarchy arose with the birth of haute couture in the second half of the nineteenth century. Ironically, with the rise of the concept of the 'fashion designer as artist/genius'—as distinct from the humble dressmaker or *couture à façon*—a new form of elitism in fashion replaced the old. This time, however, it was one determined by pecuniary rather than class dominance. Fashion historian Christopher Breward (2003) argues that this elite sector of the fashion market relied on an exclusivity necessary to sustain high prices through a deliberate glorification of the role and identity of the couturier. He concludes that: 'Fine hand-sewing, bureaucratic control and creative vision, then, underpinned the success of a couture house' (2003: 50). Haute couture demanded labour-intensive specialized sewing techniques, sustained by high prices.[1]

Arguably, haute couture in fashion was also determined by this heightened taste for luxury; however, more importantly, in economic terms, haute couture became an interface between the silk and brocade manufacturers of Lyons and the world of the aristocracy. Fine fabric, sumptuously embellished with a layering of either lace or tulle, with rich hand embroidery and beading, enticed women of high society. Certainly, couture relied on expert craftsmanship in sewing and great attention to detail and fit. To ensure a perfect fit, Worth could use up to seventeen pieces of material in a single bodice. To ensure expertise in construction, his seamstresses were organized in specialized workshops as skirt-makers, bust-makers, sleeve-makers or hem-stitchers. While the majority of Worth's garments, for example, were entirely hand-sewn, with the advent of the mechanized sewing machine there was a growing trend towards using the machine to sew the main seams of the garments. Not only were the creations made by designers who chose the fabric and determined the finishing techniques, but they also produced the models that were commercially distributed.

This advent of changing cultural values is reflected in the clientele of Paris's first haute couture designer, Englishman Charles Frederick Worth. On the one hand, he designed for members of royalty and fitted aristocrats; on the other, for grand divas of the stage. While working for the Gagelin firm, a number of Worth's garments were displayed in the famous British Great Exhibition of 1851, which promoted his reputation throughout Europe and enabled him to open his own business in Paris on the Rue de la Paix in 1858. When he was invited to create a wedding dress for the very fashionable Alexandria, Princess of Wales, in 1866, he fortuitously took advantage of the opportunity to create a 'new' silhouette that changed the direction of fashion for the next thirty years. Worth replaced the circular crinoline and introduced a narrower skirt with a bustle back. He created hundreds of garments for the influential Empress Eugenie who, after she married Napoleon III, set the fashionable taste in the royal court at a time when the demand for luxury goods reached levels unsurpassed since the French Revolution of 1789. In 1869, the empress officially appointed the House of Worth as the court dressmaker, and Worth's label bore the royal crest. The success of his fashion empire was also measured by his employment of 1,200 workers by 1870. For the opening of the Suez Canal—an important historical event—the empress felt that she needed no fewer than 250 of Worth's dresses.

Figure 1.2 House of Worth, ball gown, Paris, France *c.* 1900. Collection: Powerhouse Museum, Sydney. Photographer: Andrew Frolows. This evening gown is made of white satin, self-striped in cut velvet fabric, embossed with large floral motifs; the sleeves of lace are caught with bands of rhinestones; the bodice trimmed with tulle and lace and an artificial carnation.

Not only did Worth design clothes for many members of European royalty, including the Princess de Metternich, Princess Maria of Austria and the wife of Franz Joseph I, the Empress Elizabeth of Austria; he was also adept in marketing his work to a much broader clientele. Significantly, he was one of many of the early haute couture designers to recognize the financial opportunities inherent in the American market. He attracted the attention of wealthy patrons as well, including the American Rothschilds and Vanderbilts. When a wholesale trade was established between France and America and Australia, his gowns were shipped internationally in huge steamer trunks, as by then his name had become synonymous with Paris fashion. His clothes were purchased by department stores such as Sears Roebuck and Montgomery Ward in the United States, as well as by other major outlets as far away as David Jones in Australia, which had a buyer in its head office in London. David Jones, like many other department stores, also set up in-house workshops to copy the trends of many of the Paris models.

Herein lies the dichotomy: Worth was attempting to juggle an exclusive, one-of-a-kind garment market (which provided him with great status within an elitist upper-class society) with an international commercial fame (which led to greater financial returns). As early as the 1870s, Worth's name frequently appeared in ordinary fashion magazines, including American *Vogue*, created by Arthur Turnure in 1892. This had the result of spreading his fame far and wide to women beyond courtly circles.

As a clever business entrepreneur, he also expanded his repertoire of clients to include famous singers and actors of the day, recognizing that his garments would be seen by a much wider audience if they were worn by such popular public figures. He supplied performance costumes and personal wardrobes to famous stage performers including Sarah Bernhardt, Lillie Langtry, Nellie Melba and Jenny Lind. In 1883, Lillie Langtry—an internationally well-known celebrity—purchased enough gowns to fill twenty-two trunks for her European performance tour. So, while Worth attempted to establish himself as a creative artist who produced exclusivity for a privileged class, at the same time he compromised haute couture ideals by also catering for a middle-class clientele with no defined social currency. This social paradox will be discussed further in Chapter 2.

The influx of popular culture into mainstream society signalled a shift in the previously held elitist notion of what constituted status in society. While haute couture designers were dressing not only heads of state and socialites but also stage celebrities, to advertise their creations, artists too were using depictions of popular performers to draw the attention of the middle class to their work. In the famous Moulin Rouge cabaret in Paris, one of the star performers of song and dance, Jane Avril, was often depicted in Henri de Toulouse-Lautrec's work. While Toulouse-Lautrec was primarily a fine artist, he was drawn to the commercial processes of lithography, as it allowed him a greater spontaneity of line and more expressive characterization of his figures in his graphic design work. It could also be reproduced many times over. With the rise of the graphic design industry in the 1880s and 1890s, images of popular culture—themes, events and products—were used deliberately in poster designs to attract the new middle-class audience and to integrate 'art and life'. Ultimately, the emergence of the poster as an art form by 1900 led to a cultural shift in the visual arts. The art dealers who sold the work to the public and established a commercial market became the new artistic patrons, replacing the educated members of the academy who had previously determined the canons of taste. In a similar way to haute couture fashion, this struck a fatal blow to the exclusivity of the Salon and the art establishment.

Jules Cheret, named the French father of the modern poster, used the actor and dancer Charlotte Wiehe to create a prototype of the young, vibrant and emancipated middle-class woman of the latter nineteenth century. Cheret's elongated female figures, seen in the *Bal Valentino* poster of 1869, became famous in a series of designs he created for Job cigarette papers. These young women became known as his 'cherettes'. The girl in his 1889 Job poster not only set the fashionable mode, but also alluded to the moral licentiousness of working-class women in Paris. These posters became important sociological tools because, by being adopted as the 'new art' of the middle classes, they reflected the changing attitudes and mores of that particular society. By the turn of the twentieth century, the women's suffragette movement was

Figure 1.3 Jules Cheret, *Bal Valentino* poster, 1869. Cheret created an image of vivacious and fashionable young women in his poster, which highlighted popular culture and appealed to the feminist mores of the new middle class.

gaining momentum, and young women were trying to emulate the looks and attitudes of the emancipated women from working-class backgrounds depicted in these posters. The role and direction of art and fashion reflected this changing culture, where an evolving interaction between fashion, art and popular culture emerged.

THE RISE OF CONSUMERISM

With the rise of the middle-class consumer, economic factors implicit in the improved production systems, mass manufacture, incentive advertising and marketing techniques—including visual display and merchandising, and wider distribution markets—were influential in the evolving 'democratization of fashion'. Undoubtedly, the social and economic expansion of the middle class led to increased social mobility, which activated a shift in aesthetic considerations away from an elitist culture towards a popular culture. Prior to this, early mass-produced goods, especially ready-made clothing, were viewed with suspicion and were purchased out of necessity rather than choice. For the working classes, clothing had nothing whatsoever to do with 'dress' or signalling one's position in life, but purely served a functional purpose.

Discussing the ways in which technological development and new marketing strategies facilitated the new social mobility, early studies by fashion historians such as Ewing (1986) and Miller (1981) characteristically observe how improved production systems, wider distribution markets and incentive advertising schemes would systematically cater to a large national market. Beverley Lemire (1991) also points out that the availability of cheap, yet fashionable, ready-made attire initiated by the bourgeoisie was responsible for the bridging of this social gap. She indicates that, even in the eighteenth century, there was a great demand for 'popular' fashions amongst the working classes. This was facilitated by a dramatic increase in the production of cotton clothing 'which swept from London's court to Manchester's courtyard, with the help of newspapers and magazines' (1991: 324). As Ewing (1986) suggests, 'this was the start of a new cycle of fashion-making and fashion-selling which was to become the main means of bringing fashion to millions of women' (1986: 122). In France, the first 'good-quality' ready-made clothing appeared in 1824 with the opening of La Jardinière Maison in Paris. Within twenty years, 225 establishments were operating in France with the further democratization of fashion becoming possible in the 1850s when mechanical sewing machines were introduced, along with die-cutting appliances and the emergence of the women's dress pattern industry.[2] The Singer sewing machine undoubtedly provided the greatest impetus in the growth of ready-to-wear clothing, as it dramatically reduced the construction time required to make garments, thereby reducing production costs and lowering the price of the apparel.

The availability of ready-made clothing for both men and women coincided with the development of the department stores, and these factors were instrumental in the emergence of a 'culture of consumption' that eroded social class barriers. Large department stores such as the Bon Marché were stocking shawls, cloaks and tippets, as well as garment linings and millinery items, and this trend escalated with the introduction of a ready-to-wear department in the 1860s. According to Michael B. Miller (1981) in his historical retrospective of mass-merchandising at the Bon Marché, ready-made menswear, including shirts and ties, was expanding rapidly by the 1870s, and extensive advertising in the 1880s of 'dresses completely made' suggested that ready-to-wear was beginning to encroach even on the fashion trade (1981: 50).[3] Despite this evidence, it is difficult to ascertain the extent to which ready-to-wear was usurping private dressmaking businesses. More recent writers, including Lipovetsky (1994), also argue that the first manufactured dresses made 'according to standard measures did not appear until after 1870' and that 'the manufacturing techniques mainly produced the loose-fitting elements of dress, including lingerie, mantillas and coats; for the rest, women continued to turn to their dressmakers, and went on doing so for a long time' (Lipovetsky 1994: 83). Lou Taylor

(1999), in her study of woollen cloth in women's dress in Britain, notes that the firm of S. Hyam & Co., men's outfitters and tailors of Manchester and London, advertised riding habits that were 'matchless in price and make' to custom-made garments, and also that 'loose, outdoor garments were easily made up by the burgeoning ready-to-wear companies for the growing "fashion aware" middle-class feminine consumer market' (1999: 31). Certainly a study of the popular fashion journals of the 1870s such as *The Queen, La Mode Illustrée, The Young Ladies' Journal* and *La Mode Pratique* reveals numerous advertisements for ready-made garments by individual fashion companies and major department stores.

Arguably, by the turn of the century there was a great abundance and diversity of mass-produced merchandise available, but the stigma that they were poorly made fashion goods took a long time to dispel.[4] Significantly, in advertising at this time greater emphasis was being placed on marketing techniques than on the products themselves. Hollander, in her classic text *Seeing Through Clothes* adds that this, coupled with the fact that 'most of the designers were nameless to the general public' (1988: 358), contributed to their lack of general acceptance in the nineteenth century. While one might assume that this factor would dissuade upper-class purchasers, it is debatable whether or not it would have concerned middle-class consumers. Diana Crane (2000) argues that the process of the democratization of fashion during the nineteenth century was most pronounced in the United States because of the nature of its social structure (2000: 5). Banner (1984) noted that 'the obsession with fashion among American women in the nineteenth century has been attributed to a high level of "status competition" engendered by the "fluidity of American society, the universal striving for success, the lack of a titled aristocracy, and the modest past of the Americans"' (1984: 18, 54). Interestingly, fashion accessories such as gloves, canes and watches became obvious signifiers of middle-class male 'upward aspirants'. Watches with gold chains were much sought after by working-class men, and 'were sometimes provided as props by photographers to add momentary prestige to their customer's appearance' (Heinze, 1990: 89).

Perhaps the most important aspect of this development of consumerism, which was concurrent at the time Veblen (1965) was writing, is echoed in the following observation from James Allen's early text *The Romance of Commerce and Culture*:

> The rise of modern marketing also forced a shift in economic theory away from production to consumption—away from the idea that the value of products resides in the cost of production and towards the idea that the value derives from subjective consumer demand or desire in relation to supply. (1983: 6)

Allen's summary is central to the argument that there were three main marketing strategies developed to promote consumption: first, museum methods of presentation and display of goods; second, the use of the 'seduction theory' as a sophisticated psychological marketing approach; and third, the escalation of mass media advertising. These mass-marketing techniques stimulated 'conspicuous consumption', increased product production and generated the emergence of the autonomous consumer 'object'. In Europe, in particular, these pronounced profit-oriented sales techniques of the first two decades of the century highlighted a growing sophistication of entrepreneurial skills. Both intellectuals and artists became critical of the growing materialism implicit in business enterprise at the time. Fashion advertising, both in a literal and symbolic way, became symptomatic of the commodification and commercialization of modern society.

THE INTERPLAY OF COMMERCE AND CULTURE

The Department Store versus the Museum

Just as museums were conceived as being the repositories of the priceless art treasures of the world, it may be argued that the merchandise in the display cases of department stores became the treasures of consumerist society. For over two decades, numerous critics and writers—e.g. Bouquet, 2004; Derys, 1927 (cited in Bouillon 1991); Bayley, 1989; and Zola (reprinted) 1989—argue that the gap between art and business decreased dramatically with the rise of the department store. Anthropologist Bouquet (2004) proposes that 'department stores and museums shared many concerns in making the ordered display of valued objects visible to spectators' (2004: 197–98). In his fictional, yet journalistically descriptive, account of a late nineteenth-century department store in 1883, Zola metaphorically refers to it as 'the cathedral of modern business', which he claims was dedicated to the 'conquest of woman' (Bayley, 1989: 55). Similarly, Gaston Derys (1927), cited in Bouillon's 'The Shop Window, Museum of the People',[5] discusses the role of the department store as a more successful rival to the museum. He argues that the museum 'appeals only to the elite', and cannot 'teach beauty to the man on the street', as can the display artist working for the department stores (in Clair, 1991: 177). In other words, museums adopted mercantile display techniques and eye-catching designs to visually excite and seduce the consumer. Visitors became voyeurs, and it could be argued that the museum object was aesthetically reduced to the same level as the consumer object.

If museums have celebrated and taught the premise of materialism to the public, then the department stores led the way to the modern development of mass-merchandising. This is evident not only in the West but in the East as well. In Japan, three of the country's leading department stores, Isetan and Mitsukoshi in Tokyo and Takashimaya in Kyobashi, developed during the Meiji period from general goods and kimono stores. They sent out catalogues to exclusive buyers and advertised their summer clearance sales using advertisement inserts, called *hikifuda*, in newspapers from 1872 onwards. A similar initiative is outlined in Georges d'Avenel's (1989) essay 'The Bon Marché' (written in 1898), which deals with one of the oldest and most influential Parisian department stores. D'Avenel credits the entrepreneurial skills of Monsieur Bouçicault, the store's owner, with making this establishment the '*apothéosis*' of all modern department stores. D'Avenel points out that the success of the Bon Marché resulted from a number of factors. First, Bouçicault sold cheaper, often mass-produced, goods with a guarantee of quality—normally only given for more expensive merchandise. He relied on the premise that it was far better 'to sell in great quantity than to take much in profit'. Second, he introduced a revolutionary step in merchandising: the institution of fixed prices, which did away with 'bargaining' or determination of the price on the conspicuous appearance of the buyer. Third, clients were able to inspect the goods without an obligation to buy and, if they were dissatisfied with their purchase, a '*rendu*' would be arranged (d'Avenel, 1989: 59). Fourth, according to Artley (1976), prior to the 1850s Parisian retailers 'regarded their shops as private places or extensions of their homes', and therefore 'a new appreciation of customer psychology' had to be introduced by Bouçicault in the manifestation of an establishment extolling 'modern methods of retailing' (Artley, 1976: 6). Finally, the vastly increased expenditure on advertising, used to promote 'special sales' of goods, precipitated higher financial returns. This point is detailed by Zola in *Au Bonheur des Dames* (Ladies' Delight) (1883), a fictional account presumably based on the business ventures of the Bon Marché:

> Publicity was, above all, a tremendous force. Mouret spent as much as three hundred thousand francs a year on catalogues, advertisements and posters. For his sale of summer fashions he had sent out two hundred thousand catalogues, of which fifty thousand, translated into all languages, were sent abroad. (1989 [1883]: 56)

These new commercial merchandising techniques did not escape the attention of the avant-garde artists Picasso and Braque, who seized upon the opportunity to appropriate small sections of commercial logos into their collaged work. The *papier collé* entitled *Au Bon Marché* of 1913 is an exception in so far as Picasso appropriates a large lingerie advertisement without alteration or fragmentation from Samaritaine, a major Paris department store, and juxtaposes it with another large lingerie advertisement from its commercial rival, the Bon Marché department store. This referential and commercial juxtaposition is heightened by the aesthetic juxtaposition of the different typefaces used by these stores. The blunter and more traditional sans serif lettering of the word 'Samaritaine' contrasts visually and associatively with the more decorative and stylish curvilinear trademark of the Bon Marché.

In the collage, discordant forms visually create the illusion of a seated female figure, and Picasso has strategically placed the words '*trou ici*' near the figure to indicate

sexual suggestion. After all, he is suggesting, what more is lingerie than an entice-
ment to the boudoir? Picasso is almost certainly mocking the underlying motivations
and stereotyping implicit in fashion advertising. While this kind of direct social or cultural comment is atypical of Picasso's work, it undoubtedly anticipates the ways in
which some French and German Dadaist artists used advertising materials in their
collages to link fashion imagery and social commentary. The psychological ploys of
mass-marketing that motivated the human psyche became an inherent part of the
fashion advertisements of the day, and in turn were facetiously implied in the work of
the avant-garde artists of the early twentieth century.

The commercial success of the Bon Marché was duplicated internationally with the
advent or refurbishment of major department stores in many cities in Europe, Britain
and America. The great Wertheim department store was built on Berlin's Leipziger-
strasse by Alfred Messel between 1896 and 1899, and Samaritaine was built in Paris
by Franz Jourdain and Henri Sauvage in 1905. David Jones opened its doors as a department store in Sydney in 1877 with great fanfare, and became a public company
in 1906. Selfridge's was rebuilt and refurbished on London's Oxford Street by Daniel
Burnham and R. Frank Atkinson in 1908, and was revolutionary in having its display
windows lit up at night. In the United States, both Macy's in New York and Marshall
Field's in Chicago had been in operation for three decades by the turn of the century.

Figure 1.4   Jay's of London, brown silk chiffon
teagown with matching shawl, 1900–1910.
Collection: Powerhouse Museum, Sydney. Photographer: Andrew Frolows. Fashions were displayed at the *Exposition Universale* in Paris for
the first time in 1900. Tea gowns were shown
on wax dummies and set in salon-like settings.
Having developed from nineteenth-century
'reform dress', they continued to be popular as
a comfortable garment to be worn *only* inside
the home.

Marshall Field's department store was owned by the wealthiest man in Chicago at the time, and was designed and built by Henry Hobson Richardson, one of America's great pioneering architects. Deemed an architectural landmark, this 1892 building was six storeys high and, despite its conservative exterior, was celebrated as one of the earliest 'distinctly American' modern buildings. In 1978, it was designated a National Historic Landmark. A magnificent large Tiffany ceiling made of glass mosaic pieces—the first to be made entirely of *favrile* iridescent glass—adorned the store and added to its sumptuous display. Field himself is considered to be one of the leading figures in the development of the department store. Marshall Field's was the first American department store to establish a European buying office, which was located in Manchester, England. It was also the first American store to open a restaurant and to offer a bridal registry. Both American and European department stores fashioned their stores on the premise that, with all facilities such as rest rooms, restaurants, theatrettes or exhibition spaces provided, the customer could spend an entire day enjoying the ambience of the store.

Macy's opened its flagship store in Herald Square on Broadway in 1902, which was advertised widely as the largest department store in the world. Broadway was New York's leading street, and its first cable car lines were completed in 1893 with underground conduits to avoid having poles and overhead wires. Electric trams, or trolley cars, carried hundreds of potential customers past Macy's doors every day, and its large display windows enhanced its products' appeal to buyers. According to Elizabeth Wilson (1985: 149), the clients of the department stores 'were overwhelmingly middle class'. She points out, however, that 'this ambience of service rather than commerce gave an illusion of aristocratic life, and in this way old forms of class and personal relationships persisted in the midst of the new'. This illusion that it was the venue itself that afforded an elevated status for the bourgeois customers (one which previously only the upper classes could have enjoyed) held great appeal. As both upper- and middle-class clients frequented the stores, it would seem that—at least superficially—it led to a greater levelling of the social classes. This factor relates more to department stores in England than to those in the United States or Australia,[6] where social class distinctions were not as pronounced.

More importantly, because bourgeois culture was on display, it allowed for greater divergence of thought regarding what constituted popular culture and how social processes structured lifestyles and determined 'taste' in consumer goods. Bourdieu's *Distinction* (1984) suggests that taste in cultural goods functions as a marker of class. The shop assistant's position, for example, allowed young women a status above that of factory workers, and provided them with the means to be well dressed. It thus became far easier for a woman to 'dress above her station in life', and social mobility was possible provided one could emulate and sustain the illusion.

According to Émile Zola, this was symptomatic of the bourgeois culture which extolled consumptive virtues to the extent that it exploited and even victimized people—women, in particular. In his novel *Au Bonheur des Dames* (Ladies' Delight) (1883), he describes 'how definitions of the feminine came to be linked with such psychological disturbances as the new department store madness—kleptomania. As the modern world became more affluent and prone to overproduction, excess and indulgence, the practices of everyday life, such as shopping, were identified as sources of instability, even of insanity' (cited in Finkelstein 1996: 97–8).[7] However, Saisselin, in his book *The Bourgeois and the Bibelot* (1984: 36–9), disagrees with this proposition. Explaining a woman's relationship with the department store, he argues that whether it is in New York, Chicago or Paris, the results are the same. The advantage to the female customer is 'undeniably in her aesthetic education', and he underlines that, through the staging of theatrical effects, 'the aesthetic experience was generalized and democratized'. Elsewhere, Saisselin compares 'the striking similarities of the structures, spaces and methods of exhibiting objects in museums and department stores' despite the 'social, aesthetic and theoretical differences between the objet d'art and the consumer object' (Saisselin, 1984: 42).

Figure 1.5 A)   Paul Poiret with wife Denise at 1002nd Night's party, 24 June 1911. Photographer: Henri Manuel/Apic/Getty Images. Poiret's lifestyle was reminiscent of his interest in the exotic.

Figure 1.5 B) Paul Poiret, *Le Minaret* production costume, May 1913. Photographer: Apic/Getty Images. Worn by French comedian Cora Laparacerie in her role as Myriem in the play by Jacques Richepin, which opened in Paris. Photo printed in French newspaper *Le Theatre*, May 1913.

The impact and influence of this increased consumerism and visual display of fashion upon early twentieth-century artists such as Pablo Picasso, Eugene Atget and Marcel Duchamp is significant. The subsequent emergence of the modernist and postmodernist concepts of 'art as object' and 'art as product' become manifest in Duchamp's ready-mades and the 'café' assemblages created by Picasso before the outbreak of the First World War in 1914.

The Theatre of Fashion and Art

This conceptual comparison between museums and department stores was visually explored and exploited by a number of twentieth-century avant-garde artists. For Saisselin (1984: 42), 'the parallel between museums and department stores ought not to be overlooked', since museums—like department stores—'were spacious and often palatial and, like museums, they were divided into departments'. He adds:

> Both institutions exhibited their wares, though in the case of the stores, the wares were for sale and were not unique but mass-produced. There were other contrasts of course. The wares in the museum had reached the end point of an itinerary through space and historical time; the wares in the department stores were arranged as if on a line of departure. In a

sense the department store was an anti-museum of modern, productive, dynamic capitalist production in which 'objets d'art' were but one possible line of goods; an almost infinite possibility of commodity circulation existed since this was based on desire, which by definition of human nature knew no bounds. In the museum, art was the only line of goods exhibited. It was singled out, distinguished from other items, and thus lent a special aura that was increased by its inaccessibility and its historical pedigree. And as the nineteenth century gave way to the twentieth, more and more items were declared works of art and entered museums. In fact, the true museum of the nineteenth century might well be a department store rather than a specialized exhibition space reserved for nineteenth-century painting and sculpture. (1984: 42)

Further consideration of the marketing techniques and subtleties of the art of 'display' indicates how critical the premise of voyeurism is to this theory. Art historian Bouillon's 'The Shop Window' (1991) traces the history of window dressing back to the foundation of the Weiner Werkstätte in Vienna in 1903—one of the earliest decorative arts workshops to become an international distributor. It opened a fashion and textiles department, amongst others, and after 1910 opened retail outlets in Zurich (1917), New York (1921), Velden (1922) and Berlin (1929). Bouillon particularly emphasizes the contribution of Josef Hoffmann—one of the original founders of the workshop, which was characterized by a 'simple' sophistication that effectively focused attention upon the display of goods. Bouillon also notes that, according to the architect designer Corbusier, the *Deutsche Werkbund* organized an important conference in 1910 on 'The Decoration of Shop Fronts', which 'led to a number of revolutionary innovations taking place in Germany' (1991: 169). For example, double-façade shops allowed for greater visual exposure of the display, exemplifying a transparent, continuous space, while minimal decoration ensured that attention was focused on the consumer goods.

This new merchandising technique reached a pinnacle in Ruhlmann's shop window design for Max Furs at the famous 'Exposition des Arts Décoratifs et Industriels Modèrnes', Paris, 1925, where the glass façades 'amplified the transparency of the shop's space', giving the disquieting impression that 'the mannequins were simply taking a stroll across the bridge'. Bouillon stresses that the 'simultaneous transparency and reflectivity of its glass captivated and seduced painters and architects alike' (1991: 173). This merchandising spectacle not only brought art closer to life, but it reinforced the notion that mass-produced consumer products, such as fashion, could be viewed differently. Ready-made fashion was beginning to lose its former stigma as a 'working-class' necessity, and instead was seen as a modern response to the industrial age.

Both Bouillon (1991) and Varnedoe and Goprik (1990) emphasize the significance of the growing impact of window display, and in particular fashion mannequins and goods, upon a variety of prominent artists. As Saisselin (1984: 39) observes, the contemporaneous commercial concept of the artistic display is indicative of the sophisticated changes in the presentation of merchandise display in the consumer arena, as the dramatized tableau format in shop windows became one of the moving forces behind high-consumption capitalism, along with the distribution of goods and the promotion of desire. If advertising was to become a species of new literature, so too would the display of consumer goods and commodities become a new type of staging. Varnedoe and Goprik (1990) discuss the 'new tableau' created by the window dressers, and claim they were 'somewhat dramatized' and reminiscent of Picasso's constructions in his studio, 'where objects took on a real life as props in an implied story' (1990: 281). In his café assemblages, Picasso used banal objects to construct a new type of reality—one that questioned both the conventions of subject and the material used in the work. Picasso incorporated newspaper clippings, restaurant menus and other found objects in this work to underline the new link with popular culture.

Bouillon (1991) also cites Robert Delaunay's work *Windows* (1912) and Macke's late work *Essen* (1912), a painting of a large window, as linking consumer display to the visual elements of Cubist fragmentation of form and the overlapping spaces of Futurism through the commercial nature of its subject matter. The photographic work of Atget also clearly indicates that he became fascinated with the transparent effects of window displays, which featured consistently in his work between 1921 and 1927. His photographic imagery of headless, corseted figures in his *Corsets, Boulevard de Strasbourg* (1927) and the male liveried suits in his *Shop at Les Halles* (1925) are all reminiscent of Otto Umbehr's use of severed figures in his work and Duchamp's fascination with inanimate advertising figures.

It is worthwhile reinforcing this interrelationship between fashion display and art, as few fashion authors have explored this important link extensively. Varnedoe and Goprik (1990) argue that:

> Duchamp is the crucial figure through whom modern art's progress becomes entwined not just with commercial modes of representation, but with advertising's attempts to affect people's immediate relation to the objects themselves, by strategies of display or changes in context and scale. (1990: 270)

In fact, Varnedoe and Goprik dare to suggest that the new theatrical appeal of window display in Paris might well have prompted Duchamp's interest in transforming the art object into a display object. They also argue that the link between art and commerce was heralded primarily by the work and writing of H. Gleveo, 'an accomplished shop stylist'.[8] Duchamp remarked that the 'notions of display in art had a parallel life in the show business of everyday modern commerce' (cited in Varnedoe and Goprik, 1990: 284). Duchamp, more than any other early twentieth-century artist, directly contributed to the conception of art as a commercial product. He adopted the term 'ready-made' for his art objects, a term which refers to early machine mass-produced clothing.

For Varnedoe and Goprik: 'Duchamp's ready-mades emerged from the avant-garde thinking about the relationship between things for use and things for show and about the intrusion of commonplace objects into the category of sculpture' (1990: 270–80). In other words, Duchamp emphasized how the contextual placement of the art product within a gallery—whether it was a snow shovel, bicycle wheel or urinal—determined its artistic actuality and validity. The artist dictated that the consumer product simply became the artwork because the artist deemed it to be so. No transformation, authenticity or originality was required. Interestingly, by posing this question of what constitutes an 'original' artwork, Duchamp parodies the ready-to-wear clothing industry as well. Interestingly, Palmer White (1986) reinforces this paradox in the fashion industry when he confirms that haute couture commercialized deluxe made-to-measure garments by repeating models and selling them to French and foreign dress shops, as well as to private customers. How can one garment serve as an exclusive model and yet be sold as multiple copies at the same time? In both cases, the original and the reproduction become one and the same.

Fashion display windows used mannequins to the extent that they became a theatrical presence behind the window. Paradoxical visions of these storefront dummies all find counterparts in the Surrealist art of de Chirico, Delvaux and Magritte. The inclusion of these lifeless female figures added to the surrealist supernatural language of dreams and visions. The Surrealist photographer Man Ray photographed wooden mannequins dressed by Paul Poiret, Lucien Lelong and Louiseboulanger, posed in a variety of staged, elegant interiors taken at the Pavillon de l'Élégance at the Grand Palais, part of the 'Exposition des Arts Décoratifs et Industriels Modèrnes' held in Paris in 1925, which were featured in the French *Vogue* of 15 August 1925. This significant exhibition of the decorative arts juxtaposed with modern, industrialized fine art pieces, including paintings by Leger and other Cubist artists, mainly emphasized the mutual synthesis of the machine age aesthetic. However, Man Ray used these images 'to objectify the nature of the well-dressed modern woman by creating an ambiguity between the artificial and the real world as symbolized by the mannequins' (International Centre of Photography, 1990: 17). In the photographs, the background space was consistently empty, with a sense of the dramatic created by the manipulation of light and shade. These images appealed to both the fashion and the Surrealist art worlds.

In a more literal way, in the first decade of the twentieth century, theatrical performances of all kinds captured the imagination of the public. Hollander (1988) underlines the physical accord that occurs between the performer and the audience. In dramatic terms, when the characters utter no sounds, their clothes obviously speak more loudly (Hollander, 1988: 237). Strategically, fashion became theatre in the auditoriums and theatrettes of major department stores. Often these venues seated between 100 and 1,500 people. This was particularly prevalent in America, where elitist (and often private) presentations of haute couture collections in the designers' *maisons* were not possible. Instead, couture garments fashioned for the American market were promoted as part of a public cultural experience. Stores such as Macy's, Gimbel's and Wanamaker's attempted to blur the distinction between professional theatrical productions and department store fashion shows in order to create a pseudo-intellectual atmosphere. In 1910, Joanne Paquin sent 100 gowns, 100 hats and 100 umbrellas and mannequins to tour America, to be 'installed' in an elegant theatrical format in hotels and stores alike. Crowds were turned away at the Ritz-Carleton and 60,000 people viewed the exhibition at Altman's department store over a three-day period. In 1912, several large department stores staged more spectacular theatrical presentations of Paris couture fashion disguised under the exotic 'Garden of Allah' theme. Similarly, Paul Poiret—who had introduced oriental splendour to Parisian fashion with the introduction of harem trousers, pantaloons, wired lampshade tunics and hemlines weighted down by tassels—staged a production of *Le Minaret* during his 1913 American tour (Troy, 2003). He created an ideal of sophisticated luxury, and his presence at the events resulted in the outstanding commercial success of his collection. A year later, Poiret used the Théâtre de la Renaissance in Paris to stage a play called *Aphrodite*, where an opulent spectacle of couture fashions distinguished the actors in the five-part drama. The success of these ventures suggests that theatricality was used as a clever tool in bridging the gap between culture and commerce (Troy, 2003).

It should be pointed out that a precedent was established in 1910 when Serge Diaghilev's Russian Ballet (*Ballet Russes*) performed *Scheherazade* in Paris to huge crowds. While it was held as a cultural event, the fashion designers saw how movement, drama and visual spectacle could enhance the clothing that was worn. Not only was it the first time that the famous dancer Nijinsky had appeared outside of Russia, but it was also the first time that a European audience had seen the experimental costumes and stage settings of Léon Bakst. The dramatic impact that this single production, with its oriental bejewelled garments in brilliant juxtaposed hues, had upon its viewers would have been unparalleled in history. Poiret's exotic collections were further popularized, but more importantly the ballet's impact reverberated through every branch of the arts. The Russian Ballet 'became a catalyst of culture' and, furthermore, 'the critics found it hard to determine what to praise first—the choreography of Fokine, the dancing of Nijinsky, the dazzling costumes and sets by Bakst which exploded into Parisian fashion and interior design, or the unfamiliar music of Rimsky-Korsakov' (Lloyd, 1991: 35).

The Russian Ballet performed in Paris each year until 1929, and Diaghilev employed a cross-section of radical artists, including Goncharova and Larionov of the Russian avant-garde, the Russian Constructivists, the Italian Futurists Balla and Dépero, the Cubists Braque, Picasso, and Sonia and Robert Delaunay, as well as the Expressionists Derain and Matisse, and the Surrealists Miró, Ernst and de Chirico.

Figure 1.6 Window shopping, lingerie, 1930s. Photographer: SSPL/Getty Images. Two women admiring the spectacle of the lingerie window display, a visual marketing strategy which lead to increased sales.

THE ART OF FASHION ADVERTISING

Marketing strategists insist that the continuity of visual seduction in the fashion industry is based on the desirability of innovation and change. History has indicated that the laws of mass production and consumption decree that, in order to keep the wheels of the economic capitalist system turning, consumption has to be continuous and on an ever-increasing scale.

Throughout the late nineteenth and early twentieth centuries, 'orchestrated needs' or desires in the fashion industry were created systematically. Clothing styles not only changed from year to year, but changes in social structures—including connotations of 'status'—and developments in technology led to innovations in clothing design. Miller's *The Bon Marché* (1981) recounts that, by the 1890s, the store was selling cycling apparel for both men and women; ten years later, coats for automobile drivers were on sale (1981: 185).[9] In 1904 in London, Burberry devoted a 254-page catalogue almost entirely to ready-made sportswear. As the merchandisers discovered, consumers purchased goods for 'their visual novelty, social cachet and so on, rather than for any obvious functional benefit', according to 'the concept of "conspicuous consumption" which derives from the law of economics' (Sparke, 1987: 105). It was primarily this concept of 'conspicuous consumption' that established the visual dominance of fashion design and advertising imagery in the pre-war years.

Fashion and textile goods predominated in store merchandising from the early 1800s onwards. The growth of ready-to-wear fashion paralleled the growth of the *grands maga-sins* in Paris, which originally were 'drapery and fancy goods stores' (Miller, 1981: 34). By 1906, forty-one out of fifty-two major divisions of Bon Marché involved either fashion or dry goods. This visual dominance of fashion imagery was complemented by the wide distribution of department store and fashion distributors' catalogues, which advertised the new styles, special sales and mail-order services,[10] and by the use of full-page advertisements in the daily press.[11] Distribution figures were enormous. In 1910, Bon Marché sent out 1 million catalogues for one 'white sale' to the provinces alone (Miller, 1981: 61–2). While this sort of advertising was extensive and geographically widespread, more sophisticated techniques developed prior to the First World War marked a 'revolution in marketing'.

As early as autumn 1874, the grand London department store Debenham and Free-body produced a special mail-order catalogue directed at American visitors in London, advertising its stock of authentic Parisian mantles, costumes and millinery (Taylor, 1999: 35). In America, catalogue selling was lead by Sears Roebuck & Co., a firm that declared: 'We sell everything'. Between 1893 and 1894, the catalogue increased in size from 196 pages to 322 pages. By 1895, it was 502 pages long, and bridged the gap between rural and urban consumers. In country areas, clothing had previously been purchased for its practicality, but the catalogue offered greater choice of 'garments with style'. Like the department stores, it provided one-stop shopping and the fulfilment of wishes and desires.

Selling consumption was a matter of seduction and showmanship. Discussing the difference between the nineteenth-century mimetic catalogues, which stressed value for money and consumer choice, and the later editions, which persuasively used psychological associations inherent in the purchase of goods, Alan Tomlinson (1990: 9) observes that: 'The commodity has acquired an aura beyond just its function. The commodity now acts "on" the consumer, endows him/her with perceived qualities which can be displayed in widening public contexts.' In turn, Miller (1981) suggests that 'mass-marketing demanded a wizardry that could stir unrealized appetites, provoke overpowering urges and create new states of mind' (1981: 165–7). For Miller, 'the bourgeois culture was coming more to mean a consumer culture . . . the two were becoming interchangeable' (1981: 165). The 'image' of the product was paramount as it was closely tied with the status of ownership, whether the goods involved were fashion items or household appliances such as vacuum cleaners, electric refrigerators or automobiles. This form of conspicuous consumption, once restricted to the upper classes, now enticed middle-class individuals in the consumption of commodities.

According to de Grazia's *The American Challenge to the European Arts of Advertising* (1991), another important factor that was to greatly influence the direction of advertising in Europe in the 1920s was the influx of American business and advertising agencies such as J. Walter Thompson, N. W. Ayer & Son and Erwin Wasey (1991: 36). These firms promoted a more rational persuasive technique, commonly cited as the American 'hard sell' approach. By incorporating a 'press insert' in the advertisement, information was combined 'with persuasive reasoning'. This 'salesmanship in print' was often 'backed up by ostensibly scientific data and testimonials from prominent social figures', and sold the beneficial properties rather than the functional aspects of the product. The 'intentional blurring of the "real" reading material and editorializing for consumer products' was achieved by using similar page formatting and typographical print for both news articles and advertising sections within the publication (de Grazia, 1991: 241). From another American perspective, Ewen (1976) argues that Veblen's theories relating to the conspicuous consumption habits of the leisure class of the nineteenth century were 'now propagated as the democratic ideal' within mass advertising in the 1910s and 1920s. As Ewen subsequently observes, 'in order to sell the commodity culture, it was necessary to confront people with a vision of that culture from which the class bases of dissatisfaction had been removed' (1976: 79). Unlike Americans, Europeans were always more reluctant to accept mass consumerism as a utopian ideal—perhaps as a historical result of their more structured social class system (Clair, 1991: 238).

Many mass media critics confirm Veblen's characterization of advertising as a strategy that trades on a range of human frailties. The advertising copywriters seem to direct their persuasions towards human weaknesses at all social levels. This is consistently evident in both the popular magazines such as the Parisian *Les Annales*, as well as the more elite publications such as *Vogue*. Personal insecurities based on the dictates of improving oneself fostered the consumption of a vast array of new cosmetic and perfume products. In the early 1920s, the Helena Rubenstein cosmetic empire was built on the foundations of this consumer culture. The glamorous image of women in the cosmetic, fashion and advertising world projected a desirability that could be purchased in a mass-production economy. The quest for an idealized youth dominated facial soap advertisements, which promised rejuvenated complexions and wrinkle-free skin as a result of using their preparations. While these products offered at least short-term juvenility, cosmetic surgery and the wearing of toupees guaranteed immortality. Not surprisingly, a veiled illusion was created, as the consumers to whom the advertisements were directed were rarely specifically categorized with regard to age, marital status, ethnicity or any other characteristic—thereby sustaining a universal appeal.

Advertising—especially in the post-war era—stimulated women's needs in particular. Not only had women continued their role in the household, but they were increasingly in paid employment as well. They became a new 'niche' market as potential financially independent consumers. Advertisers appealed to the 'narcissism' of a woman's self-concept by offering goods that promised higher status and a means of increasing self-esteem, as well as intimating sexual attractiveness and helping her to maintain her security within the family structure. For both men and women, the concept of fear, which created a consequent emotional vulnerability, became the main motivating factor in advertising in the 1920s. The most pressing fears were the fear of losing one's job, the fear of failure in courtship or marriage, or the fear of what others might think or say. As class was no longer a barrier, women were enticed to dress as fashionably as their wealthier counterparts by purchasing mass-produced copies of designer garments, ensuring that they would not be considered socially inferior. In America, in particular, some advertisements not only emphasized that these ready-made garments were 'exact copies'—or at least inspired by Paris originals—but also gave them a certain exclusivity by giving them a 'name' label of their own. For example, Franklin Simon & Co. marketed the Bramley Dress as an exclusive line of ready-to-wear fashion garments that could not be sold by any other distributor.

By the 1920s, women were coerced through consumer fantasy into thinking that they could express their own individuality and personality regardless of economic limitations, class restraints and conflict. In other words, the needs of the consumer economy effectively became a woman's needs as well. The use of 'social psychology for understanding and directing consumer behaviour' investigated 'human association and motivation', and this in turn created 'lifestyle advertising'. The association of a particular commodity with a whole way of life was a remarkably successful advertising technique. The purchase of the product promised happiness, security and pleasure, and its absence resulted in personal failure and despair.

In short, whilst materialism and superficiality were nurtured by the growing advertising industry, the use of psychological associations was the key to advertisers' promotions. These marketing strategies underpinned advertising imagery and became a dominant feature of the avant-garde art movements of Cubism and Dadaism in the first three decades of the twentieth century. The rise of the fashion industry in the late nineteenth and early twentieth centuries foreshadowed a development towards greater 'democratization' of fashion. These changes were accelerated by cheaper production of goods for a mass-market; more appealing and more 'lifelike' visual display modes, which tempted the middle class consumer; more enticing merchandising methods, which attracted a wider consumer audience; and the growth of more accessible distribution centres, which offered numerous attractions for all members of the family. When this was coupled with increasingly sophisticated advertising and promotional material that catered to the weaknesses and frivolities of all classes of society, a decided shift was becoming more apparent—from what had been a relatively elitist marketing sector in society to a broader-based consumerist market. This rise in consumerism and the subsequent evolution of the fashion industry paralleled the development of anti-elitist practices in the fine arts and prefigured the development of a symbiotic relationship between fashion, culture and art.

–2–

The Democratization of Fashion: Machine Age Aesthetics

> I am no longer interested in dressing a few hundred women, private clients; I shall dress thousands of women.
>
> Coco Chanel

FLOODING THE AMERICAN MARKET: REPRODUCTIONS AND FAKES

The dichotomy underlining the work of early haute couture fashion designers forecast the inevitable growth of the democratization of fashion in the twentieth century. On the one hand, couturiers were producing extremely expensive items for elite patronage, yet on the other they were distributing copies at reduced prices to a widespread middle-class market. Suzanna Shonfield (1982) describes how, by the late 1870s, 'C. F. Worth was beginning to run his "salon de couture" on an almost industrial scale, resulting in "blatant duplication of models"' (1987: 57–8). This was due to the expediency of the new sewing machines and the use of standardized patterns with interchangeable parts, leaving only the cutting, finishing and embroidery to be done by hand. By using these divided labour practices, with the only variation being the different fabrics that were used, an unstable discourse between originality and reproduction resulted. Nancy Troy, in *Couture Culture* (2003), provides valuable insight into the commercial practices of a number of leaders in the French fashion industry, including the designers Charles Frederick Worth, Paul Poiret, Jeanne Paquin, Madeleine Vionnet and Sonia Delaunay, and underlines the contradictions inherent in their work.

Most designers, including Paquin, Worth and Poiret, recognized the important role that the American market played in achieving international and financial success. Paquin, who first opened her salon in 1891 and was considered the first important woman in haute couture, often remarked that the American market 'is the most important in the world'. Similarly, in his book *Some Memories of Paris* (1895), Worth became famous for this quip:

Some of the Americans are great spenders . . . I like to dress them, for, as I say occasionally, 'they have faith, figures and francs'—faith to believe in me, figures that I can put into shape, francs to pay my bills. Yes, I like to dress Americans. (1895: 193–4)

Troy (2003: 24–5) points out that Worth sold models designed to be copied by others—especially American dry goods and department stores—in the 1860s, which subsequently necessitated the introduction of house labels to identify genuine Worth products, as many of the garments looked identical. This was akin to artists signing their work as a means to validate the originality and uniqueness of their creations. Despite this, by the late 1880s the Worth label itself was being fraudulently copied, and imitations were flooding the market. With the consumer goods market expanding so rapidly, protection by copyright laws became mandatory, with the brand name used to authenticate the product.

By the end of the First World War, couturiers found that costs were rising, both for wages and materials (of which there was still a shortage); for those couturiers who had closed their doors four years earlier, it was difficult to cover their initial business costs. In an attempt to bolster the industry, the French government pressured the banks to extend their overdrafts. Even the larger houses were suffering financially, and it became almost a necessity to extend their markets to larger—and therefore lower—income groups.

According to Troy (2003: 10), when 'in 1916–17, Poiret decided that it would be fortuitous to establish a market in the USA', he designed a line of dresses which he named after his workshop, called *Hotel de Couture*. Their styling was particularly intended to appeal to American women, and by affixing a special label to these items of clothing, they were identified as 'authorized reproductions'. Having compromised the elite nature of his dress range, he had effectively created a new category of fashion 'objects'. Yet, when he organized a tour to America with five of his models, he found that he was unable to protect his intellectual property as his 'reproduction' designs were being undermined by an extensive system of fashion piracy that he could not control.

Within this context, perhaps it is not that surprising that, like Duchamp's work of the same period (discussed earlier), these dresses were at once 'authentic objects, signed by their creator' and at the same time 'mass-produced commodities' (Troy, 2003: 10). Significantly, Duchamp's most infamous work among his 'ready-mades' (named after the fashion term) also materialized in this contentious decade. His work *The Fountain* of 1917 (a urinal which he signed 'R. Mutt') blatantly comments on the 'signature label', which by its very essence gives the product the aura of a unique artwork while at the same time mocking the value and status ordinarily attributed to original 'sculpture'. This paradoxical notion of what constitutes an original was not only of consequence to the intelligentsia of the art world, but was of great monetary concern to the industrialists in the commercial sector.

Figure 2.1 Madeleine Vionnet, woman's wool day ensemble, France, *c.* 1930. Collection: Powerhouse Museum, Sydney. Photographer: Powerhouse Museum Photography Department. This ensemble epitomises the classic, timeless lines of Vionnet's designs.

Interestingly, another haute couture designer, Madeleine Vionnet—highly esteemed by her fellow designers for her technical and aesthetic prowess—was particularly outraged about copyists, and went so far as to include her fingerprint on her garment labels to identify and validate the original nature of the dresses. Despite this, Vionnet—like Poiret and Worth—continued to be exploited by the fashion counterfeiters who sold unauthorized copies of her designs in department stores across the United States. In another attempt to counteract this fraudulent practice, she ran a notice in the trade journal *Women's Wear* in August 1921, warning her customers that her work was copyrighted and could not be reproduced without a licence.[1] As her label was uniquely identifiable, she tried to sue a number of French and American firms and department stores for selling illegal copies. The contradiction inherent in Vionnet's actions was not that she was against selling copies of her work to the American market, but rather that she tried to devise a scheme where she received royalties for the licence to copy, thereby controlling the products' production and circulation. While the complexity of her work, based on her trademark bias cut, was very difficult to copy, it was not impossible. When, in 1923, a lawyer named Louis Dangel became Vionnet's business manager, he founded a new anti-piracy group, the Association for the Defence of the Plastic and Applied Arts, which demanded that the French government enforce an international copyright to protect the creative intellectual property of the Paris fashion designers (Troy, 2003: 330–31). Not all designers agreed to join, as they were not *entirely* opposed to the American paradigm of mass-marketing. Coco Chanel was one of those designers.

COCO CHANEL

Major changes in society, particularly in terms of social class structures and the status of women, were to impact greatly on the direction that fashion would take during the 1920s. Hollander (1983: 85) notes that: 'Prior to 1918 . . . a gentleman did not dine with his tailor, or a lady with her couturier.' The dictates of European hierarchical class structures determined that 'society had never before opened its door to couturiers, however talented they may have been, and those creative women had been relegated to the status of *faiseuses* or "dressmakers"' (Charles-Roux, 1981: 182).[2] However, Hollander (1983: 85) argues that, after the First World War, 'old social hierarchies were rearranged' and both artists and designers 'rose abruptly on the social scale'.

In the past, bourgeois fashion was merely a poor imitation of that worn by the privileged classes. As production methods became more sophisticated, the visual difference between haute couture and mass-produced fashions became less manifest. Wilson (1985: 79) argues that 'wholesale couture' or 'middle-class fashions' also developed. Several firms developed 'distinctive house styles and good design', which became 'as important as good quality'. The character and nature of commercial design was changing internationally. According to Ewing (1986: 135), in Britain for example, the firm of Jaeger claimed that 'you can no longer tell a shop girl from a duchess'. This company originally manufactured and sold garments wholesale in London in the 1890s, and in the 1920s employed professional designers to produce 'elegant, fashionable clothes at moderate prices' for the mass-market.

Increased democratization of fashion resulted in the 1920s, when three preconditions were met: a competitive pricing system, advanced manufacturing technologies which produced goods that were well made and designed, and an effective distribution network. It is widely acknowledged that the increase in the number of 'multiple stores' or chain stores in the 1920s was rivalling the number of department stores, which seemed to have reached their numerical peak. Moreover, the consumer focus of these chain stores was aimed at the increasingly large and prosperous working classes. This new means of fashion distribution targeted all sectors of society in much the same way as the department stores had done in the nineteenth century.

The chain stores offered open displays of merchandise, variable sizing, self-selection and fixed prices. A new niche marketing approach appealed directly to working women, whose numbers had increased dramatically and who were enjoying their new financial independence. Significantly, this reflected an important development in social history. As Caroline Seebohn (1982) notes, another major factor in 'democratizing the fashion industry' was that 'designers like Chanel were creating simpler, more practical clothes for women who were active, held jobs, and sought comfort instead of artifice' (1982: 184).

Undoubtedly, Gabrielle Chanel, better known as 'Coco', was one of the most influential female designers of this transitional period—a woman who rose out of a working-class background. She was the first haute couture designer to consider the functional aspects of dress, rationally deconstructing women's dress through cut, fabric and simplicity of design. Her work deliberately disrupted and overturned social class indicators in so far as it discarded the dominant concept of conspicuous consumption as a means of achieving status. Her relentless promotion of working-class attire in the early years led to a social paradox, where 'dressing down' became the epitome of elitist fashion. The foundations of elitism in haute couture were weakened further when fashion edicts dealing with uniqueness, originality, stereotyping and sobriety in haute couture were questioned by mass-production techniques and the rise of prêt-à-porter. While the bastions of haute couture had been protected and defended for fifty years by the quality of materials and garment construction, as well as the techniques employed in their work, many haute couture designers no longer applied these criteria in their workrooms.

This chapter investigates the methods used by Chanel to achieve a greater 'democratization' of fashion, and the degree to which her work reflects the influence of 1920s art and design. It will also underline how Chanel's success was based on her ability to perceive and meet the demands of a changing commercial market. It is interesting to compare how, in much the same way, fine artists such as Sonia Delaunay and the Russian Constructivists Varvara Stepanova and Liubov Popova linked fashion, as an applied art, more closely to fine art trends in the 1920s and 1930s (see Chapter 3). This underlines the notion of the synthesis of the visual arts that evolved across all media in this modernist period.

Like the avant-garde artists, both Chanel and her rival Elsa Schiaparelli (see Chapter 3) became major figures in breaking down traditional fashion concepts and institutions. Both substituted non-status or atypical materials for luxurious fabrics; both adapted male working-class attire for female wear; and their philosophies regarding reproduction superseded the need for exclusiveness and uniqueness in their work. No longer could the haute couture designers afford to work exclusively for individual clients and exclude everyone except the very wealthy.

Figure 2.2 Wilson's of Great Portland Street, jersey cardigan suits, London, 1920s. Photographer: Brooke/Getty Images. These knitted jersey outfits reflected the pioneering styles of Chanel and Patou which determined the look of the twenties.

A number of fashion and art historians have given unqualified credit to Coco Chanel for her contribution to changing the direction of haute couture. Yet Valerie Steele (1988: 245–6) suggests that many designers 'were not as paramount a force in fashion history as they have been made out to be by the inflated theories of overly enthusiastic biographers'. She concludes that 'most of the literature on Chanel is closer to hagiography than historiography'. While it would seem that Chanel undoubtedly made a major contribution to fashion's redirection—along with a number of other influential designers of the time—international monetary factors determined that the world of haute couture could no longer afford to ignore the fashion demands and economic strength of the bourgeoisie. For example, long before Chanel's name was first mentioned in an American *Vogue* magazine article in April 1923 titled 'Chanel Opens Her Doors to a Waiting World', this elitist magazine had been printing regular feature articles for several years with titles such as 'Where Modes and Moderate Incomes Meet', 'Dressing on a Limited Income' and 'Ways to Alter Your Old Fashions'. In American *Vogue* in the years following the war, it became quite common to see advertisements for copies of 'Paris originals' and lists of distributors of lower-priced ready-to-wear garments. Already by that time, the editors of fashion magazines were appealing to a potentially vast new market.

Until the end of the 1920s, it was the habit of American buyers to purchase several dozen copies of each selected model in Paris and retail them to a wealthy clientele, and then to make a thousand copies to sell at lower prices. The principal Parisian fashion houses in 1925 were listed as Patou, Lanvin, Vionnet, Lelong, Molyneux and Piguet, and the fashion export market was worth nearly 2,500 million francs. Many salons had expanded their premises and hired as many as 500 people to cope with the demand. However, after the stock market crash (in 1929), prohibitive customs duties began to make the luxury trade almost impossible, for duty of up to 90 per cent might be imposed on the cost of the model. However, models imported on a temporary basis for the purpose of copying were allowed into America duty free. These toiles (patterns cut out in linen) were sold for 100,000 francs each, with full directions for making them up.

Ironically, this practice of licensing designs, which theoretically controlled their reproduction and circulation, would ultimately lead to the destruction of the exclusivity of haute couture. Economic factors in the form of tariff restraints were also a major factor in restructuring the international fashion market, and accelerated the development of the ready-to-wear industry internationally. These restraints, imposed during both the First World War and the Depression, compounded this industrial shift.

Fashion piracy was costing the couturiers thousands of francs each year, and further hastened the introduction of ready-to-wear garments. The illegal copying of haute couture designs could not be prevented by the French authorities because it occurred in foreign countries. Infringement of copyright was the subject of the Hague Agreement of July 1928, which was promulgated 'as an international instrument of protection. It covered all designs and models registered with the *Organisation Mondiale de la Propriété Intellectuelle* in Geneva' (Palmer White, 1986: 167). Ironically, Palmer White has concluded that, despite these protective measures, in the 1920s and 1930s, 'few members of the national fashion organizations could be bothered to proceed to any such registration' (1986: 167). Significantly, in 1929, three of the key fashion houses—Lelong, Patou and Chanel—introduced their first prêt-à-porter lines. This event officially heralded the demise of haute couture and the rise of designer ready-to-wear clothing.

The Functionalist Theory and the Birth of Prêt-à-Porter

Chanel's new and innovative stylistic trends can be contextualized within the development of modernism. The modernist period in the visual arts, which spanned the 1920s and 1930s, evolved from the technological developments and inventions of the First World War period, and had an unprecedented impact upon all of the visual arts, including fashion and jewellery design. If the philosophical and aesthetic concerns of the modernist age seemingly only affected Chanel's work in a tangential way, her design direction was symptomatic of the thrust of the machine age, where function-alism and practicality prevailed. According to the 'functionalist theory' of the 1920s, the structure of the form was determined by its function and the use of superfluous decoration was considered incompatible with machine production. 'Form follows func-tion'—an edict of the extremely influential Bauhaus School of Design (established in Germany in 1919)—became the modernist slogan.

Interestingly, numerous design historians, including Neret (1986) and Sparke (1987), have compared the standardization of her designs, and in particular her range of famous 'little black dresses', with a similar production mentality that inspired Henry Ford in the automobile industry. Neret argues that a certain black dress by Chanel 'would become a sort of uniform' that women everywhere 'would want to wear'. It conformed to a universal standard that was characterized by simplicity, a streamlined silhouette and a distinct lack of unnecessary detail. He compared it to the stylistic standardization of automobile manufacture, which 'would guarantee the quality of the car' (1986: 172). In the 1920s, the industrial design emphasis was on function, and the total modularization of all of the component parts of the machine. Ford's famous retort, when referring to his Model T Ford, that 'it didn't matter what colour it was, as long as it was black' epitomizes the uniformity of the machine age aesthetic that domi-nated design in the 1920s. In October 1926, American *Vogue* proclaimed: 'The Chanel "Ford"—the frock that all of the world will wear—is of black crêpe de chine. The bodice blouses slightly at front and sides and has a tight bolero at the back'. Instantaneously, Chanel achieved the objectives that Stepanova and Popova, the Russian Constructiv-ists, were unable to realize. The key to this success was 'the impersonal simplicity of the dress' (Neret, 1986: 172) and the fact that Chanel had produced a 'standard which appealed to every taste' (Mackerell, 1992: 11).

In other ways, Chanel's innovations underlined the modernist adage of functional-ism and the use of modularization and standardization as the basis of mass produc-tion. As Wilcox and Mendes (1991) observe, Chanel was renowned for her customary attention to detail and her dressmaking skills, which she perfected over many years. She insisted that pockets could hold cigarettes and that buttons and buttonholes were functional and not just decorative appendages. While Chanel's use of expensive trimming saw her work described as *'pauvreté de luxe'*, it was very much part of the machine aesthetic of the modernist period. In terms of embracing new technological materials, Chanel used innovatory resins and plastics in her 'fake' costume jewel-lery. This new fashion style was based on the concept that jewellery no longer had to advertise one's status and wealth, but had instead become a symbol of popular aes-thetic 'taste'. Laver (1982: 130) insists that Chanel was the designer who 'did the most to displace that tradition of elegance' that dominated the era prior to the First World War, and that she undoubtedly helped to change the way status was shown through dress.

Mass production, in its true sense, did not evolve fully in the world of high fashion until after the Second World War. Chanel was one of the first haute couture designers to open a small ready-to-wear section in her *maison* in 1929. Duplicates of the same garment were offered for sale in a range of sizes, with the price including one alteration. Other designers followed suit, and by the mid-1930s the majority of haute couture salons in Paris offered similar ready-to-wear lines. Chanel's philosophy of fashion design was determined by her belief that 'a fashion is not just for one person, nor even for a group; if a fashion is not popular with great numbers of people, it is not a fashion' (Beaton, 1954: 163). She observes that 'a copy could only be a copy', but also recognizes that 'imitation was a visible sign of success' (Carter, 1980: 59). In his biography, *Chanel Solitaire*, Baillen (1973: 72) quotes a tempestuous Chanel as saying: 'I don't create fashion for three or four tarts.' As late as 1953, Chanel reiterated these feelings: 'I am no longer interested in dressing a few hundred women, private clients; I shall dress thousands of women' (*Vogue*, February 1953). This statement forecasts the future destiny of haute couture.

Chanel's sense of timing and her ability to seize the moment were crucial to her success. Chanel was 'a pioneer of the new casualness' (Hollander, 1984: 83), with comfort and practicality becoming her trademark. Chanel recognized that the rigid concept of social stratification had changed in the 1920s, as the economic instability of life at this time did not make it unusual to see Russian grandees[3] in Paris working as taxi-drivers and grand duchesses employed as models. Marly (1980) comments: 'There were some proud names who had become poor' (1980: 147). The lifestyles of the rich and fashionable were changing dramatically. Many well-to-do women could be seen riding on trams, trains and buses, and this necessitated clothing that offered greater freedom of movement. A less rigorous social stratification, and the move away from sartorial formality in dress, encouraged Chanel to extend the formal boundaries further by introducing working-class garments into the world of haute couture. Horst observed that 'In those days, fashion wasn't for elegant women only. It was a part of life. Women who didn't have much money had little sewing ladies around the corner who copied the designers . ;. . It was Chanel who made it all simpler' (cited in di Grappa, 1980: 72).

Chanel's Coup d'État: Poor Boy Fabric and Non-gender Stereotyping

Chanel achieved her stylistic *coup d'état* by two means: her choice of new materials; and the adaptation of men's clothing for womenswear. During the war, the knitted material called 'jersey', which had previously only been used for hosiery and underwear, had stockpiled in the textile dealer Rodier's warehouse. It was an improbable material for haute couture to consider, as 'it seemed totally unsuitable for tailoring, too poor and soft' (Charles-Roux, 1981: 105). Jersey was described as being a 'drab, beige colour and having a hard-to-handle weave', and was 'primarily worn by sportsmen and fishermen' (Mackerell, 1992: 22). Chanel bought the entire surplus in 1916 for a very competitive price, despite the fact that it defied 'the conventions of luxury', and consequently its adoption by haute couture 'called for purer lines and created a revolution in costume and appearance' (Leymarie, 1987: 57). Her metamorphosis of this poor man's material into a fabric caused a fashion revolution—the first time in haute couture that a cheap 'second-class' material was used as an outer garment. It was subsequently adopted as an excellent medium for mass production, expanding the ready-to-wear trade. Significantly, this humble fabric introduced an element of popular culture into traditional haute couture.

When Chanel officially went into haute couture at 21 Rue Cambon, 'her lease forbade her from making dresses'; however, as 'jersey was not considered a fabric', she was not breaking the law (Galante, 1973: 36). Devoid of superficial trimmings, these early tricot garments designed by Chanel exuded an effortless style, which emphasized comfort and ease of wearing and epitomized the liberation of youth. There was no stiffness or defined shape. Her two-piece suits featured a slightly gathered skirt and a long jacket, with the material looking limp and quite unremarkable! It was exactly this commonplace appearance that seemed so revolutionary at the time. Chanel used jersey on such a massive scale that she opened her own factory at Asnières, initially called Tricots Chanel and then later Tissus Chanel (Mackerell, 1992: 27). Other 'popular' or non-elitist materials were incorporated into Chanel's haute couture collections, such as tartan, quilting and the synthetic fabric rayon—called 'artificial' silk. The manufacture of artificial silk was perfected in the 1920s, and was eminently suitable for Chanel's 'little black dresses' because of its excellent draping qualities. Similarly, when the supply of expensive furs was interrupted, Chanel 'turned to the more modest furs, like beaver and rabbit, thus transforming the shortage into an opportunity for greater inventiveness and style' (Leymarie, 1987: 57). This broke 'the bounds of hierarchy and tradition', since 'even a woman of modest means could afford a fur stole, or a fur wrap of fox, worn casually across the shoulders' (Bailey, 1988: 130).

As an innovator in textile usage, Chanel also introduced British tweeds into the female fashion domain. She procured her fine tweeds from Linton Tweed Ltd of Carlisle, and in 1927 opened a boutique in London where she sold tweed cardigan suits 'which moved with the body and did not crease' (Mackerell, 1992: 28) as both summer and winter fashion. Fashion historians have documented that Chanel's strength lay in her affinity with the fabrics she used. Valerie Mendes (in Mendes and de la Haye, 1999: 12) argues that 'some couturiers are irrevocably associated with their favourite materials' and that 'certain fabrics can develop a symbolic relationship to the fashion trends of a particular period'. In this instance, 'textured tweeds were perfect for Chanel's classic suits'. Chanel's choice of informal and comfortable fabric suited the more active lifestyles of women, and provided suitable corporate dress as more women were working outside of the home.

Figure 2.3 Gabrielle (Coco) Chanel, portrait wearing 'little black dress', Paris, 1937. Photographer: Lipnitzki/Roger Violet/Getty Images.

Another significant contribution to the democratization of fashion was Chanel's direct appropriation and popularization of male attire, which recognized and reflected the changing status of women in this modernist era. As well as using male fabrics, she drew inspiration from divergent sources such as the straight jackets that Marines wore, men's woollen sweaters, cuffed shirts and cufflinks, Norwegian male work clothes, sailors' flared trousers and her nephew's English blazer. In 1920, she launched her masculine-style baggy yachting trousers, and in 1922 her wide-legged flared beach pyjamas (Mackerell, 1992: 33).[4] Writing from a feminist perspective, Evans and Thornton (1991: 57) argue that Chanel's contribution to women's fashion was an 'adaptation of the forms and details, but above all the meanings, of a certain type of masculine dress to that of women'. Specifically:

> Her approach to style was analogous to that of classical male dandyism—that essentially masculine cult of distinction which was crucially mediated through dress.[5] Dandyism offered the possibility of social mobility, something which was of the first importance to Chanel personally, and more generally to women in the changing social climate in the early years of the century. (1991: 57)

Cecil Beaton (1954) similarly observes that:

> Women began to look more and more like young men, reflecting either their new emancipa-
> tion or their old perversity . . . and that as a dress designer . . . Chanel was virtually nihilistic,
> for behind her clothes was an implied but unexpressed philosophy: the clothes do not really
> matter at all, it is the way you look that counts. (1954: 162)

For Hollander (1983), Palmer White (1986) and Evans and Thornton (1991), Chanel's adaptation of male attire was not primarily used to promote fundamental feminine psychology or feminist ideology; rather, it employed a lack of gender stereotyping as a seductive principle. In Hollander's terms: 'Chanel was never a feminist' and it was her view that a woman's 'practical success was never to preclude the sovereign aim of being seductive' (1983: 84).

An equally significant hypothesis is that the masculine model of power allowed greater social mobility within a male-dominated culture (Evans and Thornton, 1991: 57). If fashion is recognized as a cultural construction, then independence and equality in female dress should reflect the changing values of that society. The understated female bodies of the 1920s attempted to create a physical and social profile equitable to that of their male counterparts. Arguably, Chanel's appropriation of 'masculine power' and her 'adaptation of the meanings of masculine dress to that of women' (Evans and Thornton, 1991: 57) contrasts with Schiaparelli's apparent indifference to the seriousness and restrictions of masculine meaning in dress. For example, Chanel adapted the masculine uniform of red riding coats into evening redingotes and later into ladies' housecoats (Palmer White, 1986: 99). Yet did these clothes necessarily redress women's undermined position in society?

Interestingly, both Chanel and her great rival, Schiaparelli (see Chapter 3) created a stylized man's dinner jacket covered with black sequins. Chanel's garment was created in 1926 and Schiaparelli's in January 1931. While Chanel's version reflected her liking for 'gaudy rich ornaments on the surface of a simple structure' (Hollander, 1983: 83), Schiaparelli contributed to 'reducing the gap between the sexes' by creating 'hard chic' clothes which had 'a militant, masculine quality' (Palmer White, 1986: 97). Both garments reflected the relative financial independence and assertiveness of the post-war woman. Schiaparelli's model mimicked a more mannish mode, with widened and squared shoulders that seemingly 'concealed feminine vulnerability in an almost belligerent manner' (Palmer White, 1986: 97). This silhouette was to become the dominant look of the 1940s, and seemed to forecast the 1980s concept of 'power dressing' for women. Both designers question the representation of sexual identity in dress, and reflect the changing social mores of the 1920s.

Thus far, this chapter has outlined the ways in which Chanel contributed to the decline of elitism in haute couture by breaking down traditional concepts and ways of merchandising fashion. Chanel deviated from the elitist nature of haute couture both by creating a 'working-class look' through her choice of non-luxuriant fabric—her inspiration being drawn primarily from working-class male attire—and by embracing a philosophy of copying and mass production, which denied exclusiveness and uniqueness. In this respect, certain parallels can be drawn between Chanel's iconoclastic alternatives and the Cubists' attempts to fuse art and life. Braque and Picasso, for example, used unorthodox materials in their collaged work, incorporated the world of popular culture into their compositions, and used reproduced imagery which reflected the commercial and social stereotyping of the bourgeois world. Just as visual paradoxes informed the work of the Cubists, social paradoxes informed the design work of Coco Chanel. With her 'poor boy' fashions and imitation jewellery, she aimed to create an image of middle-class informality rather than emphasizing the affectations of the upper classes, yet her garments were consistently priced in a bracket far above the economic means of the average working girl. As Ruth Lynam (1972) points out: 'The simplest suit or dress from the House of Chanel cost as much as gold and silver embroideries of other designers' (1972: 119). Despite the apparent lack of what Veblen (1965) refers to as 'conspicuous consumption' in her garments, hems were always hand-rolled and weighted chains were inserted into the backs of the jackets. When she dressed her clients in garments of austere simplicity, she would then heap strands of costume jewellery[6] around their necks, on their wrists, hands and ears. Even if the pieces of jewellery were made of rubies or emeralds, Chanel once commented that they would do, 'so long as they look like junk!' (Lynam, 1972: 118). Was it perhaps this incongruous juxtaposition of poverty and expense that created her fashion success?

Chanel: Modernist Artist, Dressmaker or Business Entrepreneur?

While Laver (1995: 235) has alluded to Chanel as 'an important part of the whole artistic movement', it is interesting that she never considered herself to be an artist. This was in contrast to Poiret, who was insistent on promoting the illusion that he was a creative artist who was not concerned with commercialism. Even the performance of the Russian Ballet's *Schéhérazade* (1910), which exerted unprecedented influence upon the arts in general in Paris (and underlined the direction of Poiret's designs), did not impact directly upon Chanel's work. 'We're in trade, not art,' Chanel said, 'and the soul of trade is good faith' (Baillen, 1973: 75). She defined dressmaking rather as a technique or a craft—a trade by which one could earn a living. Arguably, a considerable amount of attention has been paid in biographies to her social contacts with many artists, writers and intellectuals, but there is little evidence that art ever specifically inspired her work. The Scottish Arts Council's *Fashion 1900–1939* catalogue concluded:

In fact, despite her great friendship with artists such as Picasso and Cocteau, Chanel seems consciously anti-art; even her salon was modish rather than modern; she, alone among the young couturiers, never appears in *Bon Ton* which, in its 1920 prospectus, sets out to be 'the mirror in which all the arts are reflected'. Equally indicative is her derisive comment on her arch rival Elsa Schiaparelli as 'that Italian artist who makes clothes'.

The 'synthesis' or common thread that tied the visual arts together in the 1920s was based on the 'machine age aesthetic', as it was called, which was fashioned not only by the fundamental shapes of machine imagery but by the flat planes and simple geometric shapes evident in non-Western art. Unknowingly, Picasso initiated the Cubist movement when he created a landmark painting in 1907 entitled *Les Demoiselles d'Avignon*. He introduced a new spatial language, where three-dimensional, cube-like forms were arranged in a two-dimensional space; this art movement developed well into the 1920s and impacted on the majority of decorative artists. While Richard Martin, in his book *Cubism and Fashion* (1988), cites examples of Chanel's work, he argues that it was more plausible 'that it was not the art of Cubism, per se, but the culture of Cubism that influenced fashion, just as the culture of Cubism might be said

Figure 2.4 Gabrielle (Coco) Chanel, checked two-piece suit, France, 1965. Collection: Powerhouse Museum, Sydney. Photographer: Powerhouse Museum Photography Department. A classic example of a Chanel tailored suit featuring the signature pussycat bow, embraced by the American market in the 1960s.

to align it with new ideas in theatre, literature and, eventually, the movies' (1998: 16). A year earlier, Leymarie (1987) made a similar statement when she argued that Chanel's 'consecration of humble fabrics and furs paralleled the poetics of Cubism'—just as, in 1912, Braque 'had invented the breakthrough of the *papiers collés* [collages]' into the fine arts, thereby rejecting the traditional mode of painting (1987: 57). Mackerell (1992), who is considered a major authority on Chanel's interest in art, describes how Chanel hired the Russian Futurist artist Iliazd, who had designed textiles with Sonia Delaunay in 1922 and who, in retrospect, may have strengthened her ties with Cubism. As Mackerell suggests, this involvement seems to establish some link between Chanel's fashion and the fine arts: 'Chanel's combination of pure lines and plain colours often drew comparisons with the contemporary art movement, Cubism, with particular reference to the Analytical phase which ennobled humble materials and muted colours' (1992: 23).

Otherwise, Mackerell at best rather vaguely suggests the similarity between Chanel's 'little black dresses' and both the black and white photographs produced by Steichen in 1923 and the black and white films of the 1920s that 'expressed the age' (1992: 30–1). Reflecting on the interplay that did exist between fashion designers and fine artists in the 1920s, the modernist photographer Horst P. Horst perhaps best summed it up when he stated that, at that time, 'Everybody worked together, talking fashion and art' (cited in di Grappa, 1980: 71).

Chanel's success both in the haute couture world and the international marketplace has been meticulously documented in France. Her business acumen and her sense of timing assured her both financial and professional success. Arguably, Chanel's burgeoning international reputation was bolstered not only by her design prowess: there was general acknowledgment that her great financial success resulted from her ability to respond to market demands. This capitalistic feat achieved by Chanel helped to propel fashion to the fifth largest industry in France in the 1920s.

–3–

Framing Fashion: The Artists Who Made Clothes

A most difficult and unsatisfying art, because as soon as a dress is born it has already become a thing of the past.

Elsa Schiaparelli

Arguably, all fashion is not art, but on occasion it can become art. While these words might not describe the work of Coco Chanel, they can aptly be applied to a number of other practitioners—including Sonia Delaunay, Liubov Popova and Varvara Stepanova, Elsa Schiaparelli, Cristóbal Balenciaga, Viktor & Rolf, Martin Margiela and Hussein Chalayan—who approached fashion design from an artist's perspective. This chapter will reinforce the links that tie fashion and art practice together. Many artists have turned to fashion as a 'living' art form and have applied artistic methodologies to fabric rather than canvas or clay. Fashion as art is a theme that has been embraced by numerous curators and museum directors alike, and addressed in major fashion exhibitions over the past twenty years.

MODERNIST ABSTRACT DESIGN

Design historians and critics tend to discuss the 1920s, in modernist terms, as a decade in which the successful integration of the fine arts, architecture, graphic design and the applied arts was achieved. A symbiotic relationship between the fine arts, and the applied and decorative arts, emerged and led to a more conceptually enhanced aesthetic direction in fashion. Fine artists such as Sonia Delaunay in Paris, and Liubov Popova and Varvara Stepanova in Moscow, successfully applied the dynamics of this modern visual language to a utilitarian art form: clothing. By applying their aesthetic concerns to both fashion and textile design, they pioneered the practical application of abstraction to everyday objects, and thus consolidated the link between the art and design movements of the post-war era. In fact, Anscombe (1984) argues that it was the familiarity of abstract designs on textiles that led to the acceptance of the avant-garde 'abstract' art seen in the museums. She observes the significant fact that: 'The character of the early Bauhaus textiles . . . mark[s] a departure from the textile patterns produced before the war in its abandonment of conventional patterning

Figure 3.1 Unknown designer, black georgette sleeveless dress with bands of geometric silk embroidery and couched metal thread, France, c. 1925. Collection: Powerhouse Museum, Sydney. Photographer: Powerhouse Museum Photography Department. The flat cylindrical surfaces of the 1920s garments became perfect canvasses for the two-dimensional art deco designs of the era.

and naturalistic ornament, as in Russia (Constructivism), Paris and Vienna (Weiner Werkstätte), it was primarily through textile design that the current ideas of abstract art were brought to a wider public' (1984: 136).

This modern visual language of abstraction—characterized by simple, geometric and modularized forms reminiscent of machine technology—was 'implicit in the development of modernism' (Lynton, 1980: 19) and was inherent in the design work of the three prominent women artists. Their work epitomized the ideals of the machine age aesthetic through their attention to structure and material, the underlying mathematical structure of their designs, and their use of bold, dynamic colour. These artists expanded and extended the traditional aesthetic boundaries of art and design through their fashion and textile design and fulfilled the aims of the modernist movement. Delaunay, in particular, was able to apply her colour theories (originally meant for her canvases) directly to textile designs which, in turn, were used in the production of simply constructed garments.

DELAUNAY: CUBISM

For Sonia Delaunay, painting was a form of poetry where colours were words, and the pattern of the colours created rhythms in the composition. Her early life as a painter was closely allied with that of her husband, Cubist painter Robert Delaunay, and with their experiments in colour orchestration and the founding of the art movement called Orphism in 1913. When she first moved to Paris from Russia in 1905, there was a great deal of interaction among Russian and Western European artists, and she met most of the avant-garde artists including Picasso, Braque and Derain (Heller, 1987: 122–3). A systematic development from painting to applied art and craft, fashion and textile design emerges throughout Delaunay's career. Her brilliance as a colourist is generally acknowledged, and this talent inspired her to experiment extensively in media other than pigments.

Unlike Chanel, as Delaunay viewed fashion design as an alternate mode of artistic expression, her interest in fashion as a commercial enterprise is overshadowed by her conceptual interests and her more general desire to bring material to life. When questioned about her fashion design in an interview for the *New York Times* (4 December 1977), Sonia remarked: 'I wasn't interested in fashion, but in applying colour and light to fabrics.' Based on her colour theories of 'Simultaneous Contrasts', her first *Simultaneous Dress* of 1913 was 'a creation in sheer fabric, flannel, silk and lace in a riot of colours that ranged from English rose to blue, scarlet to tangerine yellow' (Madsen, 1989: 122). Immediately, with the interplay of colours and abstract form, the leap from Cubist collage to fashion was complete. Delaunay's famous comment to Tristan Tzara, the Dadaist poet, that: 'If painting has become part of our lives, it is because women have been wearing it!' underlines this transformation (cited in Anscombe, 1984: 120). Her friendship with Tzara and her ideological ties with the Dadaist painters and poets were demonstrated in her series of *robes-poèmes* (dress poems) of 1922. The *robes-poèmes* consist of a series of abstract dress designs in which geometric blocks of colour are interspersed with lines of Tzara's Dada poetry. As the body moves, the interrelationship of colour and text becomes very fluid and creates a variety of different simultaneous juxtapositions. One *robe-poème* called *The Eternally Feminine* caressingly played with the wearer's body, with the 'I' appearing at the bend of an arm, and the 'e' at the fingers (Madsen, 1989: 180). Ideologically, her comprehension of the ephemeral nature of fashion as opposed to the enduring values of institutionalized art would have appealed to the Dadaists.

Delaunay's collaborative work with Dadaist poet Tristan Tzara extended to designing costumes for his notorious play entitled *Le Coeur à Gaz* in 1923, which featured Satie's music, Van Doesburg's sets and Man Ray's films. While the immortality achieved by this Dadaist production was due to the outrageous nature of the play, the resultant publicity brought Delaunay's costumes to the public eye. The solid cardboard costumes, which conceptually bridged the gap between dress and sculpture, did not allow for much movement (Richter, 1965: 190), and their 'direct audacity' was described by the Dadaist René Crevel in 1920 as being 'immediately impressive' (Cohen, 1978: 187). 'Sonia's costumes', as they were described by Madsen (1989), 'were renderings of stiff, formal bourgeois evening attire on cardboard encasements that parodied the clothes and characters' (1989: 189). Avant-garde spectacles like Dada performances and poetry readings[1] helped to break down earlier notions about clothing as a cover for the body, replacing them with an image of the body as a fluid screen, capable of reflecting back a present constantly undergoing redefinition and transformation (Chadwick, 1990: 257).

Delaunay's theatrical costumes have been compared with Picasso's costume designs for *Parade* of 1917. Interestingly, this analogy has been overshadowed by Damase's (1972) remark that 'Delaunay's costumes were still more original' and 'few works can be said to have such a far-reaching impact' (1972: 131)—a comment which perhaps refers to Delaunay's important contribution to modern fashion design. According to Buckberrough (1980: 64), 'the following year, cardboard costumes exhibiting the same frontal, abstract conception as those from the play (and perhaps based on its designs), were paraded before high society'. These geometric futuristic creations became the forerunners of Delaunay's textile and fashion designs of the 1920s, and in 1923 the Lyons textile manufacturer Bianchini-Ferier commissioned her to design fifty patterns for fabrics. This event launched her commercial designing career.

Figure 3.2 Sonia Delaunay, brightly coloured geometric swimsuits, 1925. Collection: Hulton Archives. Photographer: Luigi Diaz/Stringer/ Getty Images.

Delaunay's financial success resulted from the production of the initial textile designs for the Lyons textile firm. In Paris in the same year, she marketed her work in a fashion booth at the Bal Bullier. In 1924 she established a clothing boutique, the Atelier Simultané, on the Boulevard Malesherbes for printing simultaneous textiles and producing a wide range of clothing and accessories. While she primarily hand-painted 'simultaneous' fabrics and tapestries for a growing private clientele, her influence as a designer had a considerable impact on international fashion trends. Her overseas market—particularly in America—was steadily improving. Delaunay documents that 'scarves, ballet costumes, bathing suits, and embroidered coats, employing the principles of collage, were sold throughout the world' (Cohen, 1978: 211). The fusion of art and commercial enterprise in decorative design was heralded at the 1925 'Exposition des Arts Décoratifs et Industriels Modèrnes' in Paris, where Delaunay's fashions, textiles and paintings were displayed in the Boutique Simultanée, a business enterprise collaboratively run with the furrier Jacques Heim. This international exhibition reflected modern industrialized post-war culture and art. Buckberrough (1980) points out that, after this important event, 'the "modern style" typified by Sonia Delaunay's creations took precedence in the French decorative arts' (1980: 67).

Not only is Delaunay's accreditation of bringing modern art into modern life mirrored in the doctrines of other modernist movements in the 1920s—including the Bauhaus—but the creation of this universal visual language through the confluence of form and function dominated the machine aesthetic which arose out of the technological 'renaissance' of the 1920s. While some complained that Delaunay's fashion and textile designs were elitist in nature, as they were prohibitively costly and therefore aimed at the wealthy, she counteracted this claim by attempting to interface with industry by the mass production of her patented *tissu-patron*. Adapting them to commercial reproduction, these fabric patterns prepackaged the dress pattern with the textile fabric, thereby protecting the unity of the design while being marketed at a minimal cost to the consumer. While this enterprise should have been successful, in practice it was not, as the standardization of the design did not allow for individual figure variations, and consequently most women found that they needed individual alterations for a proper fit. She promoted this modernist idea in her public lecture given at the Sorbonne University in Paris in 1927, entitled 'The Influence of Painting on Fashion Design', where she emphasized the 'constructive' aspects of dress—which she stated were 'clearly influenced by painting', maintaining that 'the cut of the dress is conceived by its creator simultaneously with its decoration' (Cohen, 1978: 206). She reinforced this belief later in her autobiographical text of 1967, when she argued that the true beauty of an object is not an effect of taste, but is ultimately tied to its function. She also emphasized that the mechanical and the dynamic were the essential elements of the practical dimensions of that time.

Undoubtedly, Delaunay's major contribution to the decline of elitism is evidenced by the application of her artistic theories to design in the applied arts rather than by the practice of mass-producing her goods. Her most significant contribution centres on her prophesies for fashion production in the future. In her essay, 'Les Artistes et L'Avenir de la Mode' (first published in 1931; see Cohen, 1978: 208), she forecasts that the future democratization of fashion will 'raise the general standards of the industry', and suggests that the primary aims of industry should be twofold. First, she predicts that laboratories of research dealing with the practical design of clothing will develop in a way that closely parallels the necessities of life. Second, she suggests that industries will lower the costs of production by mass production of goods and will concentrate on the expansion of sales. Delaunay's endorsement of ready-to-wear fashion in the late 1920s is recorded in her autobiography, *Nous Irons Jusqu'au Soleil* (Delaunay, 1978):

> Before the inescapable reign of ready-made clothes, we were enjoying the last days of the 'modèle unique' before the first liberated women would be imitated by thousands of others. The ready-to-wear clothes would reclaim the conquests of the 1920s and the poem-dresses would fill the streets. (1978: 93)

And so they did.

Delaunay's contribution to the redefinition of textile and fashion design within the context of the fine arts cannot be underestimated. Until recently, Sonia Delaunay has not been fully accredited for the very important role that she played in extending and expanding the traditional aesthetic boundaries of art and design.

STEPANOVA AND POPOVA: RUSSIAN CONSTRUCTIVISM

Utopian socialist ideals directed the work of the Soviet designers, Varvara Stepanova and Luibov Popova. Stepanova and Popova were not haute couture designers, but ideologically committed artists whose contribution to modernist principles in relation to dress, aesthetics and functionality countered commercial fashion. Encapsulated in their work was the Russian Constructivists' philosophic ideal that clothing as an art form should impact directly on the masses. Before the 1917 Revolution, the new communists saw fashion as a bourgeois phenomenon, having no social utility other than that of social elitism (Stern, 2004). Pragmatically, as a fashion designer, Stepanova's approach more closely paralleled that of Chanel, whose basic concern with the union of structure and form was shared by the Constructivists. Both women came from a dressmaking background and placed great emphasis on technical skills. It seems that in both capitalist and socialist societies, this utilitarian-oriented design work led, in varying degrees, to increased industrial production and the greater merging of artistic and commercial activities. Both Stepanova (the wife of artist Alexander Rodchenko) and Popova had moved towards utilitarian clothing and textile design by 1921, as they were strongly motivated to serve the people and committed to the practical application of Constructivist ideals. Unfortunately, the influence of Russian fashion and textile design was not as extensive, nor did it have the same degree of influence, as Delaunay's work. Yet their work shared the same dynamic interplay of diagonals, the simulation of crisp, clean machine lines, and the clarity of brilliant hues, and was more in keeping with the tenets of the machine age aesthetics.

Perhaps the remarkable visual similarity between the work of artists such as Delaunay and that of the Russian Constructivists can be explained in part by historical, economic and circumstantial factors. Delaunay, while a French citizen, was born in the Ukraine (Russia), and this explains why the influence of Russian folk art is quite evident in her early work. According to Anscombe (1984) and Chadwick (1990), the post-war years reflected a time of diverse artistic activity, which advocated the identification of avant-garde art with modernist design as a means of bolstering the French economy. In Paris, after the war, there was a social milieu[2] of artists, designers, couturiers, writers and photographers in which an 'extraordinarily rich interplay of ideas existed', and which led to 'numerous collaborations in cabarets, illustrated books, ballets and schemes for interior design' (Anscombe, 1984: 114–15). Applied artists, of course, were not immune from this cultural environment, and it provided a great incentive to the applied arts as well. Women designers[3] actively involved in the applied arts benefited from this cultural environment and, turning to textile design, they supported the French textile industry's efforts 'to recover quickly from the slump caused by the war' (Chadwick, 1990: 257). Additionally, as Chadwick observes: 'The years during which Delaunay was most involved in textile and clothing design in Paris correspond to the period when Russian artists sought to find socially useful applications for their aesthetic theories' (1990: 257).

In Russia, a similar economic deprivation existed where 'crippling shortages of raw materials after the Revolution and civil war of 1918–21' prevented the actualization of many plans and theories of the avant-garde artists and architects (Chadwick, 1990: 257). According to Chadwick, the only exception was Moscow's large textile industry, which was able to mass-produce the Constructivists' abstracted fabric designs, where 'kinetic forms symbolized emancipation and mobility' (1990: 257). While this work was ideologically sound, in accordance with the Russian Constructivists' ideals, the Russian historians Sarabianov and Adaskina (1990) argue that the production itself presented its own conditions as the technology of the textile print factory was geared towards printing small repeats (1990: 302). Lodder (1983) confirms that, at the beginning of the 1920s, industrial production was at a third of pre-war levels as 'materials and technological standards were limited' (1983: 145). It seems that Tatlin, Stepanova and Popova were the only Constructivist artists who attempted to put their projects relating to fashion into operation. The establishment of a standardized pattern was facilitated by Stepanova's self-imposed limitations. She used only a compass and ruler to design her work, which usually consisted of two-coloured patterns based on the circle, triangle and rectangle. This form of reductionist, formalistic art reflected the universal rhythms found not only in the organics of nature, but also in the systematic workings of well-oiled machines. Symbolically, several interpretations have been postulated. Laurentiev (1988) suggests that 'the geometric construction can be interpreted as the mechanization of the artist's labour', that it 'reflects the world of industry in graphic form', or perhaps functions 'as an expression of the principles of technological form' (1988: 83). These mechanistic analogies clearly imply that Russian Constructivist textile work was inextricably immersed in, and directed by, the industrial process. Popova's textile designs also emphasized an ultimate simplicity printed on ordinary cotton, yet Stern (2004) argues that 'her use of geometrical forms originating in her previous abstract painting did not appeal to the masses, who obstinately continued to prefer cloth printed with floral techniques' (2004: 55). Lodder (1983) stresses that only the women's textile designs, rather than dress designs, progressed successfully beyond the conceptual stage (1983: 145–6), and she also points out that one of their greatest contributions was 'this new formulation, by a radical reassessment of the design process, which co-related the design process for cloth and clothing' (1983: 146). Significantly, it was this necessity for a total design process that inspired Delaunay to conceive her *tissu-patron*.

The Russian avant-garde's attempt to revolutionize clothing by designing anti-fashion garments only impacted upon a minority of individuals who used their dress to express their total commitment to communist ideology. By the 1930s, it had become apparent that clothing would not become an instrument of socialization, nor would it be used as a social condenser—workman's overalls would not replace traditional male garments, and individual dress would not be superseded by collective dress that offered utility, protection and anonymity.

SCHIAPARELLI: SURREALISM

In Europe, Chanel's competitor Elsa Schiaparelli created a more explicit form of anti-fashion. Like Delaunay, she was primarily a fine artist, but she found her inspiration in the use of paradoxical imagery, which often shared Freudian sexual associations apparent in the work of the Surrealists. The boundless development of novelty in her design and her unorthodox use of materials were instrumental in her ability to undermine the serious nature of traditional haute couture—a factor that often caused conflict with her peers. Chanel disparagingly referred to Schiaparelli as the 'Italian artist who made clothes'. This alluded to the fact that Schiaparelli did not have couturier training and was part of the artistic contingent made up of painters, writers, poets and film-makers in 1920s and 1930s Paris. Poiret, in his book *En Habillant L'Époque* (1931), comments on this lamentable decline of elitist practice and refers directly to designers such as Chanel and Schiaparelli, whom he considered to be instrumental in its demise. 'It has profited them considerably,' argues Poiret, 'but at the same time they have forfeited the title of couturier and fashion creator' (Ewing, 1986: 99).

Both Coco Chanel and Elsa Schiaparelli are frequently credited with playing a major part in both the aesthetic and social revolutions that occurred in fashion in the 1920s and 1930s. According to Palmer White (1988: 59): 'Schiaparelli, like Chanel, accentuated youthfulness and freedom of movement' and 'in the battle of the sexes, Schiaparelli's clothes reflected an entire social revolution: defensive by day and aggressively seductive by night'.

Schiaparelli's ability to convert something ordinary into a witty item of high fashion can be compared with Chanel's successful introduction of artisans' clothes into upper-class society. While Chanel's reputation in haute couture evolved from an initial adherence to the 'functionalist theory' of the machine age, and an astute assessment of the economics of supply and demand which emerged out of wartime restrictions, Schiaparelli's notoriety emerged from her anti-fashion. Like Dada's anti-art, which challenged the canons of the salon and the art academy, Schiaparelli questioned the notions and structures of institutions such as Parisian haute couture.

As with Delaunay, Elsa Schiaparelli's fashion career evolved from a fine art base. When she turned to fashion design, her work always retained a direct link with artistic

Figure 3.3 Elsa Schiaparelli, Butterfly evening dress, 1937. Photo: Lipnitzki/Roger Viollet/ Getty Images. Schiaparelli revolutionised evening wear by using unusual, almost surrealist motifs, like butterflies, printed on the fabrics.

methodologies. It was her association with the Dadaists and Surrealists which provided a wealth of symbolic meaning to each of her works. Throughout her designing career, she redefined and reconstituted the interrelationship between fashion and art. Despite her nonconformist attitudes and practices, she rose to an eminent position of power and influence in the world of haute couture. Like many of the Dadaists, her work 'took the form of an insurrection against all that was pompous, conventional, or even boring in the arts' (Chipp, 1973: 367). She eroded traditional and elitist practices through the use of unconventional materials, included explicit sexual imagery in the decorative detail of her garments, and used memorabilia from popular culture in her work.

A prime example of Schiaparelli's fascination with unusual materials and motifs led her to commission the Lyons textile firm, Calcombet, to produce silks and cottons with a pattern printed from newspaper clippings (about herself). The text juxtaposed fragments of articles written by fashion editors and journalists. (She included both favourable and unfavourable descriptions written about her work!) Some authors speculate that this visual displacement was either inspired by Picasso's daring collages of 1911 or by the newspaper hats that she had seen Scandinavian fisherwomen wear (Palmer White, 1986: 38). O'Neill (2005: 181) argues that 'the designer was herself keen to maintain that the overarching inspiration had been a Cubist painting by Picasso that had used newspaper as a collaged material'. In fact, he speculates that: 'It may well be that she got the idea from the Dada artist, Kurt Schwitters[4] himself, as she was well versed in modern art and was acquainted with many of the practitioners.' Scandalous as this was in the 1930s, this form of self-critique foreshadowed later postmodernist practice.

Schiaparelli's ability to combine the commonplace and the sensational into a single item is evident in her clear plastic necklace decorated with coloured insects that appeared to crawl over the wearer's neck. Not only is this a visually bizarre piece, but it stimulates a tactile sensory response. It seems that an art nouveau necklace featuring hybrid creatures, created by the famous French turn-of-the century jeweller Lalique, inspired this piece. The unorthodox subject matter and the combination of precious and non-precious materials synthesized in the piece were properties that characterized both art nouveau and Surrealist work.

Discussing the Surrealist phenomenon as 'a duality of rational–irrational', or the actual as opposed to the depicted, is manifest in the world of dreams or the imagination. This juxtaposition of opposing realities heightens the paradoxical nature of the work. In this way, Schiaparelli's work employs the conventional framework of formally tailored garments as 'the perfect foil for her gloriously adventurous embroideries', which were 'inspired by a range of historical and traditional embroideries including magnificently embroidered ecclesiastical vestments' (Wilcox and Mendes, 1991: 104). For Wilcox and Mendes, her work 'alternated between the bizarre and the lyrical' (1991: 50), and 'deliberately used provocative combinations of old and new techniques and materials' in order 'to unite the best of the fine and decorative arts' (1991: 120). In this respect, Wilcox and Mendes underline the crucial link between Schiaparelli's fashion and both art nouveau and Surrealist art practices.

In 1934, Schiaparelli first employed the firm Lesage et Cie to produce hand-embroidered belts and later necklaces, yokes and *trompe l'œil* collars in a highly coloured and baroque style. At the time, it seemed inconceivable that she could single-handedly revive this flagging industry. Palmer White (1986) consistently observes that no other couturier has ever done more to promote embroidery than Elsa Schiaparelli. Summarizing Schiaparelli's career, Wilcox and Mendes (1998) add that: 'Slowly, in a reaction to the beading of the 1920s, she returned to the use of embroidery materials employed centuries before—paillettes from medieval times—and asked for designs recalling stained-glass windows and liturgical ornamentation of the sixteenth century' (1998: 64). While Schiaparelli's collection themes determined the embroidered designs, Palmer White adds that Poiret argues that 'she conceived the garments that would enhance the embroidery' (Palmer White, 1988: 63). It was precisely the fairly unremarkable cut of her garments that so effectively allowed the ornamentation to capture the attention and imagination of the viewer.

Working closely with Albert Lesage, Schiaparelli encouraged him to experiment with innovative materials and techniques: 'Albert used . . . Murano-blown glass for little flowers; glass stones and beach pebbles; he crushed gelatino beads to lend them the appearance of hammered coins; and employed metal to reflect its new uses (in the modern machine age)' (Palmer White, 1986: 62).

These collaborations culminated in such extravagant projects as the elaborately embroidered suit of 1937, where Schiaparelli cleverly incorporated the use of ruby mirrors as part of the bodice design. These were strategically placed across the bustline, creating not only a baroque sumptuosity, but imparting a theatrical touch—mirroring the reflection of the viewer. These mirrors, perhaps used in jest as a means to divert voyeurism, were considered incompatible with high fashion.

Unlike Chanel, Schiaparelli created, by innovative synthesis, a certain eclectic and non-exclusive 'exclusiveness'. She blatantly used artistic techniques meant to 'trick the eye', and appropriated symbols from one visual context for use in another. The assimilation of optical deviations within an elitist framework of fine fabric and craftsmanship created a visual anomaly. The impact of her work was heightened by the interrelationship of the Surrealist psycho-sexual imagery with the traditional framework of embroidery, Lesage and beaded techniques. Schiaparelli, having emerged from a fine art background, embraced the artistic circles of artists, poets and writers and became a great friend to many of the Dadaist artists, including the notorious Salvador Dalí. So much of her work underscored the symbiotic relationship that has always existed between fashion and art.

Significantly, the earliest influences upon Schiaparelli's work were two major exhibitions in 1925: the 'Exposition des Arts Décoratifs et Industriels Modèrnes', Paris and the first Surrealist exhibition held in Paris. The former display of applied arts made Schiaparelli aware of the new materials that heralded the new machine age, and she subsequently adopted technological innovations and exploited the use of industrial materials such as plastics, latex, cellophane, rayon crêpe, coiled spring and wire into her work.

The Surrealist exhibition of 1925, in particular, inspired Schiaparelli to produce her earliest design sensation, the *trompe l'œil* woollen sweater, two years later. This visual deception expounds the Surrealist idea that reality is often an illusion. The hand-knitted top appeared to be decorated with a bow at the neckline. While the illusion of the three-dimensional butterfly bow was sustained at a distance, it diminished as the

Figure 3.4   Elsa Schiaparelli trying hats on model, February 1951. Photo: Nina Leen/Time & LifePictures/Getty Images. Schiaparelli became notorious for her 'mad hats' which became zany metaphors for Surrealist art.

viewer approached the wearer, forcing the viewer to participate in the joke when the visual paradox was discovered.

While Schiaparelli's use of paradoxical Surrealist imagery emerged in the 1920s, it gathered strength in the 1930s and reached its zenith in 1937 and 1938. In collaboration with Salvador Dalí, she produced the Desk Suit of 1936, which incorporated a vertical series of true and false pockets that were embroidered in strong raised relief (*bourré*) to look like drawers, with buttons for knobs. In this visual and conceptual paradox, the woman and her job become inextricably interwoven. As becomes evident, Schiaparelli's garments—like Dalí's three-dimensional pieces—should be interpreted within a social context. Through their appropriation of paradoxical imagery, her designs conjure symbolic associations that often relate to irrational feelings, sensory stimulations, totems and myths, and which seem to change depending on their environmental or social context. The symbolic associations inherent in her designs are also explicit in her choice of materials. For example, a tactile fabric that she called 'treebark' resembled its name and encompassed the body as bark enshrouds a tree trunk. Literally, the garment became a second skin, and at the same time created a visual dichotomy.

In 1943, the use of cellophane, velours, and glass fabrics called rhodophane dominated Schiaparelli's collection. *Vogue* described rhodophane as 'a brittle and fragile fabric with the transparency of glass, but it doesn't shatter like a window-pane'; glass belts 'which resembled Pyrex but were paper thin' adorned these unequivocal, sensational new garments (Palmer White 1986: 31). In this 'New Art', Schiaparelli created another conceptual paradox: a glass covering for the female body not unlike the glass display cases and windows in the department stores.[5]

When Schiaparelli appropriates fabrics and re-contextualizes them, their tactile surfaces can enhance both sexual and sensual provocation. This is evident in her dresses made in billiard table felt, and the rubber-lined hostess blouse that converts to an apron for kitchen work. This use of materials normally associated with the world of bars and brothels also juxtaposes the concept of elitist fashion in a non-elitist form. The erotic nature of the Tear Dress (1937–8) is implied, for example, in Schiaparelli's collaboration with Salvador Dalí to produce a textile that appeared to be covered in rips or tears. This illusion creates a visual fantasy that invites a tactile response to the actual fabric, something that needs to be handled as well as viewed.

In this way, Schiaparelli's work illustrates the convergence of elements of humour and provocation, in both Surrealist fashion and art. According to Palmer White, 'she ignored the sombre propriety then associated with hats' and instead 'gave them a playful and sometimes even satanic dash of humour' (1986: 100). Commenting on this tendency, Cecil Beaton (1954) refers to the 'invention of her own particular form of ugliness' which 'salubriously shocked a great many people' (1954: 184). The substantial role of humour in Schiaparelli's work is particularly evident in the Dalí-inspired Mutton Chop Hat, which went perfectly with a suit embroidered with cutlet motifs, the bathing suit with wriggling fish printed on the stomach, handbags that looked like tele-phones or birdcages, and long black gloves with clear windows for fingernails. Like certain art exhibitions, her collections were thematically presented; her Circus col-lection of 1938, for example, incorporated buttons depicting acrobats and, in one in-stance displayed (like a billboard) the words 'Beware of the Fresh Paint' on the back of a dress.

Other haute couture designers preferred overt political commentary[6] to sardonic wit. After the election of the Socialist Front Populaire in 1936, when 'strikes were declared throughout France', Schiaparelli 'brought out her Phrygian Bonnet, a sym-bol of freedom from enslavement, which the strikers had adopted' (Palmer White, 1986: 101). Historically, the Phrygian bonnet had been worn to identify freed slaves in Roman times, and was later adopted by the revolutionaries during the French Revolu-tion of 1789.

Like many Dadaist works, Schiaparelli's productions were always the result of col-laborative effort. She liaised with expert knitters, furriers, dyers, jewellers, embroider-ers and artists such as Dalí, Cocteau, Vertès, Van Dongen, Giacometti and Christian Bérard, questioning the concepts of uniqueness in both haute couture design and fine art. More generally, Schiaparelli mirrors the sentiments of the Dadaists when she refers to dress designing as a particularly transient art. This echoed Jean Coc-teau's view that: 'Fashion dies very young, so we must forgive it everything' (quoted by Steele, 1988: 251). Similarly, Laver wrote that: 'A fashionable dress is attractive (only) in the context of contemporary taste' (1967: 117). Schiaparelli (1954) declared her practice to be 'a most difficult and unsatisfying art, because as soon as a dress is born it has already become a thing of the past. Once you have created it, the dress no longer belongs to you. A dress cannot just hang like a painting on the wall, or like a book remain intact and live a long sheltered life' (1984 [1954]: 26).

> For *Vogue* editor Michael Boodro (1990), 'Perhaps the most intimate connection between art and fashion occurred during the heyday of Surrealism, when rationality was decidedly not the point'. Boodro argues that: 'Surrealist fashion was created in a spirit of fun, to amuse, to shock and—like so much else invented by the Surrealists—to question the basis on which judgements about art are made' (1990: 125–26).

Perhaps the visual paradox of Surrealist iconoclasm, initially conceived in film, was more effectively communicated through fashion and the applied arts than by two-dimensional media such as painting or photography. Fashion relates more directly to the conditions of life and to the nature of society, and this underlines its dominant appearance in the work of the Dadaists. Whereas Max Ernst used fashion imagery to elucidate, visually, the psycho-sexual associations of Freudian psychology, Schiaparelli created a more direct and dramatic paradox in her Shoe Hat of 1938—a work which refers to the 'repressed unconscious', where the 'device of displacement is at play within the language of clothes' (Evans and Thornton, 1991: 61). At the same time, it uses a sexual symbol, normally used to encase a foot, upon the head. Two other examples might include the Medusa-like head placed on the shoulder of a cocktail dress (whose writhing tendrils of hair suggest sexual provocation) and the 1937 Dalí-inspired Lobster and Parsley garment of white organdie (in which the image is strategically printed over the pubic area).[7] If the visual juxtaposition of such images elicits erotic symbolic significance, the images also serve to heighten the element of shock and sensationalism within the context of haute couture. The increasing notoriety of Schiaparelli's work not only challenged those established hierarchies through which meaning is ascribed to fashion, but questioned the traditions of one of the most elitist institutions of Parisian culture in the first half of the twentieth century. Her work provided a catalyst for later designers, including Karl Lagerfeld and Zandra Rhodes, to contribute to the neo-Surrealist revival of the early 1980s.

BALENCIAGA: ORGANIC MODERNISM

Like Vionnet, Balenciaga was renowned for his exquisite cut, tailoring and finishing techniques—the epitome of haute couture. He was without peer as an innovator in stylistic terms. Renowned as a very prolific designer who was credited with creating every major silhouette of the 1950s and 1960s, his influence on a generation of designers was unparalleled. Sir Cecil Beaton (1954), the famous fashion photographer, referred to him as the 'Picasso of Fashion'. Historical references abound in his work, and he recreated the Infanta Dress worn by the Spanish princess in many of Velasquez's paintings of the seventeenth century. His favourite model, Bettina, wore capes lined with lynx fur, which were identical to those worn in sixteenth-century Italy. His work is now in every major art museum in the world.

When Balenciaga opened his couture house in Paris in 1937, Schiaparelli's surrealistic collections were being fêted by every fashion journalist around the world. The influence of painters such as Salvador Dalí and René Magritte, who were known for their juxtaposition of 'opposite realities' to create a new visual paradox—with clocks melting over the table edges (Dalí, *The Persistence of Memory*, 1931) and steam trains emerging from fireplaces (Magritte, *Time Transfixed*, 1938)—were evident in her work. Surrealism impacted upon Balenciaga's work in a different way. His work is more attuned to other Surrealist artists—including Max Ernst, Hans Arp and Joan Miró—who used biomorphic abstract shapes to create an 'otherness' not seen before in the fine arts. The silhouettes of these organic shapes lent themselves to sculpture as well as painting. Miró and Ernst painted personal themes by using amoebic signs and symbols seemingly painted in a spontaneous way, while Arp sculpted curvilinear shapes that related to the organic forms of nature and suggested growing body parts.

This new development in the fine arts impacted upon other decorative arts, including furniture design and fashion. In design terms, it was called organic modernism. According to design historian Hauffe (1998: 106–7), after 1939 the prestigious Museum of Modern Art in New York determined 'what was avant-garde'. In 1940, it held a competition with the support of the exclusive Bloomingdale's department store entitled 'Organic Design in Home Furnishings', which consolidated the curved, flowing lines of the new organic style and the use of materials such as polyester, aluminium and plywood. Scandinavian furniture designers such as Arne Jacobsen created organic forms using new methods of layering and bending local birch and pine timber in combination with steel tube construction. His famous *Ameise Chair*, designed in 1952, was the first mass-produced Danish chair. Sleek, subtle forms became the hallmark of carved Scandinavian teak furniture in the 1950s. With the invention of polypropylene by Guilio Natta and Karl Zeigler around the same time, durable tables and chairs could be moulded to comply with the study of human ergonomics, and this was to revolutionize furniture-making and household wares.

The curved silhouette became the dominant style, as formulated by fashion designer Balenciaga in the 1940s and 1950s. Balenciaga used stiff materials that would hold their shape, but relied on expert cut to create simple, elegant forms. He is probably most famous for his evening gowns, in which the fabric was either manipulated into a distinct shape or elaborately beaded or embroidered to create a sumptuously textured surface. His greatest talent was his ability to mould garments into sculptural

Figure 3.5 Cristóbal Balenciaga, woman's silk evening dress and jacket, Paris, France, 1954. Collection: Powerhouse Museum, Sydney. Photographer: Powerhouse Museum Photography Department. Sculptural, organic shapes dominated fashion and art in the 1950s period.

creations, one of the most outstanding being his black silk taffeta Balloon or Pumpkin Dress of 1950, photographed by Irving Penn.

His sculptural work was often copied by Dior, Balmain, Givenchy, Fath and Griffe in the 1950s, and his work consistently appeared on the cover of *Vogue* magazine. While the dominant colour for eveningwear in the 1950s was black, as it effectively highlighted the silhouettes of the garments in interior spaces, popular daytime colours such as turquoise, yellow ochre, mauve and reddish brown became the decade's signature colours, drawn directly from Balenciaga's own colour schemes. Significantly, they are also the colours that have inspired many Spanish artists (including Miró), as they reflect the natural colours of their homeland—the earth, the sea and the sun-drenched stucco houses. Considering that these colours became the dominant hues of the 1950s, it is an indication of the immense influence that Balenciaga wielded over fashion. Due to the great respect afforded him by his fellow designers, he has often been dubbed the 'couturier's couturier'.

VIKTOR & ROLF: NEO-DADAISM

Throughout the 1970s and 1980s, revivalist fashion was in full swing, with the recycling of styles from the 1920s, 1930s, 1940s, 1950s and 1960s becoming monotonous.

It would seem that, by the 1990s, Western fashion had exhausted its endless appetite for change. In a constant search for novelty, some designers looked back to previous historical periods, while others found a need to react or contradict that which had gone immediately before. This lack of direction seemed to be broadcast in the growing superficiality of styles that led Suzy Menkes (2000), Fashion Editor of the *International Herald Tribune*, to call these trends 'the caricatures of fashion'. Since 1993, the work of the maverick Dutch artist-designer duo, Viktor & Rolf, has illustrated and satirized the bankruptcy of ideas prevalent in haute couture showings.

Viktor & Rolf's work highlights these stylistic absurdities and parodies the lack of originality by adopting Dadaist strategies including irreverence, affectation and sensationalism. In their 1998 collection, for example, their 'conceptual' couture fashions featured distorted figures and an exaggeration of forms as they piled one garment after another on the fashion model, until her slight form grew to enormous proportions. In both a literal and metaphorical sense, their pumped-up volumes created fashions that were larger than life. This provocative work inspires a number of postmodernist 'readings'. As an art performance,[8] it breaks away from the linear progression of catwalk models to an accumulative progression of garments from the collection using only one model. It comments on the role of the body in contemporary fashion as a non-sexual and non-gendered object. Conceivably, it also comments on the theatrical pomposity of couture fashion, which creates garments that are more suitable for the stage than they are for life.

Viktor & Rolf[9] introduced the visual pun into the shows for the Autumn/Winter collection of 2000, by parading an evening coat covered in little gold and silver bells; more bells were sewn inside the kimono sleeves of a wrap coat and, again, a tuxedo jacket was smothered with miniature bells scattered like sequins. Satirically, Menkes (2000) commented that couture was sometimes described as being 'fashion with bells on it'—this self-reflective critique of fashion was a product of postmodernist counter-couture (see Chapter 5).

Viktor & Rolf established their names as couturiers despite the fact that they sold almost nothing (Horyn, 2000a). Informed by a sense of humour, they ridiculed the pretentiousness of elitist fashion, breaking traditions and conventions by riddling their clothes with intentional errors and contradictions. In 2001, they challenged the Japanese conceptual designers (see Chapter 7) by presenting a collection that supposedly celebrated the introduction of black as a cult colour twenty years earlier. Their models wore ruffled leather blouses and black pearl jewellery, and painted their faces entirely black as well, challenging the potent and pervasive Japanese aesthetic:

> The conceptual approach of the designers means that they don't always make dresses: from a collection that consisted solely of placards painted with the words, 'V & R are on Strike' (when they were broke) to an art installation that only featured press clippings (about themselves), the designers take Warholian pleasure and fascination in knowing that printed exposure is the means by which they are understood and the means by which they continue. (O'Neill, 2005: 182)

In October 2003, a retrospective exhibition of their work was held at the Decorative Arts Museum in the Louvre to correspond to the 2003/2004 Spring/Summer prêt-à-porter collection showings in Paris. Those who look for connections between conceptual art and fashion applaud the courage (or the folly) of their work.

Often referred to as the 'kings' of the international avant-garde fashion scene, they have parodied European haute couture for its history of excessive sumptuosity, and the Japanese designers for their extremist use of black. Ironically, their Autumn/Winter collection of 2000/2001, when they brought out their Stars and Stripes collection—their first ready-to-wear collection—was their greatest triumph. While seemingly mocking American nationalism and being dubbed 'the flag bearers', they saw American culture as being globally present so they chose various American fashion icons including sweatshirts, polo necks and jeans to 'kick off' their more commercial line, a mass-produced range of clothing.

Figure 3.6 Viktor & Rolf, *Trompe l'oeil* bodysuit and body paint, *ABCDE* magazine cover. Photographer: author. This image was used for the Viktor & Rolf exhibition poster, Musee de la Mode, Decorative Arts Museum, Louvre, Paris, 2003.

MARTIN MARGIELA: POSTMODERNIST DECONSTRUCTION

Like Hausmann, Schwitters, Rauchenburg and the Arte Povera artists, Margiela chose debased and abject materials and deconstructivist methodologies to draw attention to a new type of anti-fashion. In a very objective, scientific manner, he analysed, dissected and recontextualised his garments (Plate 6). As if working with him in a laboratory, his assistant designers wore knee-length lab coats, an eccentric mode of dress that was copied by his devotees worldwide. Taking a postmodernist view of fashion design, he worked with a microbiologist in 1997 to grow mould and bacteria on the surface of a collection of garments, which was intended to eat away at the fibre of the textiles when placed outside in the weather for a period of time. A paradox is thereby created, where the clothing can be remembered as objects of beauty whilst they are gradually becoming objects of disdain. This theme was common in the 1960s conceptual art movement, when an artist might leave pieces of stale bread on the outside window sill and photograph them at various stages of decomposition. Margiela's decomposing installation of work, entitled *9/4/1615* and exhibited in the sculptural court of the Museum Bojimans Van Beuningen in Rotterdam in 1997, forced Ingrid Loschek (2009) to speculate that Margiela was comparing this process of the natural cycle of creation and decay to the consumer cycle of buying and discarding. Some read the installation as a comment on the issue of consumerism for consumerist's sake; others suggested that his work spoke about the cycle of fashion by symbolically alluding to the deconstruction of couture. At this time, the relevancy of couture was being challenged, and the world was experiencing a period of rapid, destabilizing change. A postmodernist reading would suggest that Margiela presents many different layers of meaning in his work and would advocate that individual viewers should respond with multiple interpretations.

Fashion theorist Caroline Evans describes his work as being 'much more experimental and "cutting edge" than that of many contemporary artists who use fashion motifs in their work' (Evans, 1998: 73) (Plate 6). Margiela experimented with the paradoxical concept of the 'inside becoming the outside' or at least being reproduced to appear to be part of the exterior garment. One of Margiela's most sought-after pieces by museum curators was one in which he borrowed the covering of a tailor's dummy and recontextualized it into a waistcoat made of linen canvas, which he then re-draped over the original mannequin. This, of course, takes on a surrealist perspective—a contradictory vision. The designer also deconstructs and reconstructs ideas relating to fashion detritus. When secondhand or throwaway clothing is given a new lease on life, it contradicts the traditional elements of glamour, beauty and novelty. Undoubtedly, he appropriated this notion from the Japanese contemporary fashion designers whose work reflects the notion of *wabi-sabi*, or finding beauty out of ugliness.

Margiela also rejected the age-old concept of the 'artist-as-genius' and refused to become a celebrity designer, never appearing on the catwalk, shunning public appearances and social aggrandisement of any kind in order to retain his anonymity. Similarly, both Picasso and Braque negated the idea of the uniqueness of the artist's originality as well, by signing each other's work in the early 1910s, when they were developing their objective concepts of analytical cubism. Like the Dadaists, Margiela worked collaboratively with his team at the Maison Martin Margiela and would not respond individually to queries or correspondences. He retired as the head designer of the label in 2010, following retrospective exhibitions of his work in Antwerp, Munich and London.

HUSSEIN CHALAYAN: TECHNO-DESIGN

Hussein Chalayan recontextualized the notion of the fashion 'spectacle' from one that was aesthetically based to one that was technologically based (Plate 7). Like other postmodernist artists, his cerebral work became allied more with multimedia, which offered new possibilities and new realities. His experimental work embraced avant-garde expressions ranging from sculpture to video and from architecture to performance.

In his earlier work, while investigating the theme of longevity and antiquity, he appropriated elements of Turkish costume and textiles drawn from his knowledge of his own cultural origins in Cyprus. Replicating age and decay, the garments from his graduating collection in 1993, The Tangent Flows, were buried in the garden with iron filings and took on the archaeological patina of centuries past. He referred to three of his key garments as 'monuments to ideas' as a way of linking the past with the future: the first, a dress from his Geotropics collection (Spring/Summer 1999), where a form resembling a small chair wrapped itself around the contours of the body, becoming part of the garment; the second, the Airplane dress from his Echoform collection (Autumn/ Winter 1999–2000) featured moving flaps; and the third, a remote-controlled dress made from materials used in airplane construction with solid moveable flaps from his Before Minus Now collection (Spring/Summer 2000), displayed a tulle underskirt when the flaps were raised. All of these garments related to his underlying themes of iterant existence and cultural displacement, flight and migration. According to Suzie Menkes (2005), his technical wizardry 'was designed to express refugees in flight, camouflaging their possessions' and were inspired by 'events in Kosovo and by Chalayan's childhood memories'.

Moving away from cultural meaning and memory, his later work, from 2006 onwards, centred on the dynamics of flight and notions of transformation and interaction, and became dubbed 'tech-couture'. His construction-garments became increasingly high-tech, relying on microchips inserted in the garments to mechanically program movements of different plates or sections of the clothing. Fascinated by movement, his garments used power packs of batteries attached to microprocessors to activate the transformation of hems, lapels and headwear—in other words, an entire morphing of the garment. His Airborne dress brought the latest technology—15,000 flickering LED lights combined with Swarovski crystals—to create a dazzling display in his Readings collection (Spring/Summer 2008) (Plate 7). Other collections included crystal skirts that became video display screens for projections of coloured lights or images of fish swimming underwater, hats that lit up like table lamps and full skirts that could imitate being blown about in the wind.[10] Undoubtedly, Chalayan has been instrumental in completely recontextualizing fashion within an intellectually broader sphere by fusing fashion, art and science.

In 2009–2010, at the Art of Fashion exhibition held at the Museum Boijmans Van Beuningen, the Netherlands, Chalayan's installation *Micro Geography* encapsulated a fully clothed rotating figure in a vertical tank of water that projected cross-sectioned images on a number of video screens. In the museum video interview complementing the exhibition, Chalayan commented that he had created a 'mini life' that referenced the concept of the 'gaze', much like CCTV footage—a form of documentation that became part of the visual culture. Working as a postmodernist artist, he described the installation as having layers of different meaning, yet he did not offer any possible translations. Since 2003, he has directed art projects including the short films *Temporal Meditations*, *Place of Passage* and *Aesthetics*, and in 2005 he represented Turkey at the 51st Venice Art Biennale, the world's foremost international art exhibition.

–4–

Fashioning the American Body

> Foreigners ourselves, and mostly unable to speak English, we had Americanized the system of providing clothes for the American woman of moderate or humble means.
>
> Abraham Cahan, New York immigrant, 1917

THE HOME OF READY-TO-WEAR: SEVENTH AVENUE, NEW YORK

Ready-to-wear became synonymous with American fashion, and its success grew out of diversity. It was determined by three major detrimental factors. The first was the plight of the immigrants who landed in New York, many with few skills other than hand-sewing,[1] but desperate to make a new life for their families. It also developed despite the appalling conditions in the factories and sweatboxes that housed the industry in the fashion quarter. Finally, it relied particularly on the exploitation of women workers, who were willing to work for meagre earnings.[2] In *Fashion and Its Social Agenda*, Diana Crane (2000: 74–5) provides a detailed account of how the transition from hand-made to machine-made clothing for women occurred at an earlier date in America than in Europe.[3] The major elements in this transformation were the sewing machine,[4] patterns for specific clothing items,[5] and the development of an accurate system of body measurement. Crane contends that this system of proportional measurements, and subsequently proportional sizes, made it feasible to produce ready-made clothing on a mass scale. Production of machine-made clothing expanded during the American Civil War, when thousands of ready-made soldiers' uniforms were needed, as well as cheap women's clothing, and a number of these factories continued production well into the twentieth century.

Advanced technologies and mechanization processes played a major role in the emergence of this capitalistic business empire. 'Whereas manufactured apparel was often characterized by defective cuts, careless finishes, poor quality and a lack of imagination, ready-to-wear sought to blend industry and fashion; it sought to put novelty, style and aesthetics on the streets' (Lipovetsky, 1994: 90). Factories became modernized through electrification, and the loose-fitting garments of the 1920s could be produced in standardized sizes, with minimal adjustments needed for individual figures. Egalitarian American society provided 'off-the-peg' fashion for its people, which crossed all social class boundaries and no longer carried the stigma of its previous history.[6]

While the exclusive Bergdorf Goodman store had sold Parisian dresses to wealthy New York socialites from 1925, when Wall Street crashed in 1929, this market disappeared. Not one American commercial buyer attended the Paris collection showings in the first season after the stock market plunge. The US government slapped a 90 per cent tax on all imported clothing in order to encourage local manufacturers to provide alternative models. Business entrepreneurs—often Jewish immigrants—invested their money into this new manufacturing industry. Their factories started to produce hundreds of copies of the French best-sellers.[7] Also, new synthetic fabrics were being produced by the textile mills—both in Europe and America. These fabrics were less costly, so were used by manufacturers to reduce the cost of garments, thereby giving greater impetus to this ready-to-wear market.

As many couture salons in Paris were forced to close their doors during the war, and with communications fragmented, French fashion no longer had the same influence on overseas designers. When key French fashion journals such as *La Gazette du Bon Ton* (founded by Lucien Vogel in 1912) still tried to woo American buyers in 1915 by showing garments especially designed for the American market, which featured shorter skirts promoting a more 'active' lifestyle (smartly illustrated by Georges Barbier), they did so to a shrinking audience. The war provided the opportunity for American designers to 'stand on their own feet'.

The editor of American *Vogue*, Edna Woolman Chase, had always attempted to avoid the possibility of American fashion isolation by placing American fashion within the context of Parisian culture and by encouraging the French to present their clothes within a theatrical format at various American fashion fêtes. She soon realized that a different marketing strategy had to be adopted to take advantage of the changing market. She persuaded the new director, Condé Nast (who purchased *Vogue* in 1909), that the women of American high society could be coerced into buying models from the top New York houses if the event benefited a French charity. *Vogue*'s first show attracted the cream of New York society. The display of 125 models included the work of Henri Bendel, Mollie O'Hara, Bergdorf Goodman, Gunther, Tappe, Maison Jacqueline and Kurtzman, as well as many other elite houses. This event sparked controversy in Paris, as many—including Poiret—saw it as an attempt to 'throw off the yoke of Paris' by 'instituting American styles' (Poiret, 1915). Even Worth, as early as 1912, alluded in an interview with the *New York Times* (20 December 1912) to his concern that American designers might develop a viable fashion industry of their own which would compete with the Europeans. This marked the beginning of the rise of the American super fashion consumer, whose desired image was meticulously dissected by the editors of America's fashion magazines for middle-class women, such as *Women's Wear Daily*.

Between the wars, the manufacture of ready-to-wear garments increased dramatically and Seventh Avenue in New York became the American production centre of the ready-to-wear 'rag trade'. By the 1950s, the American fashion industry had developed methods of production and distribution in ready-to-wear that rivalled those in Europe. While still driven by European haute couture design, the American fashion industry began to produce high-quality ready-to-wear that combined the casual lifestyle of the Americans with the class and repute of European designer goods. As a new fashion aristocracy arose, it allowed American designers such as Vera Maxwell to react to the dictates of previous fashion in a different way. She responded to the limitations imposed by fabric restrictions during the Second World War by designing coordinates in plain fabrics—garments that could be worn in different combinations to give the illusion that one's wardrobe was larger than it actually was.

Another pioneer in casual ready-to-wear, Claire McCardell, adopted Vionnet's bias cut in the 1940s to create simple, yet elegant, clothing that would epitomize the typically American style now associated with sportswear collections. When the American War Production Board imposed rationing for certain textiles (notably wool and silk), designers turned to cotton, using denim, cotton crêpe, mattress ticking and jersey to produce attractive, easy to wear designs (Baudot, 1999: 126). Like Vionnet, who brought crêpe out of its shadow as a lining fabric, McCardell's denim wrap-around skirt became her hallmark, establishing her as one of America's greatest sportswear designers. In these early years, other women designers—including Bonnie Cashin and Tina Lesser—contributed to the evolution of leisurewear by offering a more relaxed and informal styling that responded to American middle-class needs and values. These clothes were intended for a mass-market (for example, clothes for doing housework, retail price $6.95), and were manufactured in inexpensive fabrics such as denim, corduroy, seersucker and calico (Milbank, 1985: 352). Anne Klein revitalized the idea of sportswear separates, and also became instrumental in establishing the popularity of sportswear in America and overseas. In the 1960s, her sharply tailored sportswear made up of blazers, trench coats and trousers cut like men's trousers became her trademark; from 1974 her business successor, Donna Karan, continued the tradition. Norman Norell, known as 'America's Balenciaga', became famous for designs that came closest to bridging the gap between haute couture and the ready-to-wear industry. His trademark became a refined, clean-cut, yet glamorous (and also expensive) rendition of all-American ready-to-wear clothing.

The svelte American image that developed out of the health and fitness craze of the 1970s relied on non-restrictive comfort combined with casual elegance, impeccable grooming and a healthy, streamlined physique. 'Separates' were central to this image, and a huge sportswear industry developed from this mix-and-match approach to flexibility and variety in dress. Both celebrity and designer status fuelled the sales of body-hugging exercise clothing and sportswear. According to Breward (2003), experimental

Figure 4.1 American *Vogue* fashion model, West 42nd Street, New York, 1952. Photo: Ernst Haas/Getty Images. New York style: this photo advertises the 'New Look' fashion, automobiles and high-rise buildings—style, sophistication and glamour.

research in the Japanese textile industry in the 1960s produced stretch fabrics such as Lycra, which capitalized on the elastic properties of the fibres to allow for a new way of clothing the body. In terms of body consciousness, he argues that, with an emphasis on fitness, the development of artificial fibres including elastic, latex and Spandex 'had a significant effect on the direction of fashion' (2003: 650) and the shaping of the body beautiful, in womenswear as well as menswear.

MENSWEAR: SHIRTS

The history of the evolution of menswear follows a similar path, with the ready-to-wear industry in America also gaining a foothold in the first half of the twentieth century. As early as 1931, Arnold Gingrich published an influential magazine called *Apparel Arts*, which was the first male fashion magazine aimed at tradespeople, manufacturers, wholesalers and retailers in order to promote better design, presentation and marketing strategies for mass-produced fashion products. He also published *Esquire* magazine in 1933, which was used to show the fashion-conscious public that stylish clothes did not necessarily have to be produced by the tailors of London's Savile Row. Chenoune, in his *A History of Men's Fashion* (1993: 188), notes that by 1937, subscriptions for the monthly magazine had reached 728,000. It promoted ways to match shirts, suits and ties according to fabric, patterns and colours, and devoted long articles to the wool industry, manufacturing standards and store improvements; this, in turn, gave a major boost to the American ready-to-wear market. Interestingly, this period paralleled the rise of the industrial designer in America. Amongst the pioneers was Raymond Loewy, the man who indoctrinated America with the idea that 'style sells'. With increased consumption fuelling the manufacturing industry, the United States was to become the most highly developed industrialized nation in the world at that time. Such was their success in garment manufacture that the French menswear industry sent over a delegation in 1950 to observe and document, in a 174-page report, how American firms worked, as well as how they selected their raw materials, manufactured items and marketed products.

In terms of marketing, the shirt became a goldmine for American industry. The humble shirt, first worn as a type of undergarment, normally covered by a waistcoat and overcoat, was to become one of the largest mass-production markets in the fashion industry. It dated back to 1881 when Moses Phillips and his wife Endel began sewing shirts by hand and selling them from pushcarts to local coal miners in Pottsville, Pennsylvania. The shirt business expanded into New York City after Phillips' son Seymour formed a partnership with John M. Van Heusen, who had patented a self-folding collar in 1919. The Phillips–Van Heusen Company was formed, and introduced the first collar-attached shirt in 1929. Ten years later, the Van Heusen shirt was marketed across the country, and became a staple item in every man's wardrobe. The name became synonymous with the business shirt and, as designer Anthony Muto pointed out, 'Ready-to-wear is the American dream—the whole idea of walking into a store and walking out with something that fits is an American concept' (in Morris, 1978: 162). By 1991 it had become the top-selling dress shirt in the United States. By 2000, the Phillips–Van Heusen (PVH) brand had escalated to such an extent that the company became the top-selling dress shirt group in the world. In the mid-1960s, Arrow shirts—made by PVH's main competitor—were sold in three sleeve lengths and neck widths per size in both America and Europe to allow for a more custom-sized fit. Again, this reinforced how sophisticated and competitive the American ready-to-wear industry had become.

A FASHION ICON: LEVI'S JEANS

Another American fashion icon was Levi's jeans, a brand that first achieved national status during the Second World War, when the American government declared that Levi's were an essential commodity and sales were restricted to defence workers. Demand for the jeans skyrocketed, along with their price. This American brand icon had humble beginnings. Levi Strauss, a twenty-four-year-old Bavarian immigrant, left New York for California during the gold rush era to sell rough canvas trousers to miners. The trousers were hardwearing, with pockets that would not tear when filled with gold nuggets. While these garments exemplified the rugged hardships of the early pioneers of the West, they also symbolized the strength of the American spirit of the day. When Levi Strauss introduced his first basic pair of 'waist-high overalls' in 1853, he had no competitors. He replaced the tough canvas (which the miners complained was causing chafing) with a cotton twilled cloth from France called serge de Nîmes. This name was shortened to 'de Nîmes', from which the term 'denim' was created. It appeared in *Webster's Dictionary* for the first time in 1864. Later, in 1873, Strauss added the distinctive double-stitched pockets (which used arcuate stitching) and, with Nevada tailor Jacob Davis, patented the process of putting rivets in the trousers for strength. Branding was completed with the large, leather two-horse label that was added in 1886 and the red tag attached to the back left pocket in 1936 to identify the Levi's 501 brand at a distance. The marketing image conveys the value of the Levi Strauss brand: they are 'the real deal'—authentic, original, dependable.

By the 1950s, jeans had been further popularized by the insurgence of Western films, which promoted the adventurous and romantic image of actors such as Gene Autry and Roy Rogers. Also, jeans were immortalized as a symbol of youthful revolt in movies such as *The Wild One* (1953) featuring Marlon Brando, and *East of Eden*

Figure 4.2 Claire McCardell, identical floral print dresses, at Bloomingdales, New York, 1956. Photo: Paul Schutzer/Time Life Pictures/ Getty Images. Influenced by Christian Dior's New look, these garments offer two lengths for potential buyers.

(1954) and *Rebel Without a Cause* (1955) featuring James Dean. Increasingly, young people wearing a black leather jacket and blue jeans were mimicking the insolent casual body positions and poses of these legends of the silver screen, slouched against walls with their hands in their pockets. Jeans were adopted by typical middle-class teenagers, the offspring of white-collar businessmen. Levi's successfully capitalized on the notion that it had emerged from a working-class base, and this appealed to a generation of anti-Establishment baby boomers. In 1971, the firm of Levi Strauss was awarded the Coty Fashion Critics' Award, America's most prestigious fashion trophy. By 1992, over 450 million jeans, across all manufactured brands, had been sold for a total sum of US$8.2 billion, and they became one of the most successfully marketed clothing items in history. The company Levi Strauss became one of the world's largest brand name apparel marketers, with over 8,500 employees worldwide. In 2005, it was one of the few privately held family companies where shares of company stock, with the exception of Japan, were not publicly traded.

DECADES OF DOMINANCE: AMERICAN DRESS IN HOLLYWOOD FILM

One of the greatest homogenizing influences on global fashion has been the spread of American popular culture. Both Eastern and Western cultures became seduced by the widespread distribution of American Hollywood films. For Hollander (1988: 240), 'Movies, like Renaissance spectacles, make art out of life'. Of all of the visual arts, film-making—more than anything else—often acted as a catalyst to determine the direction in which fashion was headed. Hollywood stars are remembered for their signature dress—Greta Garbo for her cloche hat (pulled down so far that it covered her eyebrows and almost hid her eyes), Charlie Chaplin for his clown-like bowler hat, cane and fake moustache, Marilyn Monroe for her blonde hair, bright red lipstick, low necklines and billowing skirts, and Jane Russell for her tight-fitting sweaters. The cinema proved to be an inexpensive and exciting form of entertainment for mass consumption, and was an effective escape from reality during the Depression and the war years. During these stringent times, support actors were often hired for their smart hats or coats rather than their talent, as the production houses were limited to a shoestring budget. During the silent film days of the 1910s and 1920s, exaggerated appearances and gestures were necessary to provide greater dramatic appeal for the audience, so effective costumes for the heroes and heroines of the silver screen were paramount. Dress played a key role in the development of plot and characterization. The 1930s musicals provided visual spectacles that allowed Hollywood to 'transform itself into a "dream factory", where film images created suspense, humour and a distraction allowing people a temporary flight from their bleak, everyday reality . . . in 1930 alone, no fewer than seventy musicals were filmed in Hollywood'

(Gronemeyer, 1999: 78). Film designers in Hollywood produced clothes that rivalled those of the French couturiers in quality, expense and glamour, and which had an enormous influence on the public (Crane, 2000: 139). Gilbert Adrian, in particular, began his career in the garment district of New York and then progressed to Hollywood, where he worked for MGM and created the immortal 1930s silver screen look. While key European fashion couturiers were hired to design clothes for major productions, calamities often resulted—especially in the case of Erté, who never completed the costumes for the film *Paris*, and Elsa Schiaparelli, whose garments for Mae West's 1937 film *Every Day's a Holiday* were made in Paris; when they arrived in the Hollywood studios, it was discovered that they were far too small to fit her. When Chanel[8] designed her functional but drab sportswear for Jean Renoir's *La Règle du Jeu* (1939), the audiences left the theatre disappointed, as they had anticipated that they would see costumes that were more spectacular. Movie stars also became associated with particular styles of dress, which were advertised in *Vogue* and *Seventeen* magazines. Women closely followed the looks of Elizabeth Taylor, Bette Davis, Marlene Dietrich and more recently, Nicole Kidman and Sarah Jessica Parker, amongst others. Finkelstein (1996) highlights the 'Annie Hall' look from the Woody Allen film of the same name in 1977, which was the influence for a masculinization of women's clothes that saw waistcoats, ties, flat shoes, hats and oversized trousers: 'This style persisted for many years in the ready-to-wear fashion markets of the Western world' (Finkelstein, 1996: 35).

In reality, the fashions created for films simply reflected and popularized the styles of the day, but Hollywood was a formidable advocate of fashion, and extended its influence over a broad spectrum of society. Yet, when fashions changed dramatically— as they did with Dior's New Look in 1947, when billowing skirts replaced straight-line skirts and the masculine lines were transformed into the hourglass silhouette—the Hollywood producers wept, as many films they had prepared months in advance of their public screenings became redundant overnight. In other words, what was meant to be a current film became old-fashioned or 'out of style' within weeks. A new genre of American dressmakers or stylists emerged, whose names became synonymous with Metro-Goldwyn-Mayer (MGM), Warner Bros. and Universal Studios. They included Gilbert Adrian, Howard Greer, Walter Plunkett and Edith Head. Some of these designers also did some work for the wholesale trade in America. In 1932, Adrian's most successful white organdie dress with ruffled shoulders—designed originally for Joan Crawford in the film *Letty Lynton* (1932)—sold 500,000 copies in Macy's New York department store. Walter Plunkett was immortalized for the costume collection he designed for the classic epic *Gone with the Wind* in 1939, in which Scarlett O'Hara (Vivien Leigh) used the green velvet material and tieback tassels of old Victorian curtains to make a seductive gown to woo the wealthy Rhett Butler (Clark Gable). The gangster movie genre was established with *The Roaring Twenties* (1939) from Warner

Bros., starring Humphrey Bogart and James Cagney. In certain ways, these movies applauded the power and influence that the mafia leaders wielded—it was an era when the young tough guy from the slums of New York could be raised to the level of a demi-god in the eyes of his peers. His clothes indicated his tough appeal.

Just as the early American immigrants discarded their traditional clothing as soon as they disembarked, so they could symbolically start a new life by discarding their previous identities; movie producers used this same technique of changing costumes to reflect the changed circumstances or characterizations of the anti-heroes in their films. The 1943 all-black musical *Stormy Weather*, which starred Cab Calloway wearing a spectacular white zoot suit, feathered fedora and spotless white shoes, inspired other African-Americans—especially jazz singers—to adopt this new badge of identity. The zoot suit became 'all the rage' in Harlem, Chicago, New Orleans and Miami. The 'zoot suits' of the 1940s became an emblem of ethnicity and pride, establishing an identity for young African-Americans. As a subcultural gesture, these oversized and stylistically outrageous suits symbolized a statement of defiance—a refusal to be subservient to the white majority. Knee-length, double-breasted, wide-lapelled jackets with broad padded shoulders were worn over high-waisted, 'draped', tightly cuffed trousers. The suits often featured a key chain dangling from the belt to the knee or below, then back to a side pocket. They were seen as the epitome of luxury and excess, especially during the war years when material was rationed.

According to Polhemus (1994), when America needed a vision of itself, a common identity, Hollywood obliged. The Western movies of the 1940s and 1950s provided a legacy that was without equal:

> What was worn by the 'singing cowboys' on stage and screen—the boots, the Stetson, the embroidered shirt and jacket, the bootlace tie—rapidly became the street style of a subculture which was originally principally confined to the American south-west but which soon (generally sans the Stetson) spread throughout the USA. (Polhemus, 1994: 24)

In this stereotypical type of production, visual conventions define the clothing, and they conform to a rigid formula. In simple terms, white clothing symbolizes good and black symbolizes evil. Any supporting words or gestures adhere to the visual representation of the character. The film *Funny Face* in 1957 marked 'a transitional move from haute couture to prêt-à-porter, seemingly anticipating the new ideal promoted by Helen Gurley Brown' (Radner, 2001: 185). The designer Givenchy dressed Audrey Hepburn for this story of a shop girl who was transformed into an haute couture princess.

By the 1960s, the glamour and the costumes had faded and new genres of film emerged. A number of films made by young European film-makers did impact directly upon fashion photography, in particular Antonioni's *Blow-Up* (1966) and Fellini's *81/2*

(1963). However, except for nostalgia films such as *The Sound of Music* (1965), *Mary Poppins* (1964) and *West Side Story* (1961), Italian neo-realism, film noir, science fiction, thrillers and socio-political documentaries followed. Fashion historian Prudence Glynn (1978: 76) aptly summarizes that 'the moment that the cinema became visually pedestrian, the public removed its desire for spectacle to pop music . . . [where] dress was an essential part of the appeal'. As with fashion, the pop scene moved to London.

In a later film, *Breakfast at Tiffany's* (1961)—described as director Blake Edwards's cinematic masterpiece—Givenchy's costume design had an immediate and profound influence on both 1960s couture style and popular women's fashion. In the film industry, Audrey Hepburn's costumes were singled out as one of the greatest achievements in costume design. Combining high fashion style and sophistication, Givenchy produced the quintessential little black dress (LBD), which, while looking deceptively simple, was actually stuffed with horsehair and strategically placed lead weights to ensure the fabric fell just right on Hepburn's frame. In contrast, another LBD appears on Demi Moore in *Indecent Proposal* (1993), for which designer Thierry Mugler created a sexually alluring black evening garment that hid the murder weapon, thereby embodying the dress itself in the plot.

According to journalist Ali Basye on her Web site 'On This Day in Fashion' (2010), a number of other films have created iconic garments for both men and women. She cites Marlon Brando's black leathers in *The Wild One* (1954), Marilyn Monroe's white crepe halter dress in *The Seven Year Itch* (1955), James Dean's basic red jacket, white T-shirt and blue jeans in *Rebel without a Cause* (1955), Ursula Andress's white bikini in *Dr. No* (1962), the sensational transsexual dress of Transylvanian Dr. Frank-N-Furter in *The Rocky Horror Picture Show* (1975), John Travolta's white and black polyester leisure suit in *Saturday Night Fever* (1977), Julia Roberts's red evening dress in *Pretty Woman* (1990) and the immaculate men's suits featured in the James Bond movies since 1962.

Some films have immortalized a certain look that has impacted, in a more diffused way, upon street-style dressing. *Bonnie & Clyde* (1967) appropriated the 1930s styling for its antiheroic story about a pair of likeable gangsters. Both men and women copied costume designer Theadora Van Runkle's chic reimagining of Bonnie Parker (Faye Dunaway) and Clyde Barrow (Warren Beatty). Midiskirts—below-the-knee-length pencil and A-line skirts—and V-neck cable-knit sweaters and the now-iconic beret became a popular fad during the early 1970s. Along with Warren Beatty's wardrobe—a never-ending supply of three-button jackets and fedoras—the film won best costume design. 'John Fairchild, the publisher of Women's Wear Daily and a movie buff, named Bonnie and Clyde as an inspiration when he hailed the midi as the look du jour of late 1969. So convinced was he of the midi's potential that he declared

1970 the "year of the midi" in the September 14 issue of *Time* magazine' (Basye, 2010). *Annie Hall* (1977) had a similar influence on everyday fashion, reinforcing the male influence on women's dress. Richard Gere in *American Gigolo* (1980) became a show pony for Giorgio Armani and reinforced the rise of menswear in the international fashion industry.

It would seem that in the 1990s and 2000s, period costume dominated in historical films, and technological visions of the future created imaginative garments in science fiction themes, including *Star Wars*, *Back to the Future*, *Predator*, *RoboCop*, *Godzilla* and *The Matrix*, paralleling similar advancements in textile development. More casual, everyday dress dominated in 'chick flicks', including *Sleepless in Seattle* (1993), *The First Wives' Club* (1996), *Almost Famous* (2000), *Bridget Jones' Diary* (2001), and *Easy A* (2010), with some reference to vintage and street style. Specifically, films about fashion and the fashion industry that captured the attention of fashion's mass audience include *Prêt-a-Porter* (1994), *The Devil Wears Prada* (2006), *The September Issue* (2009) and *Bill Cunningham NY* (2010)—all of which document the behind-the-scenes workings of key designers, models, editors, journalists and photographers. As part of the New York Fashion Week in September 2011, Vanity Fair partnered with the Museum of Arts and Design and the Film Society of the Lincoln Center to host the first ever 'Fashion in Film' program.

AMERICAN CONSERVATISM: THE DESIGNER/STYLIST—LAUREN, KLEIN AND KARAN

American conservatism responded to the simplicity, versatility and comfort of ready-to-wear clothing. As a nation, Americans did not have the long-standing history of social class differentiation of their British counterparts. In many parts of the country—particularly the Midwest and the growing suburban areas of the large cities—they adopted a more casual, traditionalist lifestyle. In California, a relaxed 'beach style' evolved after the introduction of the Hawaiian shirt in 1946/47, together with Bermuda shorts, and the subsequent decline of business suits in favour of more ventilated and comfortable attire. New technologies resulting from the Second World War made it possible to utilize new, lightweight materials in garment manufacture.

In the first half of the twentieth century, New York was the textile manufacturing capital of America. Seventh Avenue was the hub of the fashion manufacturing and wholesale trade. Wholesalers of buttons, trims, apparel fabrics, threads and accessories opened premises within an eight-block radius, less than a square mile in total—an extraordinary concentration of industry. On a typical business day, the streets became alive with the hum of sewing machines, the wheels of clothes racks and the shouts of couriers and delivery trucks as they loaded and unloaded their goods. By 1910, some 70 per cent of women's clothing and 40 per cent of men's clothing worn in America was produced in this district. This also coincided with the first factory to produce rayon—a new, cheaper material first patented in France, which was to revolutionize the ready-to-wear industry. Today, the fashion industry sustains tens of thousands of jobs in the city; it has always been the largest single contributor to the city's manufacturing sector.[9]

In the early 1950s, while Bill Blass intentionally mingled with upper-crust society in New York to see how the people lived, he manufactured his casual daytime garments with Maurice Rentner in the heart of the garment district on Seventh Avenue. When women showed interest in the shirts and sweaters he designed for men, he opened his sportswear division—Blassport. Similarly, the internationally acclaimed Geoffrey Beene was a product of Seventh Avenue, working for Harmay, a dress house, for eight years. He explained that, for him, a designer's role was to 'make people's lives easier'. That meant introducing ease and comfort into both women's and men's clothing. His famous Beene Bag for men was an attempt to move away from the fitted look—he saw it as a transitional garment between blue jeans and the tailored suit. Even Halston, born in the Midwest and renowned for his classic, simple styling, showed his custom-made collections in an uptown boutique on Madison Avenue, yet manufactured his ready-to-wear lines—sold in department and speciality stores across the country—on Seventh Avenue. An early collection that he designed for Bergdorf Goodman was 'an attempt to bridge the gap between couture and ready-to-wear' (Morris, 1978: 92), but his *coup d'état* in ready-to-wear was the shirtwaister dress that he designed in ultra-suede in the 1970s, which was to become a classic garment in every American woman's wardrobe.

Sportswear became synonymous with a casual, middle-class existence, and it co-incided with the attitude that 'dressing down' in an elegant, comfortable manner was a subtle sign that one did not have to keep up appearances. In contradictory terms, it suggested wealth and good upbringing. Quentin Bell (1992) refers to 'conspicuous leisure' as a mode of dress that gives the appearance that one leads an entirely useless or futile life, yet is undoubtedly a sign of status. In many circles of society at the time, conventional fashion was worn as a sign of social conformity, reflecting old-fashioned ideals and values. This inherently conservative approach to design is apparent in the collections of many of the leading ready-to-wear designers, including Ralph Lauren, Calvin Klein and Donna Karan, whose international success began in the 1980s. Their work is often described as being 'classic', always appropriate and comfortably chic. American 'purist' fashion is characterized by clearly defined lines, splendid fabrics and perfect, yet formless, cuts. Fashion Editor Carrie Donovan makes a valuable comment when she argues that American designers create 'a style of dressing', as they are not interested in individual ideas but are particularly good at creating a concept. Arguably, American fashion emerged from the garment factories and from a tradition of ready-to-wear. This was in contrast to France, where ready-to-wear emerged directly out of couture.

Giorgio Armani is one of the few couture designers whose work has impacted upon American ready-to-wear. He was featured on the cover of *Time* magazine in 1982 for his revolutionary men's suits that broke away from the traditional mould. *Newsweek* (22 October 1978) described them as 'classically cut but not stodgy; innovative but never theatrical'. Armani's longer, unstructured jackets were comfortable, and suited the more casual approach to businesswear in the 1980s. As the architect of the soft shoulder, he removed the traditional padding; he also reintroduced a vintage double-breasted garment with long, deep lapels, similar in many ways to the zoot suits of the 1940s. His clothing questioned the traditional function of menswear, both artistically and culturally. He introduced the crumpled look of linen into menswear, as well as womenswear, and his shapeless, oversized clothing bridged gender stereotypes. Like Chanel, he offered an alternative way of dressing—a new freedom that appealed to international men of all ages. Ironically, Armani was inspired by the Hollywood film star Fred Astaire, whom he believed to be 'the supreme reference of elegance' in his 1930s suits. Crane (2000) believes that the American style of dress reached a pinnacle during this era, and 'had the greatest influence on 1980s and 1990s fashions'

Figure 4.3   Levi's 'Size Does Matter' game, 6 August 2008. Women run to grab a pair of jeans in New York City, hosted by Brody Jenner and Frankie Delgado. Photo: Andrew H. Walker/Getty Images.

(2000: 174). Nevertheless, Armani was the label that led the way for American menswear design to follow.

Ralph Lauren

Ralph Lauren, perhaps the number one American ready-to-wear designer, is a supreme stylist. Trained initially at Brookes Brothers, a traditional sartorial menswear establishment, he designed for clients who 'did not want to stand out in a crowd', but who wanted their clothing—based on simplistic styling and the use of fine fabric—to reflect good taste and upbringing. The subtlety of this paradigm, based on 'lifestyle' or 'concept' dressing, underlined the success of many of the emerging designers in the 1970s and 1980s. Lauren launched his Polo menswear range in 1968, and three years later turned to tailored womenswear: shirts, blazers and suits that appealed to businesswomen even though they resembled sportswear. He is often quoted as saying: 'I stand for a look that is American', and alludes to the fact that he was

Figure 4.4 Giorgio Armani fitting a man's suit jacket, Milan, Italy, 1 May 1979. Photo: David Lees/Time & Life Pictures/Getty Images. Armani was one of the leading influences upon American casual menswear design.

inspired by the *Great Gatsby* look of the 1920s. He is able to turn old classic looks into fresh, contemporary ones. Promoting this nostalgic image, his stores replicate a homey atmosphere, creating a feeling of well-being and relaxation.

While not the most original of designers, his classic good looks, at prices that the upper middle-class American could afford, were the secret to his success. He combined quality materials, excellent workmanship and attention to detail with a carefully constructed image that applied not only to his products, but to his stores as well. The image he created was determined by clothing that gave the illusion of wealth; at the same time the wearer appeared to be nonchalant about his appearance. Much like the landed gentry, he might have been walking in the countryside, sailing a yacht or riding a horse at the ranch. According to Baudot (1999), 'Ralph Lauren was a true social phenomenon. He was equally successful with his sportswear and jeans, which enabled him to reach the widest possible range of social classes and age groups' (1999: 395).

A contemporary artist, Charles LeDray (Townsend, 2002: 118–21), sees Lauren's male clothing as mirroring a conservatism usually associated with an Oxford academic, an American preppy or one who claims aristocratic heritage. In order to critique the falseness that this type of clothing suggests, LeDray constructed a miniaturized version of a characteristic Lauren casual wool sports jacket, waistcoat and colourful bow tie, then used sandpaper to fray and tear the bottom half of this detailed construction. His *Untitled* work of 1995 is 'not a mechanism that deters sentimental response, but . . . a reaction to what the clothes stand for, their social values and their repression of other, more polymorphous identities'. Townsend (2002: 119) suggests that LeDray has 'epitomized and undermined all that Ralph Lauren spent more than a decade and a slew of money to convey'.

Calvin Klein

Paralleling Lauren's career was Calvin Klein, who began working as a coat designer for Dan Millstein for $75.00 a week. 'Designing coats,' Klein often commented, 'was a great challenge as they were the least inventive of the categories of clothes.' He sold his first samples to Bonwit Teller in 1967, and quickly moved into sportswear design by combining linen blouses with flannel skirts. Unpretentious, clean-cut and charismatic, he consistently made the comment: 'I make clothes people like to wear.' His high-profile clients have included Jacqueline Onassis, Liv Ullmann, Susan Brinkley, Lauren Hutton and Nancy Reagan. His style is simple, comfortable, light and easy to wear. One collection develops into the next, and the monochromatic and minimalist conservatism that underlines his garments secured the global appeal of his label. His most effective marketing promotion, which created considerable notoriety for his label and appealed to the masses in the 1980s, was for his line of designer jeans, which were so tight that the slogan boasted: 'Nothing comes between me and my Calvin's'.

Through television commercials, the director Richard Avedon used Brooke Shields, the all-American 'girl next door' starlet, to promote the range in a very suggestive, sensual manner. In 1982, the famous American fashion photographer Bruce Weber capitalized on this blatantly sexual advertising by using highly contoured male bodies, wearing only Calvin Klein underwear, in an unprecedented marketing campaign. According to Valerie Steele (2000: 126): 'Weber created the most famous erotic photographs of men ever used in mainstream advertising.' Klein's strategic response to the body-hugging fashions of the 1980s reflected changing social mores and exploited the sexual taboos of the day.

Colin McDowell, in his *The Man of Fashion: Peacock Males and Perfect Gentlemen* (1997: 173–6), argues that Klein—as 'the first to use male sex to sell clothes'—was so successful that it was 'not inconceivable that future social historians writing about America will refer to the first few years of the 1980s as the CK era'. Branding became big business in the 1980s, and designers tried to capitalize on this growing market of 'designer label as status'. Klein, capitalizing on his underwear fame, had his name boldly printed on the waistband of his men's underpants. As jeans were worn fashionably low-slung at the time, the label was brilliantly revealed. The underwear became an international best-seller, and McDowell (1997) points out that the desirability of the garments was sustained by the risqué advertising campaigns and the seductive photography of Bruce Weber. When these fashion images of the male torso began to dominate the urban environment (an enormous billboard advertising Klein was erected in Times Square in 1982), a new form of male sexual iconography was born. The billboard advertising not only endorsed a new era in male fashion (in both heterosexual and homosexual terms), but more significantly acknowledged that the 1970s health and fitness craze had culminated in the celebration of a well-developed muscular body image of young men in the 1980s.

The conglomerate Phillips–Van Heusen Corporation (PVH) began a new era when it acquired the Calvin Klein Company in 2002, as it recognized that the brand offered incredible growth potential worldwide. Several new licensing agreements were signed in 2005, which further expanded the global presence of the prestigious Calvin Klein brands. This included handbags and small leather goods, men's and women's footwear, and 'ck'—Calvin Klein's bridge label, specializing in women's sportswear—which was distributed in Japan and South-East Asia, as well as through selected American department stores.

Donna Karan

Another key designer, Donna Karan, designed for the Anne Klein label for ten years, and during this time she developed her legendary knitted bodysuit[10] and 'seven easy pieces' system of dressing. This modular stylistic trend was embraced by other sportswear designers in the 1970s. When she established her own business in 1984, her philosophy towards designing remained the same. She explained that design was a constant challenge to balance comfort with luxury, the practical with the desirable. By creating a tailored soft look, her garments were intended to suit the lifestyle of the successful working woman—a type of no-fuss fashion. Her garments follow the movements of the body closely: jackets are made without the stiffness of linings, skirts gain greater sensuality. Karan described her objectives as wanting to make comfortable clothing that was easy, simple and sophisticated—clothes that could travel. She diversified the Donna Karan International collection to include menswear and the very successful DKNY jeans diffusion line. Her clothing image sells an American lifestyle, a trademark design philosophy.

Her flagship store located at 819 Madison Avenue is described as the ideal shopping environment. The mood it projects is very restful, with a water rock garden, soothing music and seductive lighting. She sells her work through her own retail stores and major retailers, and the company went on to become a publicly traded enterprise in 1996. Five years later, DKNY was acquired by LVMH (Louis Vuitton Moët Hennessy).

GLOBAL CONGLOMERATES

Conglomerate corporations grew from the 1960s onwards. Many high-profile designers, including Klein, Karan, Kors and Perry Ellis, amalgamated with numerous other companies to form giant international networks. Their distribution channels include regional, national and international department stores, mass-merchants, sports-related speciality stores and corporate wear distributors throughout the world. Many of these huge global conglomerates developed from humble beginnings. For example, a relatively unknown businessman named George Feldenkraus started a small apparel wholesale company called Supreme International in 1967 as an importer of guayabera shirts—a pleated, four-pocket shirt favoured by Hispanic men. The company expanded rapidly, and by the late 1990s had acquired companies including Penguin, Crossings and Perry Ellis, who had established his classic American sportswear in 1978. It changed its name to Perry Ellis International (PEI) after adding John Henry, Manhattan, Lady Manhattan (1999) and Janzen (2002). New brand names emerged, including Tommy Hilfiger (swimwear) and Nike. Between 2003 and 2005, other companies merged, including Salant, Axis, Tricots St Raphael and Tropical Swimwear. PEI traded throughout the United States, Puerto Rico and Canada, and its largest customers included Wal-Mart, J. C. Penney, Mervyn, Kohl's Corporation and Sears Roebuck. Not surprisingly, it became harder for individual designers to establish either haute couture salons[11] or smaller ready-to-wear businesses without extensive funding, in order to compete in an increasing global industry.

Figure 4.5 Donna Karan, long casual day dress, modelled by Carla Bruni, ready-to-wear Spring/ Summer, New York Fashion Week, 11 November 1995. Photo: Victor Virgile/Gamma-Rapho/Getty Images. Sophisticated, simple and seductive became key to Karan's collection's appeal.

These huge global corporate conglomerates license[12] their proprietary brands to third parties for the manufacture and marketing of various products—footwear, fragrance, underwear, active wear, loungewear and outerwear. In terms of marketing, these licensing arrangements raise the overall awareness of the brands. They use highly sophisticated 'family of brands' promotions to develop and enhance a distinct brand, styling and a pricing strategy for each product category within each distribution channel. They target consumers in specific age, income and ethnic groups. This globalization of fashion has impacted upon the apparel sector in America, as well as other countries, in four major ways. First, department stores and chain store sectors have been forced to amalgamate into a smaller number of stronger retailers. Second, larger retailers have needed to rely more on their own design expertise and to incorporate advanced systems of technology in their businesses. Third, there has been a growth in the importance of establishing strong brand names as a source of product differentiation. And finally, products are being manufactured in parts of Asia, Africa and South and Central America, where the labour costs are lower and mass production is more cost-effective.

This manufacturing shift to Third World countries was hastened, in particular, by internal problems that gained momentum by the end of the last century. For example, the New York garment district was plagued by mafia-infiltrated trade unions, which ultimately increased labour production costs and literally froze the trucking industry—which impeded the delivery of goods. It is estimated that organized crime cartels were 'costing' the district a staggering $60 million a year by the early 1990s.[13]

By the turn of the twenty-first century, the fashion system had changed profoundly. The 'global village' first mooted in the 1960s by Marshall McLuhan,[14] a Canadian philosopher and writer, had become a reality. With increased technological communication systems, the world increasingly became a smaller place, where shared ideologies grew, a consumer culture dominated and social belonging no longer adhered to the concept of clothing as an identifying signifier. Clearly, this homogenization of style did not allow for individual difference, regional bias or cultural flavour; instead, it promoted a uniformity of thinking and taste. But by creating a global aesthetic, has global fashion ultimately undermined individual and cultural differences?

–5–

Postmodernism and Fashion

We don't want to be chic; we just want to be ridiculous.

Marion Foale and Sally Tuffin, designers

A CULTURAL CONTEXTUALIZATION

Fashion and Music

The evidence of the juncture between fashion, music and dance was marked when Strauss's music inspired the waltz and gracious nineteenth-century ballroom gowns; when 1920s jazz provided the tempo to swing the lightweight Charleston-fringed dresses; and when modern South American dancing set the stage for sexually charged, tight-fitting tango garments. In the 1930s, musical theatre and Broadway shows exerted a great influence on everyday fashion as Rodgers and Hammerstein's musical scores created a new Hollywood cultural genre with its unique concept of glamour. During the Depression years, Hollywood movies became a sanctuary, a form of escapism for many audiences. The more visually spectacular the performance was, the easier it was to forget the hardships of the time. Fred Astaire and Ginger Rogers were a source of inspiration for fashion-oriented cineastes in movies such as *Top Hat* (1935) and *Swing Time* (1936), which linked Big Band music with glamorous clothing. Paradoxically, while an annual Paris Syndicale de la Couture competition awarded a coveted prize to the most sensational evening dress creation between 1935 and 1939, at the same time, dance marathons in America pushed the endurance of its unemployed competitors to the limit, while fashion companies' advertisements were used at these events to promote ritzy club fashion.

The jazz sounds of American Cab Calloway and the East Coast jazz movement in 1943 inspired black Americans to adopt the zoot suit as a form of sociopolitical comment. Baggy pants and wide-lapelled jackets contravened fabric restrictions put into place during the war, but they also formulated a distinctive and defiant 'gangster look'. Rock and roll, derived from African American rhythm and blues, dominated the postwar generation music scene. This music was linked directly with youth, rebelliousness and societal change. A more casual, energetic style of dress was required as fashion

– 85 –

became ever more closely associated with popular culture, especially pop music. Skinny trousers, checked shirts, full skirts with bobby socks and two-toned shoes dominated the dance floor. Elvis Presley and Bill Haley immortalized the image of the rebellious teenager in the 1950s, and rock and roll became the new dance form in the nightclubs.

A new era of ostentatious masculine style characterized by defiant and highly charged clothing appeared in the 1960s, paralleling the performances by Mick Jagger, Pete Townshend and Jimi Hendrix. Followed closely by disco, John Travolta in *Saturday Night Fever* (1977) immortalized the look in his iconic white disco suit and established disco as mainstream culture until the 1980s. Salsa music also became encoded in disco music as a crossover genre, acknowledging the Latino-Caribbean community within American society with its see-through clothing exuding sexuality and the exotic.

According to curator Katie Somerville, 'Popular music and its icons played a key role in establishing youth cultures in which clothes were central to "performing" one's identity' (2011: 73). In the early 1980s, hip-hop, break-dancing and techno gained mass appeal amongst the blacks and Hispanics in New York City and Los Angeles clubs. Based on very athletic and acrobatic movements, very wide-crotched and low-hung pants became the fashionable uniform worn by street-style dancers coupled with designer sports shoes made by Adidas, Nike and Puma. In Britain, Vivienne Westwood and Malcolm McLaren consolidated the relationship between punk rock and fashion in the 1980s when they promoted irreverent and confrontational clothing made of cheap and untraditional materials. Anti-fashion protest styling incorporated T-shirts with rips and tears and offensive slogans and other pieces of clothing overlaid with social references—symbols of resistance—to mainstream culture.

Music videos featuring Johnny Rotten, Michael Jackson and Madonna revolutionized the whole concept of dance, music, fashion and the spectacle. These media images not only played a major role in what youth wore but determined standards of dress, hairstyle, behaviour and cultural practices. Subtle sexual innuendo has played a key role in pop music, but now raunchy R&B and hip-hop have adopted similar methodologies to increase commercial sales. In other words, music videos consolidated the underlying image associated with the music, thereby allowing the medium of fashion to create a celebrity style. From the 1990s onwards, the boy bands, girl bands and teenage music groups were widely promoted through videos and CDs, and performers like the Backstreet Boys, Spice Girls, Britney Spears and Justin Timberlake strongly influenced mainstream fashion trends such as tank tops, low-cut jeans, visible underwear, and conspicuous gold jewellery for both males and females. It would seem that some young people just want to live the life of a rock star. But if they can't live it, they just want to look like one.

In the twenty-first century, with the cult of the celebrity pop star firmly established, Kylie Minogue, photographed wearing a Chloe green dress in 2005, led to the complete sell-out of a similar model sold in Sportsgirl within a week. At the same time, Dior's Homme designer, Hedi Slimane, toured with bands such as Air, Franz Ferdinand

and The White Stripes to gain inspiration for his design work and his book entitled *Stage*. According to the *Los Angeles Times*,

> Hedi Slimane is the man responsible for the way rock and roll looks today. His slim-line aesthetic, a cross between sleek and slacker, mod and 1980s punk, is everywhere . . . for the kickoff of the Rolling Stones 'A Bigger Bang' tour, Mick Jagger turned to Slimane to design his skin-tight blue metallic jeans, silver satin jacket and black T-shirt with red crystal embroideries. A Boston-based band, Keys to the Streets of Fear, has even released a song entitled *Hedi Slimane*. (Moore, 2005)

Pete Doherty, seen as one of the pioneers of the new British music scene, was Slimane's muse for the 2005 Spring/Summer collection and is emblematic of the new indie rock scene. The 'elegantly wasted' look he projects has been called 'skank chic' by the *London Observer* and is characterized by unshaven facial hair and a chaotic mix of clothes.

Major fashion labels partnered with leading musicians to promote their lifestyle brand. John Varvatos is another leading menswear designer who has also 'made a devotion to the spirit of rock his point of difference in a crowded American sportswear market' (Standen, 2011: n.p.). In the Spring/Summer 2012 collection, his knits were slouchy, his tunics were loose and flowing and jackets were decorated with hand-painted roses. Both Scottish singer Paolo Nutini and London rapper Roots Manuva backed sportswear label Puma in their sales campaign in 2010.

With pop musicians having to look beyond traditional record stores to sell their albums, many are selling their music in high-street cafes and fashion shops. Retail outlets like Urban Outfitters in the United States and Topshop's flagship store in Oxford Street, London play music that customers can buy in the store. Having a propensity for playing indie music, they have brokered a deal to join forces with the largest independent music store, Rough Trade, to sell CDs in store. According to *The Independent*, 'Paul McCartney raised eyebrows across the music industry when he signed up with Starbuck's label to release his 21st studio album in 2007' (Bray, 2009). While it seemed that he was the first to take the risk, Starbucks set the trend that fashion stores are now following. London band Kish Mauve have partnered with denim brand Lee Cooper, and Anna Leddra Chapman was chosen by the surf label Quiksilver to help launch its first ever range for women.

Fashion and Celebrity

The cult of celebrity has evolved as perhaps the most powerful marketing and promotional element in the fashion industry today. For 160 years, designers have relied on royalty, heads of state, theatrical performers and Hollywood movie stars to promote their work. Sarah Bernhardt, dressed almost exclusively by Worth, attained celebrity status in the nineteenth century as she performed throughout Europe to become one of the leading stage entertainers of her day and one of Worth's most lucrative marketing personalities. This celebrity status also encompassed early-twentieth-century Josephine Baker and her revealing costumes which shocked and entertained Parisian society, attracting the attention of audiences worldwide. At the same time, she proved to be a great source of inspiration for liberalizing fashion in the 1920s and 1930s. The introduction of television in the 1950s and the growing popularity of the movies increased the impact of popular culture upon the masses. With the proliferation of fashion and women's magazines and social page coverage in the newspapers, journalists constructed the glamorous, fairy-tale lives of these celebrities.

Reinforcing the substantial link between celebrity and sexuality, the charismatic Cary Grant and Clarke Gable, so often filmed in their lounging attire, built their silver-screen images on suave sophistication, refinement and glamour, while Marlon Brando and James Dean created theirs on the look of rebellious youth, whose black leather and jeans epitomized masculine sex appeal, street culture and revolution. The business suit, when worn by the refined, thrill-seeking playboy Sean Connery, reinforced the notion that its wearer was a gentleman, a modern James Bond. From the 1980s onwards, dependent on the lucrative marketing ploy of branding, designer labels became associated with media and entertainment personalities—not only including actors but sports stars and supermodels as well. At the same time, haute couture house models became identified with specific designers: Bettina for Balenciaga, Grace Jones for Azzedine Alaia, and Inès de la Fressange for Chanel. Interestingly, when models began parading clothes for a number of different design houses rather than becoming tied to one designer, their individual status and popularity as celebrities increased. While the rise of the supermodel might have begun with Twiggy in the late 1960s, the 1980s and 1990s marked the supermodels' golden age for the fashion industry. This twenty-year period produced a wave of supermodels, with the most celebrated being Linda Evangelista, Naomi Campbell, Cindy Crawford, Christie Turlington and Tatjana Patitz, whose faces appeared together on the cover of *Vogue* in 1990. The designer Gianni Versace is widely credited for promoting this celebrity status. Strategically, when Armani launched his 2011 Fall/Winter collection in China, he chose celebrated Chinese actress Shu Qi as the face of Emporio Armani with photos taken by Mario Sorrenti on location in New York. The celebrity sports star David Beckham became the quintessential metrosexual man—a term that blossomed in 1994 as a combination of *metropolitan* and *heterosexual*, referring to fashion trendsetters. According to Anna Cicolini's *The New English Dandy*, he 'almost single-handedly affected a revolution in masculine dress in Britain. Beckham is acutely aware of the importance of his appearance in the development of his celebrity status' (2005: 90).

During the late 1990s, the pendulum swung back to the Hollywood stars. American actress Gwyneth Paltrow appeared on the cover of American *Vogue* in August 1996, 'a rare distinction for a non model' (Katz, 1996: 2). Editor Anna Wintour wrote that Paltrow was 'well known as the actress every designer wants to dress' (Katz, 1996: 2). According to Gilligan, when her photo appeared again on the cover of British *Vogue* in

February 1998, her look epitomized 'the understated, classic style of Ralph Lauren, making her the ideal mannequin for his designs' (2000: 247). Luxury fashion products such as cosmetics, perfumes and jewellery were, even more directly, marketed in a way that consolidated this association between product and personality. Fuelling a multimillionaire industry, Nicole Kidman became the face of Chanel No. 5 perfume and Cate Blanchett the editor's choice for the cover of *Vogue*'s fiftieth anniversary issue in September 2009. Over the years, American fashion magazine editors, in particular, became powerful celebrities and personalities in their own right. These include Edna Woolman Chase, Diana Vreeland and, more recently, Anna Wintour, for *Vogue*. The unprecedented obsession with celebrity has led to a demand for the publication of a raft of new consumer magazines such as *Now* and *Closer, Heat, OK!* and *Hello!* as well as changes in format size of *Glamour* and *Teen Vogue* to fit into a handbag.

In many cases, legends are constructed to create dreams out of dismal realities. In death, even more so than in life, celebrities such as Marilyn Monroe, Rudy Vallee, Elvis Presley and Janis Joplin are remembered for their style of dress, their lifestyles and their public image. In a Beverly Hills auction in 2011, Monroe's iconic white halterneck 'Subway Dress' worn in the film *The Seven Year Itch* sold for $4.6 million. Over the years, no other member of the royal family attracted the obsessive interest of the media more than Princess Diana in life and in death. She encapsulated everything that was glamorous yet unpretentious, sophisticated yet girlish. This type of public adulation is constructively developed over a period of time and results from a collective media barrage that manufactures a kind of heroic appeal.

Sports brands in particular have traditionally used leading football, soccer and basketball stars to promote their lines. From the mid-1990s, they turned to 'collabs'—a slang term used where high profile designers and more underground designers work together to generate new models in fashion and footwear. When leading fashion designers produce 'special and limited edition' products in which two brands are advertised together, it successfully enhances the product twofold. According to Gill (2006), one of the earliest examples of this has been identified as German fashion designer Jil Sander with Puma.

The celebrity paradigm has now become the most crucial factor in defining success in global fashion. First designated through branding techniques based on the status of the products themselves, or the association with famous super models, or the endorsement by Hollywood stars' high-profile magazine and media featured stories, celebrity is now centred on the image of the designers themselves. Fashion films, CDs and educational videos have immortalized the lives and work of Chanel (*Chanel Solitaire*, 1981, and *Avant Chanel*, 2009), Alexander McQueen and John Galliano (*Masters of Style*, Lifestyle Documentary series CBC, 2000), Valentino (*The Last Emperor*, 2008) as well as leading individuals associated with the fashion designers and their industry, including key magazine editors (previously mentioned) such as Anna Wintour (*The Devil Wears Prada*, 2006, and *The September Issue*, 2009) and fashion photographers such as Bill Cunningham (*Bill Cunningham NY*, 2010). Becoming icons themselves adds further value to their already existing iconic brand and supports continued commercial success. Reinforcing the cult of celebrity in fashion, Jean-Paul Gaultier, inspired by popular culture, references individual celebrity icons in his fashion collections, including the 1950s Marilyn Monroe look and, in his Autumn/Winter 2009 collection, Brigitte Bardot reappears when lookalike model Lara Stone wears a black-belted mac that Gaultier calls 'Le Mépris'. In his 2011 'The Fashion World of Jean Paul Gaultier: From the Sidewalk to the Catwalk' exhibition in Montreal, Canada, he added a virtual reality mannequin depicting himself in his ubiquitous sailor-inspired suit. This blatant self-promotion reinforces the notion that designers themselves have become their own products. Designer profiles now dominate their Web sites, building digital 'journeys', citing family stories, historical accounts of business successes and opportunities for designer chats and feedback. This personalization of the Web site is intended to promote a feeling of intimacy and friendly individual attention, encouraging a perceived bonding between the designer and the customer. When a customer becomes a fashion avatar on the site and can 'try on' various garments, this promotes the idea that the client can also become a virtual celebrity.

Figure 5.1 Jean-Paul Gaultier, white and blue striped men's sailor maillot and blue pants on simulated mannequin, retrospective exhibition, Montreal, 2011. The Fashion World of Jean Paul Gaultier: From the Sidewalk to the Catwalk, presented at the Montreal Museum of Fine Arts in 2011, organized and circulated by the Montreal Museum of Fine Arts in collaboration with the Maison Jean Paul Gaultier. Animated mannequin: a concept of UBU/Compagnie de création.

By the beginning of the twenty-first century's second decade, some astute advertising firms, in an effort to appeal to male customers, are broadening their concept of who constitutes a celebrity in today's society. In terms of intellectual stakes, full-page images of successful businessmen, artists and adventurers were featured in the menswear Dunhill London label's advertisements in 2011. Captions included in the ads reveal self-reflexive comments by the men pictured that explain how each individual perceives the notion of *success* in his field. Arguably, positive associations created through brand imagery are imperative in terms of sales marketing. Transforming personalities into commodities, which, in turn, sell more products has become the sophisticated art of the marketers, promoters, media gurus, journalists and photographers.

POSTMODERNISM IN FASHION AND ART

Paralleling the emergence of global conglomerates, the term 'postmodernism' was applied to design and design movements that emerged from the 1960s to the present day. Fundamentally, postmodernism can be characterized by a number of things, seen individually or in combination with each other. First, it is essentially anti-modernist—'modernism' being a term referring to idealism and the concept of 'good taste' in design, which dominated the visual arts in the period between the world wars. In fashion terms, it could be translated as anti-haute couture or anti-fashion. This could include the use of deconstructivist sewing, pattern-making or cutting techniques, which created a less than perfect finish. On the one hand, it could reference fashion that produces a form of ugliness, breaking the codes of classical beauty. On the other hand, it could be self-mocking, a self-reflexive comment on individual taste, or upon the fashion industry itself, or the attitudes and mores of a particular society or group within that society.

Second, postmodernist art and fashion often appropriate imagery from earlier historical or cultural eras, or use material from other contexts. Revival fashion, or 'retro' fashion, revisits fashion styles from earlier decades (or even centuries) and can reveal cross-cultural or counter-cultural ideas. Combinations of a variety of ideas, styles, images, textiles, colours or patterns can create a form of *bricolage*, a range of pluralistic forms or a pastiche. Fashions might recontextualize imagery from artistic, popular cultural, industrial, scientific or mixed-media sources.

Third, art and fashion can be used as social or political markers, as they both have the capacity to advertise an individual's representation of self as well as critiquing society in general. This can be realized through the use of deconstructivist techniques, symbolic imagery, or the juxtaposition of different materials or images in the work to create a visual paradox; or simply the use of text to communicate the message. Postmodernist design often uses humour to create notions of irony, satire or parody. Humour, used effectively, enhances the power of the projected message.

Finally, postmodernist art and design embrace new technological materials and methods. Conceptual art can be recorded in digital form using electronic equipment; performance art can be videotaped; and installations can be created when a number of objects interact with each other within a defined space. Materials other than fabric, such as paint, rhodoid plastic, PVC, resin, vinyl, see-through synthetics, reflective metals or industrial materials, can be used to dress the body.[1] The fashion industry has been reliant on the technological development of new fabrics, textures and colours, as well as computers, to aid design.

The aim of postmodernist design is to be provocative—in other words, to ask more questions than it answers. In our society, what constitutes 'good taste'? In *Vogue* in 1971, a feature article asked 'Is Bad Taste a Bad Thing?' (it featured a Yves Saint Laurent collection that mixed and matched diverse patterns in combination with each other). Has all fashion become anti-fashion? Why are postmodernist fashion designers defying conventions and forcing the viewer to reassess what constitutes acceptable design in today's technocratic society? Over the last fifty years, fashion design has questioned gender differences, sexuality and moral values, addressed humanistic and environmental concerns, and asked—either implicitly or explicitly—what value history plays in contemporary dress. Has fashion become a theatrical parade, a masquerade for individuals to mask or reveal their true identities? Just as artists have questioned 'What is art?', are the designers similarly asking 'What is fashion?'

From the 1960s onwards, fashion changes have accelerated at a more rapid pace than ever before. This is reflected in the proliferation and diversity of styles promulgated until the end of the century. Peter Dormer, in his *Design After 1945* (1993), indicates that by the end of the 1950s, in terms of design philosophy, a decided change had taken place. Italian designers, in particular:

> have accepted and capitalized, through their design experiments, events and exhibitions, upon their beliefs in the dynamics of confusion and the plurality of right answers. Even in Germany and Scandinavia, 'good taste' or 'good design' is no longer a single ideology—it is accepted intellectually and intuitively that there are several right answers to any one design challenge. (1993: 200)

This unprecedented visual pluralism reflected an age of experimentation, diversified thinking and dramatic technological change with the advent of the computer age, an ever-expanding communications system and a growing popular culture.

As the litmus test of social consciousness, clothing became a metaphor that clearly indicated the anti-war and anti-Establishment feelings of the hippies in San Francisco, the nihilism of the punks in London, and the sexual revolt of women in the Western world. Clothing was used as a counter-cultural device to publicly announce an alternative outlook on society. Crane (2000) provides extensive data gathered from surveys and interviews that relate to the role of fashion in the social construction of identity. Finkelstein argues that 'clothes are regarded as the visible manifestation of entire systems of value' (1996:16). Statistics indicate that this impacts to a considerable degree upon the young, as some studies—e.g. Pujol (1992) in Gare (2000: 180)— show that, of the percentage of French men who make a concerted effort to dress fashionably (including anti-fashion—approximately 45 per cent of the sample group), the majority are classified as young (under thirty years of age) or relatively young. In the mid-1960s, similar marketing surveys in Britain indicated that more than 50 per cent of fashion and fashion products were being sold to young people in the age group 15–18 years. Designers and marketers immediately shifted their consumer focus to accommodate this swing. Not only did it become necessary to increase the ready-to-wear market so that it was affordable to younger clients, but the rapidity of change was such that it deterred wealthy clients from buying couture, as it would only be fashionable for a short period of time. Recognizing the impact that this culture of change would have, Balenciaga decided, in 1968, that it was time to close his doors. *Harper's Bazaar* Australia wrote in September 1984 that, as the greatest perfectionist among his generation of couturiers, he felt that the life which supported high fashion was finished.

The impact of American popular culture upon youth, fashion and the visual arts was universal. Teenagers had the greatest disposable income in history. There was a new kind of prosperity, especially among the working classes, and young people wanted to express their own attitudes and tastes rather than those of their parents. Crane (2000: 172) argues that the construction of personal identity is based on leisure rather than business clothes. For Crane: 'Popular culture constantly redefines social phenomena and social identities: artefacts continually acquire new meanings . . . popular leisure clothes have to be synchronized with media culture as it is expressed in TV, film and popular music.' Fashion styles change each time musical styles change, and these trends are religiously followed by a huge audience of adolescents and young adults. Youth culture determines its own codes of fashion, and these codes are carefully monitored by the popular cultural industries.

POPULAR CULTURE AND PASTICHE: QUANT, COURRÈGES, CARDIN, SAINT LAURENT AND ASHLEY

Mary Quant

Celebrity status for movie stars, television stars, pop singing idols, rock groups and fashion models increased dramatically during the 1960s and 1970s. Carnaby Street in London became the fashion Mecca for the young. Mary Quant, with no formal training in dressmaking or couture, established Chelsea's first fashion boutique, Bazaar, in 1955 with her husband, Alexander Plunkett-Greene, and Archie McNair. She epitomized a new breed of designer trained at art school, unafraid to defy mainstream ideas and an enthusiastic promoter of new ideals. The boutique capitalized on the buying power of the new, young clientele by specializing in a mode of dress that encompassed specific fashion accessories—bags, hats, jewellery, stockings, and even cosmetics. Even more significantly, she defied the fashion system—which manufactured two new styles per year—by following current fads and changing her styling every six weeks. Interestingly, the Bazaar boutique pioneered a revival of old-time shopping patterns, when small, family-owned businesses catered for personalized service—a practice that diminished when department stores were conceived. The rise of the boutique in London (Biba[2] opened in 1964) paralleled the growth of retail chain stores (which were, by then, firmly entrenched in the United States) and of Marks and Spencer,[3] which had become 'a byword for democratic fashion in the 1950s' (Glynn, 1978: 214). Gaining popularity, the store expanded in 1975 by opening a branch in Paris.

When Quant introduced the shortest skirt in history—the 'mini'—it systematically excluded older and larger women from being entirely fashionable. Youthfulness became the new feminine ideal in the 1960s, and the central market became the working girl rather

Figure 5.2 Mary Quant for Ginger Group, black linen mini dress with white revered collar and full circular skirt, 1966. Collection: Powerhouse Museum, Sydney. Photographer: Jane Townsend. In the previous year, hemlines had risen to the highest level ever seen in the history of fashion.

than the socialite of the pre-war years. It was a revolutionary, yet logical, step to take. Significantly, it signalled a turning point in fashion: the principal focus was no longer on the well-heeled, middle-aged fashion buyer; instead, the market catered exclusively for the young, who had a more limited budget. Ready-to-wear had taken the reins from haute couture, heralding the death knell of the haute couture industry. Quant became the first 'designer' rather than 'couturier' to determine the new direction in fashion.

Quant used Western movies as an inspiration for her first collection, which was presented in London in 1961, and then parodied childlike garments such as knickerbockers, pinafores, playsuits accompanied by knee-high socks, berets and pigtails. The 'off-the-peg' clothes—which initially she made herself—displayed shapes that were simple and two-dimensional. She created a visual paradox by using evening fabric for daytime wear and vice versa, combining bright, jarring colours and conflicting patterns. Her clothes were designed to appeal to those in their teens to mid-twenties, and were made from easy-care, crease-resistant, washable synthetic fabrics[4] suitable for an active lifestyle. Quant's rise in the fashion industry signified that clothes were no longer a sign of a woman's social position and income group. Hilary Radner (2001) quite rightly suggests that 'snobbery had gone out of fashion' (2001: 185). As home sewing grew in popularity with the new technologically advanced sewing machines, Quant produced designs for Butterick Patterns in 1964 to enable her styling to reach a larger market in a way that was affordable to all. Her philosophy towards dress has often been compared to that of Chanel: Chanel dressed the modern twentieth-century woman, and Quant supposedly dressed the girl. They both produced a holistic look with totally coordinated accessories.

According to Radner (2001: 186–88), 'The Look' was a term coined by Quant, made up of 'image, attitude and association' that underlined physical activity, dieting and the development of a confident self-image. Arguably, the concentration on 'self' materialized out of the reflectiveness of the baby boomer generation, and the notion of the expendability of taste, which broke fashion's rules and heralded postmodernist styling. Fashion photographers responded to this emphasis on movement and the increased interest in sportswear quite literally, by constructing the effect of spontaneity in their fashion photography. According to *Vogue*, Martin Munkasci,[5] working for Fashion Editor Carmel Snow, created in fashion photography 'a new aesthetic of urban life . . . stylistically, the genre exploits the techniques of immediacy (and disposability) that characterize the mass media in general' (Radner, 2001: 187–88). Models clung to helicopters, were dropped into haystacks and encased in plastic bubbles floating down the River Seine in Paris. Page layouts in fashion magazines were composed of images tilted on their sides to emphasize the diagonal line—which, in graphic design terms, created visual movement. The notorious photographer David Bailey helped to establish Jean Shrimpton as one of the leading fashion models, along with the boyish-figured Twiggy, in the 'swinging '60s'.

André Courrèges

Quant's competitor in Paris, André Courrèges, used similar geometric A-line shapes, but produced a more sophisticated, structured style. Having been apprenticed to the couturier Balenciaga, he became a master of cut and tailoring techniques. He was renowned for designing women's trousers for every occasion, but preferred to use gabardine (seen as a pedestrian fabric) as it shaped his garments into stylized, futuristic architectural forms. He developed a signature style through cut, channel seaming and banded hemlines, which created subtle abstract patterns on the surface of his clothing. Whereas Quant used popular London tourist sites as a backdrop for her fashion photographs, and had her energetic, youthful models hop, skip and dance down the catwalks, Courrèges preferred to stage space age showings with his models moving like robots in rigid, choreographed movements.

The 'space race' dominated the media, both in news broadcasts and in popular television science shows. The top ten movies of the 1960s included *Dr Strangelove* (1964), *Goldfinger* (1964) and *2001: A Space Odyssey* (1968), with television featuring the original series of *Star Trek* and *The Man from U.N.C.L.E.* Steele infers that Courrèges 'tended to use futurism as a metaphor for youth' (1998: 278). The look was decidedly avant-garde, and his mid-calf, flat-heeled boots became an iconographic symbol

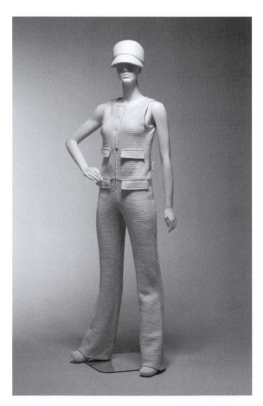

Figure 5.3A André Courrèges, acrylic and nylon jumpsuit and jacket, Hyperbole collection, Paris, 1971. Collection: Powerhouse Museum, Sydney. Photographer: Marinco Kojdanovski.

Figure 5.3B André Courrèges for Harrod's of London, mini dress in wool and synthetic fibres with matching coat, 1965. Collection: Powerhouse Museum, Sydney. Photographer: Andrew Frolows. Courrèges developed a trademark style of futuristic garments which were distinguished by shape, colour and distinctive finishing features such as banded hemlines, false pocket flaps and channel seaming.

of the 1960s. Courrèges' most famous designs were seen in his Space Age collection of spring 1964, which strongly featured silver and white PVC with bonded seams. The collection included silver 'moongirl' trousers, white catsuits and monochrome-striped miniskirts and dresses. His famous client, Jacqueline Kennedy, immortalized the Courrèges look, wearing his above-the-knee, triangular-shaped pastel coats with matching pillbox hats and flat-heeled shoes. As he fervently believed in the democratization of haute couture for the modern young working girl, Courrèges produced a large ready-to-wear collection that was widely exported. His ambition to establish workshops that produced clothing at 'boutique prices' for direct marketing was unsuccessful, but his look remained a classic icon of the 1960s.

Pierre Cardin

Professionally, Pierre Cardin followed a similar course but, by working for department store companies in the late 1950s, he developed very strategic business skills. He was the first couturier to sign a 'licensing' contract where his ready-to-wear designs carried his name, but were manufactured and marketed by another company or group of companies. As the licensing contracts expanded into a diverse range of products, his label became a great international success. His early signature fashion work was minimalist, with strong graphic lines in contrasting colours that created geometric, streamlined shapes. He incorporated decorative features as an inherent part of the surface design, making jewellery redundant. Like Courrèges, he had a fascination for technology and a passion for architectural shapes.

In 1961, Cardin opened his first men's boutique, and soon became a world leader in menswear. He designed the popular high-buttoned and collarless 'Nehru' jacket and double-breasted evening suit for men. He specialized in men's suits, which often had matching hoods. In 1964, he introduced the futuristic Moon Range to his womens-wear collection, with female models wearing tabards over catsuits, with high leather boots and space helmets. He was an expert with materials, and he became a perfectionist with pleating, mastering every possible variation—sunray, pencil and cartridge. In 1966, his moulded dresses imitated sculptural shapes and his work, like that of Courrèges, took on an austere, minimalist appearance, which epitomized the scientific space race. Both Cardin and Yves Saint Laurent worked for the House of Dior before opening their own salons. Cardin, renowned for his individualized collars, which were often gigantic and double layered, combined with geometric detail, was exceptionally experimental and innovative. Following Vionnet, he investigated the possibilities of both cowl drapery and the use of the bias, and often chose wool crêpe or jersey to create a soft and supple nonchalant look.

Figure 5.4 Pierre Cardin, collarless jackets worn by the Beatles, 1963. Photo: Harry Hammond/ V&A Images/Getty Images. An early group portrait of George Harrison, Paul McCartney, John Lennon and Ringo Starr.

Yves Saint Laurent

Yves Saint Laurent opened his couture house in 1962, and over a period of forty years was a legend of postmodernist fashion. His love affair with couture covered a gamut of pluralistic styles, and confirmed his inveterate artistic genius. As one of the outstanding postmodernist couturiers in history, his designs were a brilliant blending of ideas from many sources, which tapped the artistic, social and political feelings of our time. Saint Laurent paid homage to Chanel in his 1964 collection, reiterating her simplistic shapes and eye-catching accessories in deference to her celebrated coordinated look. In both fashion and art, the revival of the 1920s experimentation with colours, lines and optics (taught at the Bauhaus School of Design and reflected in art deco styling) was fundamental to the development of hard-edged graphic lines juxtaposed with large, flat areas of colour. In the decorative arts—especially furniture and household design—bold, bright primary colours were used to highlight the properties of plastics and resins, new technological materials that had emerged from experimentation during the Second World War.

The designers of the 1960s, in general, mirrored the work of the hard-edged painters such as the American artists Ellsworth Kelly, Kenneth Noland and Frank Stella, who were producing huge canvases saturated with flat, juxtaposed areas of colour formatted in minimal compositions. Bridget Riley's op art canvases of undulating lines, and Victor Vasarely's studies of geometric shapes, interpreted the extensive colour studies that were undertaken by the Bauhaus's Johannes Itten and Wassily Kandinsky. Vasarely investigated spatial properties in conjunction with his 'colour forms'—in which shapes, related to colour, form units of a more complicated grouping. The juxtaposition of complementary colour schemes creates a kinetic visual movement, when after-images are created by the eye itself.

Arguably, these art and design movements impacted directly on the work of Yves Saint Laurent. The art of illusion influenced the textile designs in his op art collections. His Mondrian Dress of 1965 was designed to commemorate the work of the de Stijl artist of the same name, whose non-objective painting helped to revive neo-Bauhaus optical colour studies in the 1960s. The creation of this famous garment paralleled a number of retrospective exhibitions of Mondrian's paintings in the Sidney Janis Galleries (1962 and 1963) and the Allan Frumkin and Marlborough-Gerson Gallery (1964) in New York, followed by an exhibition at Galerie Beijeler in Basel, Switzerland in 1965. After the opening night showing of Saint Laurent's collection, thousands of copies of the Mondrian Dress were reproduced by Seventh Avenue manufacturers. In 1966, three major exhibitions of Mondrian's work were held in The Hague, Toronto and Philadelphia. He appropriated pop art into his 1966 fashions, inspired by his friend Andy Warhol's op art in 1972, and for the next thirty years he paid homage to many of the great twentieth-century artists, including Matisse and Picasso. In the

1980s, he employed the famous company of French embroiderers and embellishers, Lesage et Cie (founded in 1922) to copy, in sequins, Van Gogh's *Irises* painting, as it had just been sold for the highest auction price ever paid for a work of art. Being entirely embroidered by hand, it was said to be made from 250,000 sequins in twenty-two different colours, 200,000 individually threaded pearls and 250 m (273 yd) of ribbon (Frankel, 2001: 206). Within the fashion industry, the irony implicit in this metaphoric work—the highest price paid for a garment as well—was appreciated by the audience and received top media coverage. The fashion press loved the eclectic nature of each successive Yves Saint Laurent collection. The only constant element in his pastiche collections was change—characteristically, in keeping with postmodernist trends. Even in his early work, he challenged the seriousness of couture by introducing 'fun' clothes mimicking the beatnik look, followed by the sailor look and the gypsy look. Later, he drew heavily from many other sources, including history, travel, cultural events and the theatre.

Just as the performance of *Schéhérazade* by the Russian Ballet inspired artists and designers alike to recreate an exotic and colourful array of theatrical costumes in the early years of the century, so did its influence impact upon Saint Laurent, a lover of theatrical costuming. This was particularly so throughout his 1960s collections, which were characterized by bright colours and rich brocades. His African collection followed, being made up entirely of rows of beads revealing the flesh below, and underlining the cross-cultural nature of his work. As Yves Saint Laurent continued his involvement with theatrical costuming throughout his career, he designed garments for his friend Catherine Deneuve for the Surrealist director Luis Buñuel's 1966 film, *Belle de Jour*, and also designed Isabelle Adjani's clothes in Luc Besson's film *Subway* in 1988.

The revival of interest in historical films inspired a return to historical dress. The classic film *Dr Zhivago* (1965), for example, set in post-Revolution Russia, motivated designers to create collars and cuffs trimmed with fur on their winter coats. Yves Saint Laurent produced a Catherine the Great collection in the late 1970s, which featured sumptuous, richly coloured brocaded garments trimmed in black fur. His Russian collection of Autumn/Winter 1976–7 was considered to be one of his most magnificent in years, and was captured on the front page of both the *New York Times* and the *International Herald Tribune*. During this decade, classic cinema initiated a host of fashion revival styles, as movies of the 1920s, 1930s and 1940s were shown to audiences who enthusiastically engaged with the nostalgia of classic screen productions.

Saint Laurent was one of the first haute couture designers to openly acknowledge his interest in popular culture. Interestingly, when asked in an interview for *Dazed and Confused* (March 2000) what his greatest influence was, he replied, 'The fashion of the street.' He watched what the young were wearing, where they were going and what they were doing. According to Steele (1999), he was the most successful designer, in the long term, to combine couture with street style. He designed an American Indian protest uniform in sympathy with the student riots in Paris in 1968, complete with headband and fringe. The headband later became identifiable with those persons participating in demonstrations against the Vietnam War. Just as he had introduced turtle-necked sweaters with black leather jackets in 1960, he continued to heed the dictates of the street. In Spring/Summer 1978, he showed the Broadway Suit—a man's suit with short, full trousers worn with a straw hat. 'I wanted to bring some humour into fashion: adapt the street humour, its freedoms, the arrogance of punk. But of course with dignity, luxury and style' (Saint Laurent, 1978, quoted in *Yves Saint Laurent Retrospective*, 1986).[6]

In retrospect, Saint Laurent will be remembered as most famous for introducing the 'midi' trench coats that were worn over trousers, his tuxedo suits for women and the peasant dresses that he designed from 1973.

The combination of feminine features, such as frills, with a tailored masculine style created an ambiguity which many felt reflected the dual role of women in our society. This is particularly obvious in his T-shirt dresses and his *Le Smoking* (black tie) garments, both designed in 1966. With a see-through blouse and trousers tailored from a man's tuxedo, *Le Smoking* was to be worn at sophisticated evening parties and

Figure 5.5 Yves Saint Laurent, embroidered cotton peasant ensemble, Rive Gauche range, France, 1976. Collection: Powerhouse Museum, Sydney. Photographer: Powerhouse Museum Photography Department. The peasant look became one of YSL's seminal prêt-a-porter collection themes. This series was sold in Rive Gauche specialty stores.

reappeared many times during the course of the next decade. Saint Laurent sensed that women in trouser suits, for both daytime and evening wear, would become a major fashion statement over the next four decades. In *Paris Match* (4 December 1981), he commented: 'If I had to choose one design among all I have created, it would be Le Smoking. Every year since 1966, it has been part of my collection. In a sense it is the Yves Saint Laurent trademark.' In the same year, he opened a number of Rive Gauche boutiques, which sold his designer ready-to-wear line. Like Cardin, the *maison* of Yves Saint Laurent was consolidating its financial standing in the industry.

In significant terms, Saint Laurent made a decided contribution to the changing role of women in the 1960s. A feature article in the *New York Times* (13 January 2002), entitled 'When Trousers were a Statement', pointed out that 'people had forgotten what a big deal it was' when women started to 'wear the trousers in the family, along with men'. While the first famous woman to be photographed wearing trousers was Sarah Bernhardt in 1899 (see Chapter 6), and they featured in Paul Poiret's *Les Choses de Paul Poiret* illustrated by Georges Lepape in 1911, it was not until the 1920s that they were introduced into fashion—primarily for sportswear purposes. They became a functional necessity during wartime, when women took on men's jobs in the factories, fields and ammunition depots, but it wasn't until the 1960s that evening trousersuits were designed for women to wear for formal occasions. Interestingly, in the 1970s, the New York fashion retailer Ellin Salzman, wearing a tweed Saint Laurent trousersuit, was barred from Claridge's Hotel in London. (She defiantly removed her trousers and walked in wearing only her jacket!) While women in trousers were outlawed in many upmarket venues in the mid-1960s, by the 1970s most establishments had come to regard trousers as suitable attire for women. Saint Laurent, following in Chanel's steps forty years later, appropriated men's fashion in order to break down established gender codes in his creation of elegant women's trousersuits.

Laura Ashley

Popular culture not only influenced designers such as Saint Laurent; when television sets became available to large sectors of the community in the 1960s, television programmes, as well as cinema, began to impact upon the stylistic direction of fashion. Series such as *Little House on the Prairie* (1974), set in the days of late nineteenth-century American settlers, kindled a historical revival of Victorian working-class dress. Classic books describing nineteenth-century life became popular, and reprints of old favourites such as *Little Women*, *Pride and Prejudice* and *Tess of the D'Urbervilles* flooded bookshops. Perhaps inspired by a reaction to an age of accelerating change which proliferated advancements in technology, this nostalgia for the past and a revival of idealized romanticism had a substantial impact upon both the literary and visual arts, including fashion. The British designer Laura Ashley revisited the look of the long pioneer dresses of the late 1800s. Ashley's business began in 1957 when she was making 'country overalls' for women, which evolved into long, country-style dresses. By the mid-1960s, they had become a fashion fad amongst the young. By using textiles covered in small floral designs, reminiscent of Victorian wallpaper designs from the Arts and Crafts movement, the dresses recreated a romantic simulacrum of the image of a simple, uncomplicated lifestyle. These loose-fitting garments, which allowed for total freedom of body movement (no undergarments required), were quickly adopted by students and artists alike, and proved to be an ideal form of 'alternative dress'. This 'granny' dress preceded the 'peasant' dress, and soon flowing, hand-painted and embroidered ethnic-look garments were entering high fashion in the couture houses of Yves Saint Laurent, Bill Gibb and Zandra Rhodes.

According to Laver (1995), the early 1970s paved the way for the stylistic pluralism of the 1990s:

> Individuality and self-expression were paramount. Clothing was often customized with embroidered, appliquéd and patchworked designs. Tie-dyed T-shirts became popular. Colours were muted and textiles predominantly made from natural fibres. In Britain, at the top end of the market, Bill Gibb became famous for his stunning appliquéd and embroidered designs and Zandra Rhodes for her exquisite, ethereal, hand-screened silk and chiffon garments. In Italy, the Missonis did much to elevate the status of knitwear in fashion, incorporating subtle patterns and blends of colour. (1995: 266–67)

Valerie Steele's *Paris Fashion* (1999) insightfully comments that the 'obsession with British and American popular culture'—seen across Europe and Asia in the proliferation of Saint Laurent's pea jackets and pop art dresses, and Cardin's use of industrial zippers—was actually generated from ideas that came out of Seventh Avenue rather than Paris.

THE T-SHIRT: A BLANK CANVAS

From humble beginnings, the T-shirt, like Levi's jeans, transformed itself from a basic working-class, utilitarian garment into a postmodernist signpost that advertised and expressed personal interests and individual beliefs. Constructing identity through lifestyle is determined by 'the type of popular cultural products we consume, and the creative uses to which we put these products or commodities' (Kidd, 2002: 109). Just like the T-shirt, new products—like the beanbag (designed by Gatti, Teodoro and Paolini in 1968–9)—spoke to one's emotional and sensual, rather than functional, needs. The quest to define 'self' amongst postmodernist youth culture was paralleled by the popularity and rise of the T-shirt. The new consumerist-led society relied on diversity and changeability, which was precisely what the inexpensive T-shirt offered.

Like blue jeans, T-shirts have become cultural icons, and are usually discussed within a paradigm of capitalism, sociability and leisure lifestyles. The visual pluralism that they offer includes expressions of social or political beliefs or affiliations, and likes or interests, and they easily become an advertisement for commercial products or a medium for self-expression. They replace postcards or photographs, depicting the places that one has visited, as well as acting as a souvenir of one's travels. The 'I ♥ NY' slogan by Milton Glazier has been copied by cities around the world, but originated in New York—the home of the quick message. Madison Avenue, famous for its 'ad men', used T-shirts in the 1940s to gain support for the presidential elections. Long before anyone else, they comprehended the potential of clothing as a new form of visual dialogue.

The T-shirt has been described as a form of 'political poster', and as a tattoo that 'acts as a second skin'. As a graphic tool, it has become a mandatory means of sartorial protest for the young. Protest campaigns about Civil Rights and the Vietnam War were referenced in the visual arts. Graphic designers such as R&K Brown (1969) in their appropriated *Iwo Jima* photograph, and George Maciunas's (1969) *American Flag* poster protested about genocide committed by American troops in conflicts over the century. In 1968, Japanese artist Hirokatsu, as a reminder of the Second World War, created a poster entitled *No More Hiroshimas*, and Ron Borowski's sardonic photograph of a black American, with an American flag superimposed over his face, read: 'I pledge allegiance to the flag of the USA . . . where all men are created equal'. T-shirts were worn to street marches as a sign of peaceful protest, with their verbal and visual references acting as effective communication tools, bridging language and cultural barriers. Both the hippies of the 1960s and the punks of the 1970s used the T-shirt as a means of protest and propaganda, with perhaps one of the most controversial being produced by fashion designer Vivienne Westwood in 1977. The image of Queen Elizabeth with a safety pin through her nose was a bold political statement that enraged the British, and was seen as an unforgivable act of rebellion.

With the invention of Pastisol in 1959, a plastic printing ink that couldn't be washed out of fabric, plastic transfers and spray paint, the mass production of T-shirts gathered speed in the 1960s. By 1965, marketing professionals had begun to recognize the T-shirt as a medium for exploiting product branding internationally. As a walking billboard, they provided unpaid advertising for companies such as Budweiser, Coca-Cola, Disneyland and, later, sporting companies such as Nike and Slazenger. The use of constant repetition as a tool, adopted by commercial television advertisements to hypnotize viewers, inspired Warhol's silkscreen multiple prints of Campbell's soup tins.

In much the same way that Warhol's images were seen as a blatant comment on consumerism and the manipulation of the public by advertising agencies and media corporations, the T-shirt serves a similar purpose. They use both irony and satire to critique the superficialities of society. Most effectively, they are used as a means of expressing cynicism about the dominant culture. They can make provocative statements about racism, gender, violence and obscenity. Postmodernist artists use humour extensively to point out the contradictions and complexities of modern life. As a form of self-expression or self-branding, the T-shirt conveys messages to others indicating one's preference for a particular style of music or band, and acts as a conversational catalyst for like-minded people. Musicians and rock groups use T-shirts as 'memorabilia retailing' for their tours, seen as an important part of the promotional fanfare. Slogans such as 'I'm High on Life', 'The Anti-Everything T-Shirt' and 'Born Free' were popular in the 1960s and 1970s.

Fashion historian Leslie Watson (2003) explains how the 1980s ushered in political correctness and social awareness in London. She notes that designer Katherine Hamnett launched a T-shirt collection called Choose Life—clothes with a social message, including 'Stop Acid Rain', 'Preserve the Rainforests' and '58% Don't Want Pershing'. The last-mentioned shirt (a protest against the deployment of American nuclear weapons in Britain) was worn by the designer herself when she met Prime Minister Margaret Thatcher at Downing Street in 1984 (2003: 125). Ecological T-shirts were made of cotton that had been grown without the use of pesticides or from recycled materials. It seems that the greater the commitment to a cause, the more blatant the message becomes.

Clothing speaks to both strangers and observers (Finkelstein, 1996: 79). In art, like fashion, the T-shirt has been used to reflect the culture of the street and the everyday, and has turned T-shirts with slogans into art objects. Artist Jenny Holzer produced an 'Abuse of Power Comes as No Surprise' T-shirt, while graffiti artist Keith Haring used T-shirts to bridge the gap between the street (the subway, actually) and the museum. These T-shirts—also Hamnett's protest shirts—were exhibited at the Documenta VII exhibition, held at the Fashion Moda Gallery in East Village New York in 1982. Chris Townsend, in *Rapture: Art's Seduction by Fashion* (2002), remarks that: 'For a while, both art and fashion were unified in making the billboard for the body'. He elaborates:

> The model of artist-driven retailing developed by Fashion Moda, with its roots in Claes Oldenburg's pop art project *The Store*, would persist as an enterprise to which young artists could resort to sell their ideas, turned into low-priced editions. The T-shirt as cheap medium for artwork, made by that art into a statement of individuality, would likewise remain a staple of such activities. Amongst the most notorious of such enterprises was the shop run by Tracey Emin and Sarah Lucas in East London in the early 1990s. The self-deprecating irony of their 'Complete Arsehole' T-shirt neatly summarizes a shift in concerns over a decade of art practice, from the ideological earnestness of the early 1980s to a micro-celebrity culture where individual identity was paramount, even in its mocking erasure. Fashion, as much as art, could readily accommodate both extremes. (2002: 47)

Figure 5.6   Dolce & Gabbana, grey James Dean T-Shirt, 2011. Photographer: author. Celebrity icons never go out of fashion.

DISPOSABLE FASHION

The idea of cheap, disposable fashion as well as disposable art became manifest in the notions of postmodernity. It was the message and not the medium that was of primary concern. Fads or 'short-lived' fashions challenged the concept of permanence, classic styling and practicality. Neo-Dadaism, as it was called in artistic circles, reignited an interest in Duchamp's early work. This renewed interest in conceptual art was initiated by Duchamp's first exhibition in New York in the early 1960s (which included his famous 1917 ready-made, a urinal entitled *Fountain*). It was held at Alfred Steiglitz's gallery, Gallery 291 on Fifth Avenue (after it had been rejected by mainstream institutions). In 1963, the first great Duchampian retrospective was held in Los Angeles, and it reinforced the notion of the ready-made, which not only influenced the development of pop art but also helped to consolidate interest in conceptual art. It evolved around the Fluxus movement, and was inspired by a number of post-war artists who, in the 1950s, effectively exhibited nihilistic work that questioned the nature of the art product itself. New York artist Robert Rauschenberg exhibited *Erased De Kooning Drawing* (1953), which was a piece of blank paper. In 1957, Yves Klein declared that his paintings were now invisible and to prove it he exhibited an empty room. It was called *The Surfaces and Volumes of Invisible Pictorial Sensibility*. The birth of the conceptual art movement, which dated from approximately 1967 to 1978, formally acknowledged that the idea or conceptual process was more important than the end product, or artefact. It was the means, rather than the end, that mattered. Arguably, an end art product was not necessary at all, and the event or the art process could be recorded for history through photography or video.

By the end of the 1960s, 'happenings'—which were seen as a type of art 'performance'—gathered strength, and they became integral to the anti-materialistic views of the hippie movement. They embraced social change and emancipation for women, students and children. They were tied to 'the extraordinary productions of pop concerts—from the Rolling Stones to The Who, from Roxy Music to Alice Cooper—the new performance became stylish, flamboyant and entertaining' (Goldberg, 2001: 154). Contemporary performance art evolved from these conceptual beginnings. Art could be ephemeral and transient. 'Live gestures have constantly been used as a weapon against the conventions of established art' (Goldberg, 2001: 7).

It is more than coincidence that paper dresses were very much a fashion fad between 1966 and 1968.[7] The Victoria and Albert Museum in London holds paper dresses in its collection, categorized under 'Subcultures'. With paper dresses, the purchaser could use scissors, crayons, paint and stickers to customize the garment. Paper clothing had all the attributes necessary to be truly democratic fashion—it was affordable, accessible and appealed to the young. In *Art History*, Whitely (1989: 82) discusses how the low cost of manufacturing and printing paper garments was in keeping with the pop art sensibility of 'enjoy it today; sling it tomorrow' consumerism. He adds that, at a time when fashions changed so rapidly in order to be up to date, it didn't matter if the fashion consumer purchased inexpensive, flimsy garments because by the time they were worn out, they were also out of fashion. Commenting on the Boutique Paraphernalia, Warhol characteristically quips: 'Almost everything in the store would disintegrate within a couple of weeks, so this was really pop.' In the 1960s, people's expectations were that disposability was the way of the future (Healy, 1996: 28), and as paper could not last for more than one or two wearings, this contributed to its up-to-the-minute fashionability.

In the world of science and technology, society was increasingly developing a throwaway mentality. NASA had considered paper clothing for space travel, and the Scott Paper Company released a psychedelic paisley dress in 1966 as an advertising gimmick to promote a new line of table napkins in the United States. They offered readers a paper dress for $1.25 and, in less than six months, 500,000 dresses had been sold. The dress was very fragile and light-sensitive, as the material was made from binding wood pulp and rayon mesh. Mars Manufacturing Corporation, America's leading producer of paper dresses, used the wonder fabric Kaycel, as it was both fire- and water-resistant, and the dresses were labelled 'Waste Basket Boutique'. France produced the paper bikini, designed to disintegrate upon contact with water, and Dispo in London sold throwaway paper dresses that could withstand three washes and three ironings. Campbell's brought out the Souper Dress—a sleeveless paper shift which featured repetitive Campbell's soup cans (à la Warhol) as a promotional piece of fun clothing. American graphic designer Harry Gordon designed a series of poster dresses (one was a close-up shot of an eye with long eyelashes), with images screen-printed on to an A-line mini dress that fastened at the shoulders with Velcro straps.

The designer Paco Rabanne was commissioned by Scott Paper to make paper dresses to complement his better-known plastic and metal creations designed for the Paris catwalk. Alexandra Palmer (2001: 85–105) explains that paper clothing, which appeared to be nothing more than a very short-lived fad, had a considerable impact upon the fashion of the day. She offers an extensive catalogue of the large variety of garments worn by both ordinary people and an array of celebrities. Among others, she lists the Beatles' custom-made neon orange jackets worn on their Los Angeles visit, the paper saris of Air India's hostesses, plus numerous garments worn by the rich and famous at high-profile paper balls and dinners. She elaborates:

> The extensive interest generated by paper garments is exhibited by the diversity of places where the clothes were worn and by the spectrum in age and social position of those who wore them. A benefit in Washington had the guests trade in their Dior clothes to be auctioned, and in return were given paper dresses to wear . . . the highly fashionable Mrs Kennedy was one of the guests . . . the Duchess of Windsor, who was on the 'Best Dressed' list, wore a paper dress thus providing a role model for older and more conventional women to wear them. (2001: 85–105)

The mission of the pop artists was to take art 'out of the galleries into the streets', the main objective being to make art part of life, as it had been until the eighteenth century. Undoubtedly, in terms of cultural significance, this was the main contribution of the paper dress. With its novelty value, it became a metaphor for the concept of disposability in a modern industrialized society. By reinforcing the potential for the successful substitution of materials, it attested to the unlimited possibilities for fashion within the new technological world.

YOUTH CODES: THE HIPPIE MOVEMENT

The hippie movement embraced the anti-consumerist appeal of ethnic clothing. This became a passive form of anti-fashion—or at least a counter-cultural dress that was seen as integral to the hippie movement and the anti-war protests of the late 1960s and early 1970s. Despite the fact that this look was inspired by a raised social consciousness, it was quickly adopted by designers at the high end of town, as well as the mass-market manufacturers on Seventh Avenue. In the United States in the 1970s, 'artwear' was concerned with charting an identity separate from fashion and the clothing industry. One-of-a-kind artwear, intended exclusively for a gallery or museum audience, and produced by designers such as Zandra Rhodes and Vivienne Westwood, gained recognition in the cultural framework of the 1970s.

'Street style' fashion became synonymous with hand-made cloth, individually handcrafted wooden jewellery, macramé belts, crocheted tops, and hand-embroidered images and lettering that were used to create unique, personalized jeans. The hippie culture placed emphasis on the primacy of the personal connection of the artist and the patron, and reinforced a cultural link between the art clothing and the wearer. In summary, it was a rejection of industrial and technological processes. This form of street style dress manifested the concerns of the times and, like a banner, publicly announced the dissatisfaction of American youth with the conservative mainstream values of American society, the participation of the American government in the conflict in Vietnam, and society's ideas about masculinity. Both young men and women wore caftans, jeans, cheesecloth tops, velvet cloaks and Afghan coats that were hand-embroidered with slogans such as 'Make love, not war'; such clothing not only advertised their political views and their libertine philosophy towards marriage and raising a family, but also indicated changes in sexual morality.

As Yves Saint Laurent had consistently noted, clothes were a form of protest. Handmade peace motifs, the marijuana leaf, love beads and headbands became symbolic expressions of a subculture that resisted the influence of mainstream American society. The hippie culture adopted multicultural styling, including Afro hairstyles, facial and body painting and adornment. Tribal customs such as ceremonial love-ins reinforced members' constructed identity as belonging to a rebellious and non-conforming social group. The hippie movement began in San Francisco's Haight-Ashbury area and spread quickly across the country. This subculture group refused to work, own property or material objects (other than a guitar), nor were they prepared to embrace the Great American Dream. 'Dropping out' became a romanticized, alternative lifestyle for the young, and denim and patched dungarees became appropriated as a symbol of working-class, socialistic ideologies. Second-hand and vintage clothes were worn with hippie pride. The hippie movement had an unprecedented influence on global fashion, and very rapidly became a worldwide phenomenon. Haute couture designers, jumping on the bandwagon, sold the look—though not the dogma—to the highest bidder.

Zandra Rhodes

Zandra Rhodes, a British designer, was one of the first to capitalize on this new street style. Zandra's colourful guise echoed her own creations. She emerged from a textile art background, first studying at the Medway College of Art and then receiving a scholarship to continue her studies at the Royal College of Art in London. Like Quant, she set up her own boutique, making up her own garments in the Fulham Road Clothes Shop. She capitalized on the labour-intensive ethnic look, with hand-dyed chiffon and silk fabric in brilliant rainbow colours with hand-beaded or embroidered features. These ethnic dresses suited progressive upper middle-class women who wanted to demonstrate their high-mindedness or their individualized personas. Rhodes, a perfectionist down to the last detail, researched the themes of her collections thoroughly before she started to design specific textiles for each range. Her diverse influences, like those of Saint Laurent, came from history, nature, her travels, street styles and other designers' work.

Her ranges have included the Chinese collection, the Ayers Rock collection, the Shell collection, the Zebra collection and the Conceptual Chic collection. She became famous for her punk fashions, which she—like Vivienne Westwood—appropriated from the street. She designed a range of wedding dresses made up of ripped white fabric, creating holes and frayed edges that were pinned together with 18-carat gold safety pins from Cartier.

Rebellion Becomes Mainstream

Like so many of the street style fashions that were slowly absorbed by the fashion houses, copied by industry and then sold back to middle-class consumers, both the hippie and the punk fashions proved to be highly successful business enterprises. For McDowell (2000), hippie fashion 'brought with it a new form of status, that of dressing down to please oneself rather than dressing up to please others' (2000: 467). Identification with a particular group in society is considered one of the prime motives for wearing a particular form of dress. Polhemus and Procter (1978) argue that adornment allows us to assert ourselves as individuals, but it also allows us to identify ourselves as part of a social collective. Similarly, Batterberry and Batterberry (1982) contend that, for the hippies, self-expression in dress became an article of faith in their code of rebellion. In socio-political terms, their dress mirrored what they stood for. In other words, meaning inherent in their clothing became paramount to their social and political protest, and when Western designers embraced this look, its social value or currency was diminished. By the end of the 1970s, and well into the 1980s, at least superficially, most fashion had become a form of anti-fashion, following the directions of a proliferation of subcultural modes of dress.

–6–

Anti-Fashion

Clothes make the man. Naked people have little or no influence in society.

Mark Twain

THE DEVIANCE OF FASHION

Until the nineteenth century, any deviance from the established social class differentiation, in terms of dress, was viewed as a serious threat to an ordered society. Throughout history, it seems that there has always existed the wish to 'dress above one's station in life', but doing so often had dire consequences. In the Middle Ages, such behaviour was punishable by death; during the Renaissance, the 'imitator' would be placed in stocks in the town square, at the mercy of passers-by.

According to Hollander (1988), anti-fashion or non-fashion should not be defined in opposition to fashion, but as 'a periodically fashionable attitude' in the history of dress (1988: 350). Anti-fashion has often been defined as a form of nihilism, in much the same way as a revolutionary break with tradition in the fine arts has been labelled 'anti-art'. When this deviation becomes accepted as mainstream, the notion of the avant-garde disappears. While the early dandies, such as England's Beau Brummel, gained cultural capital by using their appearance to raise their status in society, they were in fact inventing a new social order. Brummel's impeccably tasteful dress and personal demeanour were highly regarded, even amongst the aristocracy, and proved to be more influential than class identification. However, when women attempted to wear unconventional dress at the same time in history, it was seen as a cultural affront to the bourgeoisie. When the actress Sarah Bernhardt was photographed wearing trousers, she explained that she wore them only in her sculpture studio, for practical reasons. She appreciated that if women wore trousers or loose-fitting smocks, without corsets, it would be regarded as a counter-cultural assault on modesty, decency and femininity. According to Barwick (1984: 121), these clothes were 'outrageously different, contemptuous of convention, escapist, theatrical, for the Edwardians the whole Bohemian effect was outrageous'.

Finkelstein (1996) reiterates: 'Throughout the history of women's social and economic struggles, dress signals an individual's politics or morality' and that the wearing of trousers and bloomers 'has been regarded as a blatant signal of female sexual abandon and rebelliousness' (1996: 70). Beginning in the 1850s, women's rights advocates and health reformers began to provide women with more practical and healthy dress. Trousers worn under skirts constituted the initial effort. This was followed by underwear reform and the adoption of aesthetic dress. Usually worn without corsets in the home, these empire-waisted garments were often constructed of layers of soft, drapable, transparent silk fabrics. They sometimes shared design elements with classical Greek or medieval clothing. The earliest visual examples of this clothing can be seen in the photographs and drawings of the family members of the pre-Raphaelite painters. The adoption of aesthetic dress was supported in large part through the efforts of the Liberty Company beginning in 1884.

The turn-of-the-century suffragettes purported to use 'male' strategies to lobby for their cause. When they attempted to burn down empty factories as a form of sexual protest, these acts outraged conservative members of society, who indicated that 'not only were they violating their feminine roles', but that they were 'advocating a

Figure 6.1   Sarah Bernhardt wearing a pantsuit in her sculpture studio, c. 1899. This is one of the first photographs of a female celebrity wearing trousers.

range of unorthodox, even criminal practices' (Finkelstein, 1996: 70). When several members of the feminist group in London, including Emily Pankhurst, were jailed, they subsequently staged hunger strikes as a form of protest. Again, these actions readily provoked hostile reactions from the general public, who saw these women as 'terrorists'.[1] Not only was the name of the suffragette movement blackened, but it discouraged the average woman from adopting its dress reforms. It is ironic indeed to note that, by the 1920s—when women in most Western countries had gained the vote, the right to own property and the right to be educated—this style of casual dress had become fashionable.

PUNK FASHION: RHODES AND WESTWOOD

Punk fashion used visual violence rather than political violence to prompt a response from middle-class society. Elements of contrast and contradiction proliferated in the costumes of the street punks, with tribal and ritualistic body accessorizing which suggested metaphoric links to earlier primitive societies. Effrontery in dress, obscenity in language and offensiveness in behaviour characterized the urban punk warrior. Popular music performs an important role in identity creation for contemporary adolescents, because it is the most available and accessible form of media culture for them and, as such, a rich source of cultural meanings and standards to assimilate or resist (Crane 2000: 188). Punk music formed the backbone of this counter-cultural movement, which used dress to display its defiance of the establishments, the institutions and the canons of mainstream society. A study of historical fashion quickly reveals that, in revolution, the mode of dress becomes a badge of political affiliation.

Postmodernist fashion, as discussed earlier, relies on a hypothetical visual paradox: propriety in dress can be replaced by a total lack of respect for status display and value systems. Historically, dress has responded in similar ways to social, political and economic instabilities. In order to highlight the relatively few instances where fashion has responded to anything other than a dominance of sumptuosity, which identified the wearer as having wealth, status and social class standing, only three key periods in history can be cited: first, in the fifteenth century;[2] second, in the seventeenth century, during the Thirty Years War;[3] and finally, in 1780s and 1790s France during the French Revolution,[4] when a sector of society—primarily comprising the young—known as Les Incroyables and Les Merveilleuses displayed extremes of dress as a means of expressing their horror of the 1790s Reign of Terror period.

A return to this exaggeration and distortion in dress emerged in the late 1970s and 1980s,[5] when British punk recreated the most nihilistic fashion worn since the French Revolution. Clearly, it seemed that there was one dominant aesthetic emerging in fashion—a look of poverty, which dominated street style clothing. Yet it was more than poverty; it was aggression, a demand for attention. In Britain,[6] the young railed against the dominant ideology and punks replaced their more passive hippie counterparts. The economy in the early part of the 1980s was in recession, issues of global poverty dominated,[7] and the disparities between rich and poor—even in the wealthiest nations—continued to rise sharply. England, by 1975, had reached its highest level of unemployment since the Second World War, with the young being the hardest hit—especially those who were the least educated and who lived in the lowest socioeconomic areas of London. Britain's economy took a turn for the worse when Harold Wilson's Labour Party came to power and immediately imposed IMF (International Monetary Fund) restrictions on citizens, which many believed cut public expenditure and increased the cost of living. Angry working-class Britons felt that they had been betrayed by their own party. It was a time when youth reacted heatedly against the hypocrisies of the Establishment. Unemployment breeds a sense of worthlessness and desperation. This socio-political disorientation contributed to a social backlash in their music, their fashion and their lifestyle.

The Sex Pistols, the leading punk band in Britain, criticized the autocratic nature of the country with savagery and bitter humour through the lyrics of their *God Save the Queen* single: 'There's no future in England's dreaming.' John Lydon (also known as Johnny Rotten), lead singer of the Sex Pistols, complained: 'If you weren't born into money, then you might as well kiss your life goodbye; you weren't going to amount to anything . . . you were told at school, you were told at the job centre, that you didn't stand a chance; you should just accept your fate and get on with it' (the Sex Pistols' documentary, *The Filth and the Fury*, 1996). When London's streets filled with rubbish due to the continuing strikes of the mid-1970s, Lydon decided that it would be fitting to wear torn trousers and garbage bags cut up to make T-shirts as an outrageous method of presentation—a new aesthetic. On a more conservative note, Barnard (2002) argues that: 'The punks produced their own music and clothing in opposition to the music and fashion system that had become monolithic, unadventurous and predictable' (2002: 136). A number of young artists alternated between art performances and punk performances, and one group called COUM Transmissions held a scandalous exhibition in London's Institute of Contemporary Art in 1976 called *Prostitution*, which documented Cosey Fanni Tutti's activities as a model for a pornographic magazine and resulted in the group being banned, unofficially, from holding any more public exhibitions in England. The following year, the Sex Pistols' records were also blacklisted by radio stations (Goldberg, 2001: 182).

Art and fashion school students helped to define the new look, which became immensely design-conscious. Shiny gold industrial fabrics and plastic-coated cottons were used, along with metal fastenings including zippers, studs, spikes and safety pins. Zippers and webbing used for pockets were placed everywhere on the garment—the more bizarre the position, the better. For some, it was a revival of the 1950s look, with straight-leg drainpipe Teddy Boy trousers worn by men and voluminous mohair sweaters worn by women. For others, the look was unisex—functional but sinister. Punks became increasingly hostile in their dress, adding tribal mutilations, body piercing and swastikas as tattoos and accessories that symbolized their obsession with bondage and other sadomasochistic interests. They wore lavatory chains around their necks, used tampons as decorative accessories and featured pornographic imagery on their T-shirts. Their clothing was dirty, usually tattered and ripped, defiled with obscenities, and held together with pins and string. For the punks, fashion became ugliness—an external form of visual intrusion. They sourced their eclectic clothing and accessories from charity shops and found objects, produced home-made items, and even shopped at sex shops and army surplus stores. This insolent, anti-authoritarian presence appealed to disaffected youth around the world, and quickly became a global phenomenon. Interestingly, with time, this defiance ate through the very fibre of the entire fashionable world.

At first, punk fashion seemed quite distasteful to the *beau monde*. No one really wanted to be reminded of the pain of poverty, or the undignified way that it morally attacked individuals and families. For Bell (1992), this look might have been called 'conspicuous leisure'—in other words, 'visible evidence that one is leading an honourably futile existence' (1992: 32); however, for the punks, honour played no role. The punk aesthetic was steeped in shock value, and it revered what was considered distasteful. As an anti-fashion statement, it was designed to disturb and disrupt the complacency of wider society. Statistics have indicated quite clearly that this fashion was a product of social economics. Historians thought it would be short-lived—merely a fad—but it has mutated over and over again, tied to a global recession that has continued for almost twenty years. In the early 1990s, it was called neo-punk; in the mid-1990s, it evolved into a generic 'grunge' street style.

By 1993, unemployment had reached a peak of 5 million in Britain and, of that total, 1 million were aged between sixteen and twenty-four years (New Policy Institute and Joseph Rowntree Foundation, 1993). Significantly, Valerie Mendes—then Curator of Fashion and Textiles at the Victoria and Albert Museum in London—hosted a fashion exhibition called 'Street Style' (curated by Amy de La Haye) in 1994 which, she contended at the time, received hostile criticism from London's conservative press as being quite an 'inappropriate' exhibition for such an old and prestigious institution. Yet it attracted the largest audience of any 'specialist' exhibition in the history of the museum—35,000 people walked through the turnstiles in the first three days. During these stringent times, it clearly struck a chord with the British public.

In both Zandra Rhodes's and Vivienne Westwood's collections, highly priced slashed and torn garments symbolized an economic irrationality—a social paradigm where a new ethic was embraced and the deconstruction of the fabric reflected, quite literally, the deconstruction of past values. There was an intrinsic irony in the adoption of this aesthetic into designer wear—an industry that fetched high prices as it seemingly mocked this underprivileged sector of society. Rhodes's collections, in particular, caused controversy. Polhemus (1996: 94) disparagingly comments that: 'The European fashion centres are churning out chic imitation punk garb and Zandra Rhodes—"High Priestess of Punk"—fattens her bulging bank balance by selling the punk image to Dallas, New York and Chicago.' He argues that the punk fashion was about anti-fashion and anti-commercialism—both of which Rhodes ignored. He insists that her garments defied the unexpected nature of true punk fashion, as everything she did was calculated and created with the intention of being aesthetically pleasing. While Rhodes's Conceptual Chic collection is decidedly glamorous, Steele (2001: 47) argues that Westwood was the direct inspiration for Rhodes's designs. Unremittingly critical as Polhemus was, Rhodes's appropriation of images, themes and symbols from a different cultural context was inherent to postmodernist practice.

In contrast, Westwood's threateningly aggressive and visually provocative form of dress shocked the fashion audience in the 1970s just as much as it did in the 1980s—albeit in a much more direct way. Mulvagh (1992) claims that Westwood was the only designer who directly researched gang cults among the young, and designed to suit this taste, while other designers such as Rhodes, Mugler, Montana and Gaultier merely applied the style to their collections—which was particularly evident in 1977 (Mulvagh, 1992: 344, 356). Not only did Westwood initially imitate the punks' eclectic DIY look, appropriating imagery from a diversity of sources, but she was able to sustain her anti-Establishment reputation throughout her career.

With Malcolm McLaren, she opened her SEX boutique in London, and McLaren became the manager of the Sex Pistols. Johnny Rotten wore Westwood's clothes, and the Sex Pistols helped to put punk rock into the popular media with their loud anti-music and their obscene behaviour. Some of Westwood's most innovative work came from these early years, when she used underwear as outerwear—a postmodern trend that was seen later in the collections of Gianni Versace and Jean-Paul Gaultier, amongst others. This move also highlighted the role of fetishism in sexuality—an issue that was assuming greater importance in critical thinking about the cultural construction of sexuality. Considering that the feminists of the 1960s and 1970s were full of rage and strictly anti-sexist in their views, the rebellious nature of Westwood's blatant use of sexuality did not seem to fit well with their ideological focus. Arnold (2001: 47) argues that Westwood pioneered a fashion for young women that was threatening and overtly hostile, thereby freeing them from the need to aspire to a particular fashionable ideal of beauty.

Women artists in the 1970s and 1980s also adopted a much more blatant and provocative stance in their work. Judy Chicago became infamous for *The Dinner Party* (1974–1979), where a large, triangular table was set with symbolic ceramic plates representing thirty-nine famous feminist guests of honour. However, as the work was in homage to women's history, the plates featured a floral-like sculpture that was sup-posed to represent the female vulva. According to the artist, *The Dinner Party* aimed to end the ongoing cycle of omission in which women were written out of the historical record. The scale of the installation—14.5 m (48 ft) on each side—visually symbolizes the magnitude of female achievement traditionally reserved for men.

As pottery, textiles and craft skills were seen as women's work at this time, these seemed to be the most appropriate media for parodying sexist society. American Barbara Kruger used graphic design to create a series of provocative posters that challenged the perceived stereotyping that women had endured for years. *Untitled (I shop therefore I am)* of 1987 portrays the previously held belief that consumerism creates identity.

Cindy Sherman uses clothing and performance art to depict stereotypical roles that women play in society in her *Untitled Film Stills*. Her methodology is based on con-structing individual personas to reconstitute the identity of self and to mimic mass me-dia's configurations of femininity. The series is both humorous and devastating at the same time. In another series, she questions the notion of the ideal female body when she uses prosthetic body parts procured from a medical supply shop to create garish robotic figures that mimic human actions. Also, her photographs of large, old, sagging women comment on a new ideal of beauty, and she deliberately turns genital imagery into a form of pornography. Cindy Sherman's practice (in the early 1980s) witnessed fashion's entry into art's discourses (Townsend, 2002: 50). Dressing up in designer clothing (from the collections of Gaultier and Kawakubo, amongst others), she bridged the gap between art and business. Townsend argues that:

> Fashion has for some time taken its cues from art, not Hollywood . . . [and yet at the same time] art's response had largely been to incorporate fashion into its own histories . . . [Sher-man's] costumed performances within the photograph referenced the emergence of a new generation of designers such as Jean-Paul Gaultier, one of whose jumpsuits was worn by the artist in *Untitled # 131*, 1983. Sherman also directly interpolated her imagery into the discourse of imagination and consumption, that she analysed by producing it in collaboration with a New York retailer, Dianne B, who used a range of the images for advertising purposes. What was, at one level, a critical commentary, became, through the process of its creation, an extension of the subject of its critique. (2002: 52)

Not surprisingly, her ambivalent photographs were among those included in the Spring/Summer 1993 issue of *Harper's Bazaar*.

Both Sherman and Westwood share a similar sense of irony and irreverence, and combine an interesting aesthetic and concept in their work. Westwood reportedly stated: 'The only reason I'm in fashion is to destroy the word "conformity". Nothing's interesting to me unless it's got that element.' Her breakthrough came in 1989, when John Fairfield, the publisher of *Women's Wear Daily*, named her as one of the top designers in the world, amongst Yves Saint Laurent, Giorgio Armani, Emmanuel Ungaro, Karl Lagerfeld and Christian Lacroix (McDermott, 2000: 10). In 2004 the Victoria and Albert Museum chose Westwood's work for a travelling exhibition—an honour rarely accorded to a living designer. She received an OBE (Order of the British Empire) for services to fashion in 1992, and in 2006 she was made a Dame.

FASHION AS IDEOLOGY: BENETTON, MOSCHINO AND GAULTIER

Fashion spending can be part of a new political platform that is sympathetic to the ambitions of various eco-movements, as well as those against racism and sexism, and those forms of local politics that advocate national pride and tribalism (Finkelstein, 1996: 76). The highly successful Benetton label was based on the marketing strategy that individuals use branding to identify with social or political 'causes'. Benetton's advertising rarely shows an image of the product, because the product becomes secondary to the social 'consciousness' that it sells with its clothing. The photographs used in Benetton's advertising campaigns rely on visual shock to gain and sustain the viewer's interest. The memory of the visual image of a black woman suckling a white baby makes a statement regarding racial integration, while a young man dying of Aids, surrounded by his family, reinforces the humanitarian need for compassion for this affliction. These sentiments become associated with the label, which is intrinsically linked with the actual clothing. The consumers are buying a social placebo, which signifies that they share a common philosophy and are monetarily contributing to a cause—thereby justifying the expense, as it is akin to making a charitable donation.

Franco Moschino used a 1960s neo-pop approach to create anti-fashion statements. Using irony as a postmodernist tool to critically comment on fashion orthodoxy, his work was considered both avant-garde and fashionably provocative. Within a similar visual arts framework, the Italian Moschino used both text and design to humorously communicate parodic messages. For example, he blatantly designed a ticker tape rendition that wrapped the body but left the buttocks exposed. With text running across the back spelling out 'C–H–E–A–P' in large letters, he produced a zany but tasteless comment. On another level, he combined Duchamp's conceptualism with baroque extravagance. He capitalized on the 1980s obsession with designer labels by creating a unique signature style for his customers, whom he said 'had their own distinct personalities'. At the same time, he produced pastiches of the work of other designers—commenting, for example, on the banality of much commercial fashion of the Calvin Klein type by producing his own line of underpants, worn on top of trousers and bearing the waistband slogan 'To Be Shown in Public' (McDowell, 1997: 199). For *Uomo Vogue* fashion journalist Mariuccio Casadio (1997): 'Through art, performances and a passion for the provocative and unconventional, ever present in his designs, as well as through a unique conception of exhibiting space and an understanding of gesture and pose, Moschino still holds a prominent intellectual position in fashion' (1997: 19).

Unpredictability was a strong element of Moschino's work, and his fashion shows turned into performance art with an underlying ironic critique. T-shirts and other garments printed with 'Now is all there is', 'IN LOVE WE TRUST' and 'You can't judge a girl by her clothes' used verbal puns that were characteristic of his humour. Moschino 'highlights the cruelties and paradoxes of contemporary culture, the endlessly regenerated power of the ready-made and the din of forms and banality by which we are controlled and surrounded' (Casadio, 1997: 30).

In the late 1980s, Moschino embraced technology, using short videos to highlight a selection of the clothes in his collections. In a revisiting of the 1960s, he designed

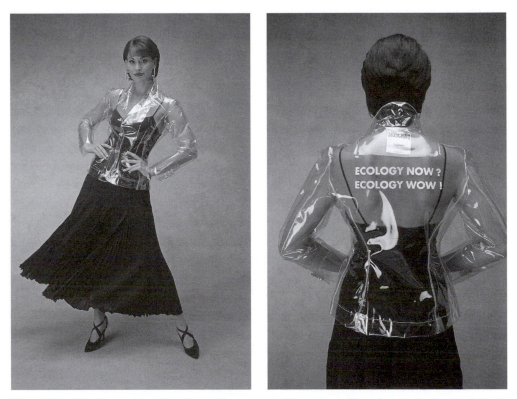

Figure 6.2 A & B   Franco Moschino, black silk slip evening dress worn with a clear plastic fitted jacket with white stitching, front and back view, Eco-culture collection, Italy 1994. Collection: Powerhouse Museum, Sydney. Model: Joslyn Baxter. Photographer: Andrew Frolows. On the back, printed in white, are the words: 'ECOLOGY NOW? ECOLOGY WOW!' This led to Moschino's Ecoculture collection, launched in the same year, the first ecological collection designed with environmentally friendly materials and dyes.

a dress constructed from plastic-coated cards that were linked together, in much the same way as Paco Rabanne did, but overlaid them with printed images and synthetic materials (such as fake hair) not normally used in high fashion. He pumped up jackets and stoles by using inflatable PVC materials in his Couture! collection. He appropriated fun imagery from film, animation, media and pop culture, to which the young at heart responded. To a greater extent, his work is reminiscent of Schiaparelli when he uses a *trompe l'œil* effect to create visual paradox. His Organic Bikini (which was made by sowing and watering real grass), hats in the form of wedding cakes, and white handbags dripping with melted chocolate, all paid lip service to the visual irony of neo-Surrealism, which reinvented itself in the early 1980s. The Label Queen dress, created from shopping bags for a window display in his New York boutique on Madison Avenue, made a reflexive statement about excessive levels of consumerism in society—a consumerism generated by the fashion industry in particular.

Similarly, the Swiss artist Sylvie Fleury collects shopping bags featuring designer labels, which become part of her museological installations. In her work *Delicious* (1994), Fleury entices her audience to make associations with wealth, glamour, style and status. The contents remain untouched as they sit on the gallery floor. Labels such as Chanel, Armani, Tiffany & Co. suggest the purchase of luxury items such as clothing, perfume and jewellery. Jessica Berry (2005: 39–43) suggests that the artwork centres on the process of shopping and discarding, and constructs the notion that the act of acquiring, for fetishist collectors, is vital to their enjoyment of the object. She argues that, unlike the pop artists of the 1960s and 1970s whose work critiqued consumerism, Fleury presents the fetishized commodity collection as positive and desirable. Her work underlines the irony of the museum as 'department store'—an issue debated by art historians Emma Barker (1999) and Mary-Anne Staniszewski (1998), who agree that many museums have become indistinguishable from shopping malls in order to promote interaction between object and viewer.

Gender issues from the 1960s resurfaced in the 1980s. The women's liberation movement had lobbied for equality in employment in terms of pay, benefits and promotional opportunities. In the 1980s, despite the fact that an equal opportunities act was enacted in many Western countries,[8] women in professional careers used fashion as a political language to illustrate their expectations of power and position in the management structures of large corporations. Ironically, as the more casual, loose-fitting garments popularized by Armani, the Americans and the Japanese avant-garde designers were embraced by male executives, the fitted tailored suits traditionally worn by men found refuge in women's businesswear.[9] Visually, at least, there appeared to be a role reversal. This style of dress was worn particularly by women who were trying to 'break through the glass ceiling'—a common feminist cliché. 'Hard chic' was slick, high-fashion look—competent and cut-throat. It allowed women to look professional, high-powered and successful, and it didn't matter if they actually worked or not. Power dressing relied on mimicking the male silhouette, with square, padded shoulders, narrow skirts or trousers with belts, and tailored blouses (that in many ways resembled Arrow brand business shirts). Well-cut jackets exuded a sense of confidence and authority.

Philip Morris cigarettes launched Virginia Slims (1967–86) in the late 1960s. Advertisements for the product promoted the idea of slimness being equated with smoking, rather than eating. The ads played on themes of freedom, independence and women's emancipation, and the product adopted the ideal slogan: 'You've come a long way, baby'. While the promotion enraged feminists, it became one of the company's most successful cigarette marketing campaigns in history, as the number of young women smoking rose dramatically.

Jean-Paul Gaultier's designs for menswear also reflected changing attitudes towards gender representation in the 1980s and 1990s. While the canons regarding suitability of dress for men had altered slightly, Gaultier aggressively contested gender stereotyping by consistently presenting cross-dressing in his menswear collections. His male models wear feather boas, bejewelled bodices, corsets and furs, and skin-tight trousers that do not deny masculinity but offer an alternative vision of sensual male attire. His clothing—both for men and women—could be described as fetishistically obsessed, reflecting a social deviance and defiance. He made body piercing and tattoos acceptable on the Paris catwalk by using models that he had chosen from the street—real people. Often described as the 'bad boy' of fashion, Gaultier's subversive designs had a considerable influence on contemporary twentieth-century fashion. Other designers followed suit, including Vivienne Westwood, Thierry Mugler, Dolce & Gabbana and America's John Bartlett.

STREET STYLE

Karl Lagerfeld has suggested that Mary Quant became the first symbol of street fashion because of the great diversity in her collections. However, by the 1990s, according to Polhemus (1994: 131), 'the history of street style . . . [had become] a vast theme park'. In the 1980s, nostalgia opened the floodgates for revivalism of many of the past street styles—'neo-mods, neo-Teds, neo-hippies, neo-psychedelics, neo-punks and . . . neo-New Romantics' (1994: 130). He also argues (1994: 131) that this 'supermarket of style' first emerged in Japan, and that every piece of attire worn 'comes as part of a complete semiological package deal' (see Chapter 7). Collage aesthetics, consisting of a juxtaposition of words and images, multiply meanings and associations, which contributes to formulating a multi-layered 'reading' of the work or a diversification of identity for the fashion wearer.

Polhemus (1994: 130) insists that: 'Street style . . . [in the 1990s] is characterized by the extent to which it exists within the shadow of its own past.' More critically, social historian Dick Hebdige (1987) sees British street style as 'the decay of the present while viewing the past'. He argues that design uses objects that have been detached from their original sources and reused in such a way 'that history is turned into personal memory'. He alludes to the fashion charade of neo-punk, which 'exists everywhere but comes from nowhere', and tacitly comments that punks now expect to be paid to be photographed. Cynicism prevailed in the fashion of the 1990s. By the middle of the decade, fashion journalists had become highly critical of the constant rehashing of appropriated styles, as well as the lack of originality and sincerity in design. They, amongst many others, signalled the demise of the haute couture empire. Ailing economies and the Gulf War, with its rising oil prices and halting trade with Arab Emirate countries, contributed to the fall in sales of high fashion and perfume.

Only a few designers avoided the pastiche and nostalgia that was overworked in design terms, and overpriced for many who could not see the value in buying 'underprivileged' clothing. In particular, Mendes and de la Haye (1999) include in this list Issey Miyake (see Chapter 7), Shirin Guild and Asha Sarabhai—designers whom they argue 'reworked their own cultural clothing traditions in a reductionist aesthetic which resulted in modern, functional clothes that were in many respects trans-cultural' (1999: 255). Cultural authenticity was applauded in the work of these Japanese, Iranian and Indian designers. Also, young Belgian designers took deconstruction—which seemed to emerge most convincingly from the design studios of the Japanese Rei Kawakubo and Yohji Yamamoto in the 1980s—to new heights. Trained at the Royal Academy of Fine Arts in Antwerp, Martin Margiela, Ann Demeulemeester, Dirk Bikkembergs and Dries Van Noten made their mark on Parisian fashion. Margiela and Demeulemeester, in particular, 'produce clothes that critique clothes'. Exposed seams highlight the fabrication process, lining is revealed, loose threads hang down like tentacles, fabric draws your attention to surface renderings, and the 'objectification' of the garment encourages a reflexive analysis of the work's meaning. Just as postmodernist art envies fashion's media exposure and glitz, postmodernist fashion searches for greater intellectual credibility. Margiela's Size 74 collection, Spring/Summer 2000, features ridiculously oversized coats, shifts, lingerie and men's business shirts. These larger-than-life clothes dwarf the wearer and make the body appear to shrink in size. By challenging the visual proportions of high-fashion garments, the viewer is forced to 'see' the clothes differently. Irony, inherent in the sizing, is created by the paradoxical idea that sample designer clothes are usually too small to be worn by the average woman, as they range from American size 6 to 8 to fit a model's figure. Margiela's clothes, in comparison, are gigantic! The viewer must conceptually scale down the clothing, and in turn, this clever contradiction demands critical reassessment of the fashion system as it makes implications about the illogical and superficial nature of the industry.

Like fashion, the visual arts adopted a postmodernist 'anti-aesthetic' and 'shock tactics' in their work. Instead of fashion's grunge, neo-punk or heroin chic revealing this anti-aesthetic, artists chose to use detritus materials such as garbage, rotting food and old car bodies in their work. Post-conceptual artist Damien Hirst exhibited his *The Physical Impossibility of Death in the Mind of Someone Living*, a shark in form-aldehyde in a vitrine, at the Saatchi Gallery in London in 1992. In 1999, Tracey Emin was nominated for the British Turner Prize; at the exhibition she showed a work enti-tled *My Bed*, consisting of a dishevelled bed surrounded by detritus such as condoms, bloodstained underwear, bottles and her bedroom slippers. Both fashion and fine art received criticism for these tactics, though fashion was probably targeted more fiercely due to its perpetration of negative body ideals. Comparatively speaking, fashion had only recently defied conventional codes of propriety (emerging in the 1960s along with sexual permissiveness), whereas the fine arts had a long history of defiance and revolt.

Quite literally, by the end of the twentieth century, fashion had become seamlessly allied with grass-roots human issues. Global issues such as homelessness, personal welfare and safety created anxieties that were quickly addressed by leading design-ers, both Western and Eastern. Mendes and de la Haye (1999) elaborate: 'The Italian company Superga created bulletproof clothes, with built-in air pollution masks, acid rain protection and infrared, night-vision goggles. Lucy Orta, a Paris-based conceptual designer, addressed world conflict and the destruction of urban life. Her Refuge Wear range, introduced in 1992, featured multi-functional survival clothes which adapted to form tents and sleeping bags' (1999: 256).

The House of Prada, originally established in 1913, brought out a minimalist range of nylon bags and rucksacks, which became a staple accessory for both men and women in the 1990s. Even Issey Miyake, inspired by the new trend, designed a man's vest that could be converted into a backpack. Younger Japanese designers such as Hiroaki Ohya created *The Wizard of Jeanz* in 1993, a series of twenty-one books that folded out into clothes. The notion of permanence associated with books, which trans-fer knowledge from one generation to another, inspired this idea. Louise Mitchell, curator of the 2005/2006 exhibition *The Cutting Edge: Fashion from Japan* at the Powerhouse Museum in Sydney, Australia, featured his work amongst others. She explains:

The *Wizard of Jeanz* is a technical tour de force, a feat of skill that allows a book to transform into a ruffled neckpiece, a pair of jeans or an elegant evening dress. In a similar experimental mood, Shinichiro Arakawa created a series of garments that are framed like paintings but, once out of the frame, put on and zipped up around the body, become real wearable clothes. Transformable themes are also seen in Aya Tsukioka's wrap skirt, with its apron front screen-printed on the reverse with the image of a vending machine similar to the millions found on Tokyo's streets. When the wearer unties the waistband and lifts the apron above her head, she can 'hide' behind this image. The designer's aim is to provoke laughter by creating clothes that encourage the viewer to recognize the need for moments of respite from the pressures of everyday life. (Mitchell, 2005: 9)

One of the roles chosen by artists since the pop art movement has been that of questioning and challenging consumer desires for the new and improved. Textile artist Miriam Shapiro also claims that young female artists, in particular, are interested in using costume as tent, home, protection and theatrical design. She uses fabric as a metaphor for life—a material that becomes more fragile with age and, as it fades, becomes a reminder of the limited time we have to enjoy life. Miro Schor's work *Dress Book* (1977) is an earlier example of how a dress, formatted as a book, can be used to narrate a story, to act as a diary which records personal feelings and document one's journeys in life. The fragility of the paper can represent vulnerability and the viewer can turn the pages of the dress, reading 'her' like a book. This cross-referencing of similar themes in fashion and art reinforces the importance of identity and meaning to designers and artists alike. Caroline Broadhurst, whose colourless line drawings of skeleton clothes (in the late 1980s) illustrate the link well, explained: 'Clothing holds a visual memory of a person, and it is this closeness to a human being that I am interested in' (Colchester, 1991: 141). Her work communicates the intimacy of clothing, the idea that they have been shaped not just by fashion, but by somebody's life. Undoubtedly, these provocative statements—evident in both fashion and art—question the role that the visual arts play in today's society. Coupled with technological advancements in textile development, personal notions of insecurity, anonymity and tribal affiliations reinforce the concept that fashion actually came from the street and not the catwalk.

−7−

Japanese Conceptual Fashion

Each period, each generation, decides what avant-garde is.

Rei Kawakubo (Comme des Garçons)

Cross-cultural influences, which further melded fashion design with a different form of street style, were introduced by the Japanese designers. Their Zen-based philosophy, based on a preference for simplicity and naturalness, led them to create works of art of a beauty unaffected by the shifting tides of fashion. The subtlety in their work and their distinctive stylistic philosophy have been sustained for decades on the catwalks of Paris.

ISSEY MIYAKE, YOHJI YAMAMOTO AND REI KAWAKUBO

Since the 1970s, the Japanese fashion design of Issey Miyake, Yohji Yamamoto and Rei Kawakubo of Comme des Garçons has had an unequivocal impact on Western dress. Offering a new and unique expression of creativity, they have challenged the established notions of status, display and sexuality in contemporary fashion. Ignoring stylistic trends, these Japanese designers work within a postmodernist visual arts framework, appropriating aspects of their traditional culture and embracing new technological developments and methodologies in textile design. Yet, at the same time, they infuse their work with meaning and memory. The subtleties inherent in their textiles and forms promulgate a new aesthetic in Western dress. Miyake, perhaps the most revered designer in Japan today, has consistently propagated new ideas, new materials and new design directions, which accommodate the modern lifestyle of contemporary women. While the work of Yamamoto and Kawakubo was initially framed as another form of anti-aesthetic, their contribution to the evolution of twentieth-century fashion has been more profound. Their understated work underlines the notion that culture, conceptualization and experimentation can be integral to fashion, as they are to art. By the end of the century, they had helped to change the face of fashion irrevocably.

Figure 7.1 Yohji Yamamoto, Isetan department store display, Tokyo, Homage to Dior collection, Japan, 1997. Photographer: author. At a time
when the house of Dior was looking for a new
head designer, Yamamoto presented this tongue-
in-cheek, deconstructivist tribute to the fine workmanship of traditional Dior garments.

THE AESTHETICS OF POVERTY

Postmodernist fashion relies on visual paradox—underclothing becomes outerwear,
new is replaced by old, and propriety in dress is replaced by a total lack of respect
for the display of status and value systems. Highly priced, slashed and torn garments
symbolize an economic irrationality. A social paradigm is created and a new visual
ethic is embraced. The literal deconstruction of fabric and finishing techniques seemingly reflects the deconstruction of past values.

Harold Koda, Fashion Historian of the Metropolitan Museum of Art, referred to this
new concept of dress, as seen in the work of Yamamoto and Kawakubo, as the 'aesthetics of poverty'—a phrase that seemed to aptly describe the new dress code. This
duality of an extravagance (designer fashion) masked in the garb of noble poverty creates a paradox particular to the Japanese culture. In the traditional tea ceremony, the
highly refined and polished are fused with the rough and the natural. The aim is to
create an effect of sublime beauty, expressing naturalness and ease. The Japanese
preference for understatement is coupled by a love of old things that imply accretions
of time. In their poetry, for example, they acknowledge that perishability is a necessary
element of beauty and the words exemplify their grief over the fragility of both beauty
and love. In their pottery, they choose simple and irregular forms, perhaps cracked,

as they represent both humility and an appreciation of the traces of the individuality of the potter. These aesthetic sensibilities are integral to the work and philosophy of these contemporary Japanese fashion designers.

In Western terms, Koda compared the 1980s trend with the 1890s, a time that also 'saw decadence as an aesthetic ideal' (Martin and Koda, 1993: 97). In ideological terms, dress design has undoubtedly responded to social, political and economic instabilities throughout history. In the 1970s, 1980s and 1990s, global events such as high rates of unemployment, youth revolutions, anti-war sentiment, global poverty and environmental catastrophes impacted greatly upon the conscience of society, and became implicit in postmodernist visual arts practice. While cultural differences existed, both punk fashion and the work of Japanese designers Yohji Yamamoto and Rei Kawakubo reflected this practice. The Japanese fashions were characterized by torn, ripped and ragged fabric, and uneven and unstitched hemlines—a disarray that was quite subversively calculated. Subsequently, due to their unprecedented influence, a new form of anti-fashion emerged as the dominant aesthetic in the early 1980s.

For centuries, Western fashion has doggedly adhered to a structured and tailored fit, which extols the virtues of sexuality, glamour and status—the mainstay of European haute couture design. Fashion historians have frequently coined the well-worn phrase 'conspicuous consumption' (first used in 1899 by Veblen, in *The Theory of the Leisure Class*), as this term underlines the key motivational role that the display of wealth in dress has played throughout history. Visual sumptuosity reflected individuals' standing in society, their status in a hierarchical order, and defined their position within a social class system. While Veblen questioned the need for this perceived pecuniary emulation, he argued that this material display of wealth reflected a 'status anxiety'. Arguably, this nineteenth-century notion of social class elitism gradually lost momentum as waves of middle-class consumerism blurred the distinctions between the classes throughout the course of the twentieth century. As history has shown, this growing 'democratization' of fashion eventually led to a contradiction of modernist ideals and practices.

What defined modernist haute couture fashion—the uniqueness of the design, fine finishing techniques, unblemished surfaces, exquisite tailoring, and hand-sewing— gave way to the predominance of mass-produced prêt-à-porter clothing. Yet this new culture of dress presented by the two Japanese designers actually appeared to mock the exclusivity of the earlier modernist fashions. In fact, according to fashion historian McDowell (1987), the Japanese designers Kawakubo and Yamamoto 'made few concessions to traditional Western ideals of dress, chic or beauty' and their clothes were 'as much a statement of philosophy as they were of design' (McDowell, 1987: 178).

These avant-garde designers produced clothes that appeared radical to Western eyes, and could almost be seen as a homage to their country's past and a challenge to the increased Western influence there (Carnegy, 1990: 20). Interestingly,

Figure 7.2   Rei Kawakubo, Comme des Garcons, deconstructed three-piece ensemble, ready-to-wear Spring/Summer collection, Paris Fashion Week, 19 October 1984. Photo: Daniel Simon/ Gamma-Rapho/Getty Images. A photo of one of Rei Kawakubo's early collection showings in Paris.

both Yamamoto and Kawakubo—who are now in their sixties—grew up in post-war Japan. It is important to remember that, during and immediately after the Second World War, Japan suffered years of austerity, and this impoverishment was imprinted on the minds of many. Their early 1980s collection showings in Paris can be better understood if viewed within this context. It could also explain the media reaction to their collection in 1982, when the derisory fashion headlines screamed 'Fashion's Pearl Harbor' and Kawakubo was described as a 'rag picker'. Their models, dressed in black deconstructivist clothes, looked cadaverous, with either shaved heads or seemingly dirty, unkempt hair, with pasty white faces that were 'devoid of make-up, apart from a disturbing bruised blue on their lower lips' (Mendes and de la Haye, 1999: 234). Arguably, the fashion press saw this work as a political statement—and perhaps it was.

While punk fashion in Britain could be discussed within the context of a generational protest—one that relied on provocation, visual obscenity and hard-core sexuality—deconstructivism in the garments of the Japanese designers could symbolize, in a more passive and discreet way, their reaction to Japan's historical position in the post-war years. For two decades, in the 1930s and 1940s, Japan had suffered a very stringent economic environment. Japan was one of the poorest countries in Asia, and these years are commonly referred to as *kuraitani*—the Valley of Darkness. Arthur Golden's *Memoirs of a Geisha* (1997) describes, in an anecdotal passage, the feeling of desperation in 1945:

> Anyone who lived in Japan during this time will tell you that it was the bleakest moment in a long night of darkness. Our country wasn't simply defeated, it was destroyed—and I don't mean by the bombs, as horrible as they were . . . During the period of a year or more, I never once heard the sound of laughter. I've often observed that men and women who were young children during those years have certain seriousness about them; there was little laughter in their childhoods. (1997: 349)

Yamamoto has been described as a designer who is driven by an existentialist philosophy, and whose work elicits an intellectualism that ties form with meaning and memory. In his autobiography *Talking to Myself* (Yamamoto, 2002) he asserts: 'Dirty, stained, withered, broken things seem beautiful to me'. The Japanese term *hifu*[1] refers to a form of anti-style, and is seen as an undeniable element of Yamamoto's dressmaking. According to Yamamoto, one can actually feel *hifu* clothing—its confusion, shabbiness and disarray—as if it were reflecting a meagreness of spirit or sadness in the people wearing the clothes. In other words, the disarray of the fabric mimics the emotional fragility of the wearer. This merging of the emotional, intellectual and aesthetic encouraged many viewers to see Yamamoto's collection showings as a form of performance art.

He describes his work as being 'contradictory' to the commercialism of Western fashion. He creates clothing that has a universal appeal, a timeless quality—clothes that are meant to last a lifetime. In the 1980s, he was greatly inspired by the 1930s photographs of August Sander, taken in the American Midwest during the Depression years. Images of farmworkers ploughing the dusty fields in their faded and tattered work clothes, and women and children huddled in shanty doorways, elicit an honourable dignity that he tried to emulate in his own collections. Yamamoto observes: 'I like old clothes . . . clothes are like old friends . . . What makes a coat truly beautiful is that you're so cold you can't live without it. It's like a friend or member of the family. And I'm terribly envious of that' (quoted in Chenoune, 1993: 305).

By placing Yamamoto's work within the framework of postmodernist visual arts practice in the 1980s and 1990s, it is difficult not to consider the work of other artists such as Messager, Boltanski and a number of the postfeminist artists, who used clothing as a means to evoke an emotive response in their work and to link art with the everyday. Messager placed worn-out dresses under glass in wooden display boxes and hung them on the wall like paintings. Her *Histoire des Robes* (History of Dresses) series in 1990 is an affirmation of the feminine, and dramatically evokes a sense of melancholia and lost identity. Boltanski used actual lost property from railway stations to memorialize the unknown owners. These personal effects relate to the themes of loss, death and memories that have been buried. They are meant to remind us of the experience of remembering.

Authors often compare the work of Yamamoto and Kawakubo, as they were great friends and soulmates for ten years. Kawakubo also finds beauty in the unfinished, the irregular, the monochromatic and the ambiguous. Placed within the context of Zen Buddhist philosophy, this translates as an appreciation of poverty, simplicity and imperfection (Leong, 2003). Kawakubo asserts that she does not have a set definition of beauty:

> I find beauty in the unfinished and the random . . . I want to see things differently to search for beauty. I want to find something nobody has ever found . . . it is meaningless to create something predictable. (quoted in Kawamura, 2004)

Kawakubo's conceptualization is inherent in her philosophy towards design, as she is always projecting forward to the future—pushing boundaries. 'It's not good to do what others do. If you keep doing the same things without taking risks, there will be no

Figure 7.3 Rei Kawakubo, Comme des Garcons, deconstructed silver-grey pleated skirt, 1999. Photographer: author. Courtesy of the late Paul Jellard, Fiveway Fusions, Sydney. The temporary basting at the waist became a permanent feature of this deconstructed garment.

progress,' she said (*Undressed*, 2001). Kawakubo relies on spontaneity in her work: 'I could say that my work is about looking for accidents. Accidents are quite important for me. Something is new because it is an accident' (*Undressed*, 2001). While her work is uncompromising in its anti-fashion directions, like that of Yamamoto, it is still very personal and self-reflective. 'When I am designing, what's important to me is to express what's happening in my own life, to express my personal feelings through my designs' (*Undressed*, 2001).

A CULTURAL HERITAGE

Another strong link that ties both Yamamoto and Kawakubo to Miyake is the truth of their Japanese heritage. This embracing of their indigenous culture could be read as a backlash against a previous celebration of 'outsider' popular culture. According to a contemporary Kyoto textile artist, after the war American popular culture exerted a growing influence of on Japanese society. It seemed that the Japanese people were no longer selectively focused on their cultural heritage, instead desiring new and novel consumer items rather than cherishing traditional pieces. The kimono, for example, has always played a significant role in the culture of Japan. The great value attached to kimonos and textile design is evident in the involvement of some of Japan's most famous artists in the design of the garments, such as the nineteenth-century print-maker Utamaro. Kimonos are handed down from generation to generation, and they have defined and contributed to the Japanese tradition of beauty.

All three designers insist that the underlying influence of the kimono in their work is profound. They agree that it is the space between the fabric and the body that is most important. This negates the blatant sexuality of fitted Western clothes, and introduces the possibility of layered or voluminous clothing that becomes a sculptural form of its own. Kawakubo comments on the 'gender-neutral' design of her kimono-inspired constructions: 'Fashion design is not about revealing or accentuating the shape of a woman's body, its purpose is to allow a person to be what they are' (*The Story of Fashion*, 1985). This is abundantly clear in her Spring/Summer 1997 Bump collection, where padded sections were added to the clothes to distort the back and hips of the body, thus critiquing the notion of the perfect female shape. This is very much in keeping with postmodernist practice, where self-critique and reflection challenge accepted norms of life and society. Does sexuality always have to be determined by body shape? Kate Betts (2004) argues in *Time* magazine that Kawakubo invites an open interpretation of her work, but also suggests that this collection calls for some level of self-awareness. Not surprisingly, Kawakubo commented in 1983 that she saw the New York bag lady as the 'ideal woman' to dress, and in 1984 that a woman who 'earns her own way' is her typical client. Another often-quoted statement of the 1990s refers to how she designed clothes for 'strong women who attract men with their minds rather than their bodies'. This inherent feminist critique—obvious in both her words and her work—was echoed not only in many different forms in arts practice in the 1980s and 1990s,[2] but also in literature, media advertising, film and dramatic production.

Miyake's work comments on the recontextualization of the kimono to create a different aesthetic milieu. Miyake rejected the traditional forms of Paris collection clothing. Through the inventive use of fabric and successive layering, he developed a concept of fashion based on the use of cloth—or rather, the 'essence' of clothing: the wrapping of the body in cloth. He created anti-structural, organic clothing which takes on a sculptural quality that suggests a natural freedom, expressed through the simplicity of its cut, the abundance of new fabrics, the space between the garment and the body, and its general flexibility. Miyake stated: 'I learned about space between the body and the fabric from the traditional kimono . . . not the style, but the space' (Knafo, 1988: 108). Like Kawakubo, Miyake's designs also have parallels with architecture. His structures in bamboo recall Samurai armour, a rigid house for the body. These constructions exemplify ideas of the body moving within a space beneath an outer space (Holborn, 1988: 120).

Similarly, Yohji Yamamoto redefined male clothing forms when he introduced his Autumn/Winter 1985/1986 'unstructured' men's collection with baggy, pleated trousers—a draped look that approximated Turkish harem trousers. Suit jackets lost their tapered waists, linings and padding were removed, and the way sleeves were mounted changed the male silhouette dramatically. Different textiles were used, such as soft, elastic fabrics made of viscose and crêpe yarns, and this new redefined form heralded the direction towards comfort and simplicity. Perhaps more importantly, Yamamoto saw this new aesthetic as a reflection of a new 'ideal of clothing'. He said: 'People don't "consume" these garments: they might spend their entire lives in them . . . that's what life is about. Real clothes, not fashion' (Chenoune, 1993: 305).

TEXTILE DESIGN

Another major factor that unites the postmodernist work of Yamamoto, Kawakubo and Miyake is their interest in experimentation in textile design. The Japanese fashion empire is built on the framework of its textile industry—just as, for centuries, the French industry has been. This experimentation was evident in Kawakubo's 'lace' or 'Swiss cheese' sweaters, when weaver Hiroshi Matsushita reformulated the actual fabric on the loom to create various-sized holes that appeared as rips or tears. Some textile designers believed that, with growing industrialization and complex technologies, a more humanistic approach was needed in the creation of new textiles. In Japan, when one defines imperfections in fabrics, it is called 'fabric hand', as these aberrations are considered precious (Niwa, 2002: 238). This is used as an inherent criticism of the mechanical uniformity in textile production and experimentation with new methodologies in textile design. Matsushita refers to this technique as 'loom-distressed weaves'. In postmodernist terms, it is called 'deconstruction'.

Miyake is renowned for his research in textile technology. In his ongoing series of collections using pleats, Pleats Please, which he started in 1993 and worked on for over ten years with Minagawa,[3] Miyake has created a kaleidoscope of colour in his surface patterning, akin to the fragmentation of colour as seen on a computer screen. The interplay of pattern and colour is heightened by the technique of heat-setting pleats in the synthetic garment, resulting in an origami of pleating. As the wearer moves, the colours start to dance before your eyes. Pleating became Miyake's obsession—he would design a pure shape first, and then press it into a pleating machine. *Interview* magazine quotes Miyake as saying: 'Pleats give birth to texture and shape all at the same time. I feel I have found a new way to give individuality to today's mass-produced clothing' (Saiki, 1992: 34). The series attests to Miyake's desire to produce adaptable clothing that is both functional and reflective of modern simplicity in an egalitarian society.[4]

Textiles reference Miyake's cultural heritage in many different ways. He included *shashiko*—a Japanese technique for quilting cotton—for coats, and he also used a fabric called *tabi-ura*, formerly reserved for the bottoms of the fitted Japanese sock. Paper, originally used as a lining for winter coats worn by the ancient farmers, has been reintroduced in his collection showings. 'There are no boundaries for what clothes can be made from. Anything can be clothing,' he says. Miyake is inspired by the natural forms of shells, seaweed and stones. The oil-soaked paper used so commonly in the traditional Japanese umbrella is re-employed to form a translucent coat:

> The model glows through this golden paper skin, like an insect set in amber . . . One of Miyake's most innovative images is found in the bark of a tree. The body can move inside a tube of fabric as if in a caterpillar skin. He asked: 'Did you know there's a tree in Africa where the bark comes off completely? It's round, just like a tube of jersey. I wanted to make something woven that was warped like African bark. (Penn, 1988: 15)

Architect Isozaki compares this to the hollow, seamless, sacred garments woven for the gods—which became the prototype of human clothing. It becomes an archetypal dress, a universal, circular form (Holborn, 1988: 120). Perhaps this served as an inspiration for his APOC (a piece of cloth) collection in 1999, an ongoing series, where Miyake introduced a flat tube of white fabric that could be cut into a variety of garments—literally a capsule wardrobe.

Miyake's contribution to the invention of new synthetic fibres cannot be underestimated. In *Miyake Modern*, Simon (1999) remarks that one of the most remarkable aspects of his work is determined by 'an understanding of textile fibres, both natural and synthetic, and of fabrics, both hand-woven and traditionally dyed, as well as high-tech textiles that are not woven at all' (1999: 45). Mitchell, Curator of Fashion in the International Decorative Arts department of the Powerhouse Museum in Sydney, suggests that Miyake's work aims 'to rediscover the traditional beauty of a Japan which is disappearing; to emphasize the importance of industrially produced clothes by using synthetic materials' (quoted in English, 1999). It all offers fashion a focus as it walks backwards towards the twenty-first century, and offers suggestions for the future (Benaim, 1997: 7).

CONCEPTUALIZATION

Both appropriation and recontextualization play a key role in the definition of postmodernist practice. Miyake's book *East Meets West* (1978) includes an essay by his close friend Arata Isozaki, the architect of the Museum of Contemporary Art in Los Angeles, which consolidates Miyake's link between his fashion design and architecture. The publication underlines the close association Miyake has always maintained with other art practitioners. For example, Leni Riefenstahl's photographs of the Nuba stimulated Miyake and fellow art director Eiko Ishioka. They both viewed the Nuba as magnificent specimens, wonderful human surfaces, as abstract as these African tribesmen's body designs. In 1989–90, Miyake used a stretch fabric to create a series of tattoo-like bodystocking garments that fitted the body closely. By embracing ethnic beauty, he treats the garments as a second skin. His collaborations with other visual arts practitioners have not only created a culturally diverse interface in Miyake's work, but have also infused it with a richness of symbolic reference and meaning.

All three Japanese designers rejected change for change's sake, and instead chose to work on the refinement and evolution of previous collections. This evolution of an idea was the basis of Japanese fashion. The conceptual process of serialization, revisited by many conceptual visual practitioners since the 1960s, is integral to the Japanese approach to design.

Miyake, Yamamoto and Kawakubo are often described as niche designers—designers who do not follow stylistic trends or directions. Unlike their European and American 'stylist' counterparts, they have not exclusively embraced the revivalist or popular cultural imaging that has inundated Paris catwalks for decades. The riotous and multifarious themes that we see in the repertoire collections of Alexander McQueen, Jean-Paul Gaultier and Vivienne Westwood find no place in the work of the Japanese designers. Nor is it likely that these designers will ever be nominated as possible head designers of other 'mega' fashion houses. Obviously, the uncompromising nature of the Eastern designers' work eliminates their suitability for such a role, despite the fact that the international press voted Kawakubo the leading designer in Paris in 1987.

The conceptual underpinning in their design work also explains why, in the early 1990s, their reputation as leaders in the international fashion arena was consolidated

(English, 2004). It could be argued that Miyake, Kawakubo and Yamamoto all offered a meaningful alternative to the superficial, regressive and over-designed work of so many of the Western designers in the 1990s. Their work—more closely allied with postmodernist practice—did not fall neatly within the dictates of the established fashion industry, and as a result was not consumed by its self-imposed boundaries. Perhaps this is why it has appealed to noted art photographers such as Irving Penn, Nick Knight, Robert Mapplethorpe, David Sims and Inez Van Lamsweerde, whose photographs underline the notion that fashion can step beyond its immediate frame of reference. For example, the publication entitled *Issey Miyake: Photographs by Irving Penn* is a collaborative effort between the Japanese designer and the Western photographer, printed by Nissha in Kyoto (Penn, 1988). Three tons of Miyake's designs were shipped to New York, where Penn made his own choices. Penn, like Miyake, 'employs an art of reduction—his fashion photographs are emptied to allow the geometry of his clothes to be the sole uncluttered force. Penn's photographs are contextless, the subject without the surround' (Holborn, 1988: 118). In a similar way, Japanese landscape and woodblock print artists also concentrated their images by juxtaposing them with bare, unadorned elements. Penn presents Miyake's clothing as flattened, near-abstracted images in a white nothingness. The clothes disclose nothing of the bodies underneath, and sexuality often becomes ambiguous. Penn places Miyake's clothes within a neutral space to underline the notion that fashion can be seen as a reconsidered form.

Kawakubo worked collaboratively with American postmodernist artist Cindy Sherman in 1994 to promote her Comme des Garçons clothing (Glasscock, 2003). She sent

Figure 7.4 Issey Miyake, screenprinted and pleated polyester dress, artist's series, Pleats, Please collection (with Yasumasa Morimura-printed self-portrait), Autumn/Winter 1996/1997. Collection: Sherman Galleries, Sydney. Reproduced courtesy of Dr Gene Sherman.

Sherman garments from each of her collections to use as she wished. Sherman pro-duced a series of unconventional photographs, which 'centred on disjointed manne-quins and bizarre characters, forcing the clothing itself into the background'. Sherman presented Kawakubo's clothing in masquerade settings, but the confrontational, the-atrical images are not about clothes. They are about performance art. Sherman is re-nowned for her interpretations of mass media stereotypes of femininity. Her critique of 'fashionable' photography is in keeping with Kawakubo's approach to the business of fashion design, which is strongly inspired by the values of the contemporary art world.

Kawakubo also deconstructed accepted merchandising strategies by participating in the design of her shop interiors and exteriors. Her minimalist approach encompassed cracked concrete floors, warehouse tables for display of folded goods, and old refrig-erator cupboards for storage. In 1999, she designed an architectural landmark build-ing as Comme des Garçons' home base in Tokyo, with a curvy 30 m (98 ft) expanse of street-level glass screenprinted with blue dots. From the outside, it creates a pixilated effect, with the customers appearing to be moving across a huge television screen like actors on a set. This type of self-reflectivity considers the notion that media advertis-ing not only reinforces mass-market consumerism, but also becomes a reality in itself.

Japan's willingness to embrace the avant-garde is evident in its fine art, architec-ture and fashion design. Japanese design had an unprecedented impact on Western design during the twentieth century. The designers Miyake, Yamamoto and Kawakubo produce work that is imbued with the history of the past, yet looks dynamically towards the future. They have become leaders in the international fashion industry. Their cloth-ing has created a visual language that strengthens the converging line that exists be-tween fashion and art. Miyake is amused when his work is so often referred to as an art form, stating that: 'Clothes are more important than art.'

Younger designers, who are apprenticed to these leading fashion masters, take many years to develop their trade under the tutelage of their employers. In Japan, it is called *enryo*—a supreme void of ego that demonstrates complete dedication to the group. For Westerners, it is a kind of learned humility. Naoki Takizawa, designing for Issey Miyake, combines a mixture of new and different materials to discover un-expected forms. Using a disciplined approach, he experiments with space age ma-terials, some developed by NASA scientists, and combines them with natural fibres. Making clothing that conforms to Miyake's functional philosophy towards design has allowed Takizawa to continue the evolution of the company's Pleats Please collection. In 1993, he was the key designer of Issey Miyake menswear, and in 1999 he became head designer of the Issey Miyake label, leaving Miyake to concentrate on his APOC line. Like his mentor, Takizawa collaborates effectively with other renowned visual arts practitioners, and in his Autumn/Winter collection of 2004/2005, entitled Journey to the Moon, he incorporated the popular cultural images of Japanese artist Aya Takano. In this collection, distinctively Japanese animé figures set in pale blue and pink futur-istic landscapes embody eccentric street style imagery.

Plate 1 Changing room at the Zwieback Department store, Vienna, Austria, c. 1910. Photo courtesy of Oesterreichsches Volkshochschularchiv/Imagno/Getty Images. The dressing rooms of early department stores were large, elegant and luxurious.

Plate 2 Victorian balloon-sleeved dress, red russet silk from the David Jones department store in Sydney, Australia, 1890s. Collection: Powerhouse Museum, Sydney. Photographer: Penelope Clay. Many department stores had their own dressmaking and tailoring workshops. This silk brocaded day dress with removable sleeves was possibly a copy of a Paris original.

Plate 3   Paul Poiret, oriental-inspired clothing at Richelieu-Drouot auction house, Paris, May 2005. Photographer: Jean Ayissi/AFP/Getty Images.

Plate 4   Madeleine Vionnet, satin hand-draped wedding dress, 1939, Les Arts Decoratifs museum exhibition 2009–2010, Paris. Photographer: Francois Guillot/AFP/Getty Images.

Plate 5 Cristóbal Balenciaga, flamenco-inspired evening dress, white cotton pique cut bodice with soft black silk flounces, 1951. Photographer: Bill Brandt/Getty Images.

Plate 6 Martin Margiela, *The World According to its Creators* installation, Museum of Costume and Fashion, Paris, 6 June 1991. Photographer: Pool Benainous/Marouze/Gamma-Rapho via Getty Images.

Plate 7 Hussein Chalayan, garment made of crystals and over 15,000 flickering LED lights entitled *Readings*, 'From Fashion and Back' exhibition, Design Museum, London, 21 January 2009. Photographer: Dan Kitwood/Getty Images.

Plate 8 Ralph Lauren, Autumn/Winter collection, New York, February 2012. Typically conservative American 'preppie' styling. Photographer: Timothy A. Clary/ AFP/Getty Images.

Plate 9 Billboard on Broadway, New York, featuring Kate Moss modelling Calvin Klein (CK) jeans. Photographer: Richard Corkery/NY Daily News Archive via Getty Images. Many of these advertisements were considered too provocative for public consumption.

Plate 10 Pierre Cardin, silver and black outfits, Cosmocorps line, 1963–4. Photographer: Keystone-France/Gamma-Keystone via Getty Images.

Plate 11 Zandra Rhodes reclines on bed with model wearing wedding dress, 1985. Photographer: David Montgomery/Getty Images.

Plate 12   Vivienne Westwood, blue super-elevated gillies, made of alligator leather, cork, and silk, Anglomania collection, London, Autumn/Winter 1993/1994. Collection: Powerhouse Museum, Sydney. Photographer: Sue Stafford. While at first the shoes seemed like a humorous parody, they became the most famous shoes of the twentieth century and an icon of fashion footwear.

Plate 13   John Galliano for Dior Haute Couture, black deconstructed and beaded evening dress, Spring/Summer, Paris, 2000. Photographer: Daniel Simon/Gamma-Rapho via Getty Images. This collection was inspired by the homeless people of Paris.

Plate 14 Rebecca Patterson/Megan Salmon for SpppsssP label, fabricated dissolve wool dress, Deconstructivist/Reconstructivist Rubens series, Perth, Australia, 1999. Collection: Powerhouse Museum, Sydney. Photographer: Leisa Hunt. Reproduced courtesy of Leisa Hunt. The Japanese *shibori* technique has been used to dissolve sections of the fabric.

Plate 15 Issey Miyake label, fashion collection showing, ready-to-wear collection, Fall/Winter 1997/1998, Paris. Photographer: Daniel Simon/Gamma-Rapho via Getty Images.

Plate 16   Yohji Yamamoto, men's street style-influenced collection, Autumn/Winter 2012/2013, Paris, January 2012. Photographer: Francois Guillot/AFP/Getty Images. The heaviness of the shrouded coats reinforces the notion of fashion noir.

Figure 7.5 Comme des Garcons boutique, Isetan department store, Tokyo, Japan, 1997. Photographer: author. A deconstructivist example of interior design. The boutique has a floor of bare, cracked polished concrete, fold-up warehouse tables and second-hand refrigeration units painted red and used as cupboards.

After twenty-five years, Kawakubo's protégé, Junya Watanabe, has become one of Japan's leading fashion designers. His design work is aesthetically challenging and he, like Takizawa, has continued the traditional heritage of experimental textile development. His work relies on complex construction techniques, tactile surfaces and a sculptural interplay of light and shade. While he extends Kawakubo's conceptual approach to fashion, his work responds to existing stylistic trends more directly. He pays tribute to historical revival, and playfully paid 'witty and irreverent homage to Coco Chanel with ropes of pearls entwined in the necklines of dresses or stitched to the hems of ever more complex ruffled and draped creations' (Lowthorpe, 2000) in his Autumn/Winter collection of 2000. Political reference aggressively appeared in his 2006 Spring/Summer collection, where 'violent head coverings created out of ripped gaffer tape, tattered mohair, studs, pins and nails were the order of the day' (Frankel, 2006).

A new generation of Japanese designers—many of them graduates of Central St Martin's in London—have joined the ranks of existing design studios, or have ventured to create new businesses of their own. Tao Kurihara joined Comme des Garçons in 1997, and—working initially on the Tricot line—'studied' directly under Watanabe for eight years before she was allowed to create a modest collection in 2005, at the age of thirty-one. Her collection, inspired by lingerie, was described as a confection of wool and lace translated into coquettish corsets and shorts. She now works with her own team of six designers.

In contrast, Jun Takahashi launched his Undercover label in Japan in 1994, which attracted a cult following in Harajuku, a district of Tokyo renowned for the street style fashions worn by the local teens. According to *Gap (Japan) Press*, the well-known prêt-à-porter fashion magazine, commenting on the 2002/2003 Autumn/Winter collection, Takahashi's appeal emanated from his independent vision, which employed a 'twisted' aesthetic. His new shop, opened in Tokyo in 1992, featured stuffed animals and one-offs that had been taken apart and remade, displayed in a glass showcase. The theme of his collection that year was Witch's Cell Division, where items were disassembled through fasteners and put together in different combinations, similar to robots with interchangeable parts. Black etchings, like tattoos, covered parts of the models' faces; moons, stars and witchery images decorated the garments—creating a unique and somewhat bizarre collection. In the same year, he launched his collection on the catwalks of Paris, under the sponsorship of Rei Kawakubo.

Another Japanese label, 20471120, created by Masahiro Nakagawa and Azechi Lica, uses recycled materials from clothing previously owned by specific groups of people. Nakagawa recycles the memories that are associated with their clothing when he constructs a new garment from old clothing. He suggests that too many memories are being discarded with the clothing. Indirectly, the clothing comments on excessive consumerism in Japanese society.

Figure 7.6 Masahiro Nakagawa and Azechi Lica for 20471120, dress made from synthetic fabric recycled from a garment of the UNIQLO brand, Spring/Summer 2001, Japan. Collection: Powerhouse Museum, Sydney. Photographer: Sue Stafford. Nakagawa gathered clothes that belonged to fashion journalists and art professionals, which he tore apart, reassembled and returned to their owners. He literally reconstructed memories that the owners associated with their clothes. The project was intended to comment on the overwhelming consumer culture in Japan and to suggest that frugality was the only answer to Japan's ailing economy.

HARAJUKU STREET FASHION

Japanese youth were introduced to European street fashion by Shoichi Aoki and Noriko Kojima, through the publication of a magazine called *Street* in 1985. Paradoxically, they promoted these overseas trends in Japan and, in turn, Aoki became famous for documenting the visual response of Tokyo's youth to these new trends. For his monthly *FRUiTS* magazine, launched in 1997,[5] Aoki photographed the self-designed street style dress paraded through the streets and parks of the trendy neighbourhoods of Shibuya and Harajuku.

Designers of Japanese street style shared the DIY philosophy of their British punk counterparts, and adopted the use of plaid material, T-shirts advertising punk bands, ripped clothing and studded accessories. Unfazed by mainstream designer trends, they embraced the hyper-celebrity culture of Japan and recreated illusions of *manga*— a popular cartoon art form aimed at adults—and animé characters in their clothing. This subcultural form of dress was contextualized within a popular culture that was always transformative, dynamic and fundamentally linked to trends of disposability. A diversity of custom-made 'looks' burgeoned over a five-year period. These included girls—known as *wamono*—who wore a collage of traditional elements of Japanese ancient dress with kimono, sashes and *geta* sandals combined with second-hand and home-made items; the cult of 'cuteness' or *kawaii*, which encouraged a childlike appearance complete with plastic jewellery and toys worn as accessories, highlighted by an overabundance of the colour pink; the baby doll Lolita look, with frills and flounces; and the Gothic Lolita look, sometimes dominated by black Victorian mourning dress, which created an air of elegance and a nostalgia for an entirely fictional past. Blatant sexuality—manifested in fetishwear of red net stockings, black leather skirts and leopardskin-patterned fabrics, perhaps influenced by Westwood and Margiela—became another version of street fashion. Further appropriations of the Western cowboy look (*ganguro*), the tanned and blonde California girl or Mountain Witch look (*yamamba*), and the black American hip-hop look for young men, added to this aesthetic chaos. Not only did these borrowed looks take traditional meaning away from the original cultural referents, but they also recycled them into a meaningless fashion pot-pourri. Such styles were dubbed 'dressing up', 'putting on a show', 'playing at costumes'—these words described an outsider's reaction to the new direction of fashion. More critical commentators described this devotion to fashion as self-indulgent and dishonourable. Gothic Lolita, for some, signified a 'nostalgia fetish' or 'a form of drag'. The wearing of black vinyl kimonos or full punk bondage gear with whitened faces and blackened eyes conveyed a much more sexually aggressive appearance than their doll-like counterparts. Any public display of youthful intimacy or sexuality, whether in the community, on poster advertisements or in the media, was considered immoral before the late 1980s, and was not tolerated. The press referred to young women wearing 'Harajuku styles' as the 'Sirens of Tokyo'.

Whether this individualized styling represents a candid critique of the role of women in Japanese society and culture is difficult to ascertain. Kinsella (1995) argues that 'this practice of performative dress-up provides a hyper-real form of what the Japanese call "cosplay" (or "costume play"), as well as a nexus between the old, the new and various connected ideas about identity in relation to culture, gender and youth' (1995: 247–8). If we agree that diversity in dress is complicit with street style, and therefore depicts identity as subject to constant change, then the Harajuku street style emphasizes the way different images of femininity show how tenuous commodity identity can be. Most commodity-oriented subcultures have become complicit in the niche marketing of their own identities (Kinsella, 1995: 226). Entire stores in the Harajuku area, for example, cater for a total Lolita transformation—the consumer's link to an alternative lifestyle.

In highly populated urban Japanese cities, where loss of individual identity becomes inevitable and highly dominant, traditional male structures exist within the society, street style dressing offers teenage girls and young women in their early twenties a form of escapism. The notion of attracting attention, yet hiding behind the safety of a group, suggests a personal insecurity that can both challenge and reinforce consumerism. As the notion of feminism is relatively unexplored in Japanese society, the diversity of street style dress allows for an investigation of different models of the feminine. Clothing can be a form of identity, an expression of creativity, a form of entertainment or performance, but at the same time it can act as a subtle mode of non-conformity—a passive critique that counters the Japanese ideology of order, control, uniformity and impersonality. According to Hebdige (1997), subcultures are both a play for attention and a refusal to be categorized:

> Subculture is, then, neither simply an affirmation nor a refusal, neither simply resistance against symbolic order nor straightforward conformity with the parent culture. It is both a declaration of independence, of Otherness, of alien intent, a refusal of anonymity, of subordinate status. It is an insubordination. At the same time, it is also a confirmation of the fact of powerlessness, a celebration of impotence. (1997: 404)

The Japanese ability to synthesize the ideas and practices of other cultures is central to its success in the international design industry. Appropriation, pluralism and fragmentation are inherent in postmodernist practice, whether it is in the decorative, applied or fine arts. The visual anomalies or contradictions evident in Harajuku street style fashion are peculiar to the Japanese culture. More importantly, the style evolved from individual choice; it was not determined by designer trends or dictated by conglomerate ready-to-wear markets. The notion of difference, based on the adaptation of so many diverse local contexts combined in Harajuku street style fashion, suggests that this way of dressing was one of the very few which was resistant to the stereotypes of globalization.

–8–

Global Practices—1980s Onwards

Great fashion is like a one-night-stand; because it is short-lived, you can remember it forever.

Karl Lagerfeld (1985)

This chapter summarizes the main developments that have characterized the last decade of fashion in the twentieth century, and outlines key issues that have arisen from major changes taking place during the course of the twentieth century. In turn, these issues pose implicit questions that only future events can answer. Each issue has been addressed in a mutually exclusive format. This does not deny that an inter-relationship or overlap exists but, rather, attempts to highlight topics that are worthy of individual consideration by today's fashion reader.

THE DEATH OF HAUTE COUTURE?

By the mid-1990s, it seemed that French haute couture was no longer sustainable. What had happened to Western designers by the early 1990s? London journalist Juliet Herd (1991) wrote of the unbridled indulgence that sounded 'the death knell of haute couture' at the start of the 1990s. This 'extinction of the Paris couture industry' was reaffirmed by Pierre Bergé, the high-profile head of Yves Saint Laurent, when he stated that 'Haute couture will be dead in ten years' time' (Herd, 1991). The French prime minister, who believed the French fashion industry 'needed an overhaul' in order to survive, called a summit meeting to discuss the troubles of the ailing $3.3 billion export industry. It seems that the exclusivity of the Chambre Syndicale, the industry's powerful authority, prevented the inclusion of the younger, more avant-garde design-ers in the 'club', and that wealthy young clients were turning to prêt-à-porter as haute couture 'seemed to be running out of ideas'. Herd argues that 'the lack of originality among top designers was highlighted at the French collections', where one fashion expert observed that 'many top couturiers appeared to be wandering up blind alleys, uncertain of their role'. Significantly, there were twenty-one haute couture houses in Paris at this time, according to the Chambre Syndicale, which regarded haute couture (and not prêt-à-porter) as the backbone of their business.

Figure 8.1   Philip Treacy, The Featherbone Dandelion, cockerel-feathered hat with grosgrain ribbon, London, 1992. Collection: Powerhouse Museum, Sydney. Photographer: Andrew Frolows. According to Isabella Blow, Treacy was fascinated by birds, and he captures the concept of flight effectively in this creation. His postmodernist hats are unique, one-of-a-kind creations in the true sense of haute couture.

Similarly, the 7 November 1991 issue of *L'Express* asked a pointed question: 'Who broke the desire machine?' Historian Chenoune (1993) argues that: 'Many people have begun to feel that the current *fin de siècle* is marked by an unhealthy atmosphere. The problems of Aids, unemployment and economic recession are complicated by the political upheaval and ethnic nationalism resulting from the recent collapse of communism and the Soviet empire' (1993: 316).

Placing this phenomenon within a social and historical context, could it be that Western fashion had exhausted its endless appetite for change by the 1990s? In their constant search for novelty, some designers looked back to previous historical periods, while others found a need to react to or contradict that which had gone immediately before. This lack of direction seemed to be broadcast in the growing superficiality of styles that led Suzy Menkes, Fashion Editor of the *International Herald Tribune*, to comment on the bankruptcy of innovation and new ideas (Menkes, 2000).

Crane (2000: 143) suggests that, by the late 1980s, there were two groups of couturiers: 'one group included older designers . . . who produced collections that often consisted of restatements of ideas and motifs from the history of designer fashion'[1] and who took 'few risks, varying their collection just enough to keep in step with the times'. The other group, she adds, consisted of younger designers whose work was more unconventional and 'who were recruited especially for their originality or the entertainment value of their designs'. In other words, they were hired because of 'their skill in attracting the attention of the media'. When the selling of haute couture garments is no longer a priority, the more outrageous the collections are, the more publicity is generated for the designer brand—which, in turn, sells more profitable auxiliary products. Large-scale fashion shows called 'Défilés' were held in Paris, in which the big names—including Mugler, Lacroix, Gaultier and Lagerfeld—created spectacular designs; however, few were ever transformed into real fashion (Lehnert, 1998: 171). Bernard Arnault, the financier behind Dior, Givenchy and Lacroix, tactfully described coutureas 'the research and development laboratory of Paris style' (Steele, 1999: 288).

Yves Saint Laurent haute couture was losing $20 million a year when it closed its doors in 2002. There were only eleven elite haute couture *maisons* remaining in Paris, as few clients were willing to pay in excess of $90,000 for a made-to-measure garment. Saint Laurent had 120 remaining regular customers, including France's first lady, Bernadette Chirac. Bergé, the company chairman, finally admitted: 'Let's not kid ourselves—haute couture is finished and it's better to get out before it disappears completely' (quoted in *The Australian*, 2 November 2002).

LVMH: THE SUPER SYNDICATE

From the 1980s onwards, with the growing uncertainty in the global financial markets, fashion designers and others sought to consolidate their business interests by taking refuge with other firms. Of these commodity chains, by far the largest and most influential is Louis Vuitton Moet Hennessy (LVMH), a global fashion conglomerate in which the centrality of branding of luxury goods is the dominant competitive strategy for success. During the 2000s, the luxury market nose-dived, along with the stock market, and conglomerates like LVMH looked to divest themselves of unprofitable companies, and subsume larger, more secure companies under their banners in order to weather the financial storm. By 2011, LVMH had expanded to an international retail network of more than 2,500 stores and 80,000 employees worldwide. It viewed itself as a patron to the arts, committed to supporting young artists and designers, including John Galliano, Alexander McQueen, and Marc Jacobs, who seemed to have the versatility and skill to reinvigorate older, more staid labels. Its marketing strategy was based on the idea that haute couture, while not cost effective itself, has had an unparalleled influence on brand profile and publicity. The concept of successful branding, a philosophy upon which the empire was built, resulted in the LVMH group acquiring a unique portfolio of more than sixty prestigious brands (Plate 18). Monsieur Bernard Arnault,

CEO of LMVH, a very powerful player in global identity politics, determines the head designers of the fashion houses under his banner. He selectively chose designers who could refresh and yet sustain the branding image of older fashion houses, which needed to meet the forces of an increasingly competitive market. Galliano revived the House of Givenchy and was then moved on to the House of Dior, leaving the Givenchy position to McQueen, another outstanding postmodernist designer of the time.

BRANDING: THE DESIGNER AS PRODUCT

Just as actors, sportspeople, musicians and models have become global celebrities, so have the fashion designers themselves. In the past, individual designers sometimes shunned their own fashion shows because they were too private, camera-shy or aloof to attend. Traditional French haute couture relied on intimacy, privacy, select customers, elite venues and extreme subtlety in business transactions, and certain designers—such as Balenciaga—preferred to stay in the shadows. This not only hindered image profiling, but often restricted sales as well. In today's market, the presence of a designer will not only boost sales at collection showings, but at store openings and perfume launches as well. Their image becomes synonymous with their product. In turn, the 'designer as product' maximizes brand awareness. Armani will appear on stage dressed down in white T-shirt and jeans. This downmarket image not only advertises his 'diffusion' line, Emporio[2]—created for a younger clientele—but also reinforces that the white, single-pocket T-shirt is the ultimate universal casual statement for men—in fact, the best-selling line since the Second World War.

Reinforcing their designer label's image, Calvin Klein has become the master of image creation and—like a chameleon—has metamorphosed his image from the suave man about town to the sophisticated and more mature suited businessman. Yohji Yamamoto wears understated black—historically the symbolic colour of intellectual pursuit—and signifies his perceived reluctance to promote his creative work as commercial enterprise. Tom Ford and Karl Lagerfeld, both always immaculate, exude a confidence through their self-assured manner, which mirrors their success in the industry. For designers, remaining in the public eye is central to the marketing success of their fashion goods.

Haute couture collection showings cost a designer hundreds of thousands of dollars, which is never retrieved in sales; however, the opulent displays generate pages of free advertising, keeping the designer's name constantly in the media. The post-war French haute couture firms became corporate entities as they were only able to survive with massive financial investment and management. Dior's business, for example, was backed by a textile magnate and run by a business manager, while the designer himself was allotted a share of the profits. Licensing is a very effective way of reaching a mass consumer audience with little effort or expense on the part of the designer. The licensing of many additional types of products has become a major source of income. When a designer agrees to let a manufacturer use his or her name on a product, the designer receives a royalty (usually 7–8 per cent of the gross profits). This could include goods such as sunglasses, millinery, textile goods (towels, sheets etc.) or other household items. Pierre Cardin was the first designer to sign a licensing contract to mass-produce ready-to-wear for a vast audience in 1959. Significantly, by doing so he established the commercial mechanism by which the industry thrives today. At the time, this outraged the *Chambre Syndicale de la Couture Parisiènne*, a syndicate of haute couture designers whose main aim was to uphold the exclusivity of individual design. As retribution, he was denied membership of the elite group for a while (which meant that he couldn't show his collection as part of the Syndicale's Paris Fashion week), despite the fact that his garments had become headline news as trendsetting design. His aim was to produce fashion for everyone, not just the rich, and he soon began to make brand-name furniture and later gave his name to over 900 products, including carpets, floor tiles, frying pans, restaurants, cars, boats, olive oil and orthopaedic mattresses (*The Age*, Melbourne, 1 August 2003). He has become a global billionaire through licences that carry his name in ninety-seven countries, including New Zealand, China, the United States, Canada and Russia. Undoubtedly, Cardin is a world leader in developing an individual brand-name portfolio.

Other product and interior designers have followed his lead. Philippe Starck is seen today as one of the key lifestyle product designers, who links his products with his own image. In his promotional photograph he appears with his Salif juicer, topped with a lemon, being worn provocatively as a hat. In other advertisements, he stands on a ceramic plant base holding two pot plants. Interestingly, as a member of the New Design group in Paris, he founded a firm in 1968 which made inflatable objects; the next year he became Art Director with Pierre Cardin. In 1975, he began designing interior and product designs independently. He was not interested in protest or provocative design, as were most members of the New Design group in France—including Gaultier—but was commercially oriented towards relatively inexpensive items for mass production. While anti-design was popular in the consumer goods industry, Starck was pragmatically oriented towards the classic industrial design model, as promulgated in the philosophy of America's legendary Raymond Loewy. According to Hauffe (1998), he has not hesitated to borrow elements from past design styles—streamlined dynamic lines, organically formed handles, chair legs reminiscent of art nouveau, and more. His preference for unusual combinations of materials, such as plastic with aluminium, plush fabric with chrome, or glass with stone, is also characteristic of his design (1998: 164).

By the 1980s, the royalties gained from the licensing of fashion labels, as well as the sale of perfume, cosmetics and other fashion products, became the main source of profitability for many designers, including Yves Saint Laurent. For many of these products, the value resides only in the name of the product; otherwise the item has no social currency. In contemporary society, class differences are no longer visually conspicuous. Multinational corporations have globalized fashion and fashion products to such an extent that branding has become essential to create an illusion of status—to create a difference in objects which otherwise appear to be very similar.

In the last chapter of *20th Century Fashion*, by Valerie Mendes and Amy de la Haye (1999), the authors provide an exceptionally detailed account of the proliferation of designers and fashion styles that brought the twentieth century to a close. From futuristic clothing inspired by technological advancements to the plurality of ethnic styles and historical revivals, the 1990s produced eclecticism unrivalled since the 1890s. They recount the changing names of de facto head designers in the leading couture houses, such as McQueen at Givenchy, Galliano at Dior, Lagerfeld at Chanel and Ford at Gucci. By 2006, McQueen had moved to Gucci and Tom Ford to Yves Saint Laurent. In each case, the designers are assessed by their ability to appropriate the details, themes or 'looks' of the *maisons*, and to capture the essence of the original designer's work.

Yet one of the most significant trends, according to Mendes and de la Haye, was the move from prêt-à-porter—which has become more expensive—to diffusion lines

Figure 8.2   Marc Jacobs (in collaboration with Stephen Sprouse) for Louis Vuitton, travelling bag, women's leather goods collection, Spring/Summer, France, 2001. Collection: Powerhouse Museum, Sydney. Photographer: Sue Stafford. The use of graffiti-like text as image links this fashion accessory to similar practices in fine art and reinforces the importance of using designer labelling as a symbol of status.

aimed at global audiences. Just as haute couture was used to advertise and promote a designer's ready-to-wear lines, now ready-to-wear lines are used to promote diffusion lines. The cheaper diffusion lines were not widely advertised in the 1980s, but by the 1990s they were being paraded down the catwalks. America again took the lead in this new marketing venture, and when Donna Karan brought out her diffusion line, DKNY, it became an immediate success. More often than not, these lines were simple, conservative and inoffensive—a 'fashion understatement', but they have since expanded into formalwear. According to Frankel (2001: 56), designer Issey Miyake doesn't approve of diffusion lines, which he says are insulting and patronizing to the wearer. He says, 'I don't want people to think of my clothes in terms of money, to feel they can only afford second best.' Instead, he claims that, with his Pleats Please line: 'I worked on how to keep the price down.' For Miyake, it seems, success translates as more than making money.

Even Cartier Jewellers (established in 1889 in the Rue de La Paix in Paris), which had sold jewels to the crown heads of Europe, succumbed (in 1973) to producing a diffusion gift line called Les Musts de Cartier, which included spectacle cases, leather goods and luxury lighters that could be purchased for two hundred dollars. Not only did this strategic move stabilize the company's financial affairs, but it also revived the luxury goods market. The directors did not see it as a democratization of the brand name, but as an opportunity to provide the public with greater access to luxury goods without detracting from the prestige of the Cartier name.

For many, the media's constant bombarding of the public with advertising imagery reflects the malevolence of mass consumerism.[3] By using manipulative devices, advertising seduces the buyer of limited means to purchase imitation 'status' luxury products including pseudo-designer labels and perfume brands. This fuels the production and sale of 'knock-off goods', or cheap fakes, by Asian manufacturers, amongst others. An article in *Bazaar* (April 2005) argues that China continues to be the main source of counterfeiting; however, in the aftermath of negotiations by the United States–China Joint Commission on Commerce and Trade in 2004, the Chinese government announced the formation of a new counterfeiting task force to attack the problem.

Reproducing designer label goods for mass profit has been evident internationally since the turn of the century (Mah, 2006). In 2006, Louis Vuitton—one of the most pirated brands in the world—had forty full-time lawyers and 250 freelance investigators, and spent 15 million euros to fight counterfeiting. In the same year, LVMH, Prada Holdings, the Burberry Group and Pinault-Printemps-Redoute's Gucci successfully sued a Silk Alley landlord in Beijing, China for copyright infringement. Despite the court ruling, newspaper journalists rationalized that it would not increase the sale of the luxury goods, as buyers in the counterfeit market usually could not afford 'the real thing' anyway. According to Indicam, an anti-counterfeiting coalition based in Italy, worldwide production of counterfeit goods has reportedly jumped 1,700 per cent since 1993, and according to the ACG, the number of fakes seized in the European Union has increased tenfold in the past five years (Thomas, 2005: 75). In the United States, law authorities (in a report to the US Congressional House Committee on International Relations, 2003) argue that they are now recognizing the connection between the financing of terrorists and intellectual property crime. In France, where anyone found guilty of producing, importing or exporting fakes as part of an organized gang can receive up to five years in prison and a fine of 500,000 euros, even tourists passing through with counterfeit goods bought elsewhere risk a maximum fine of 300,000 euros and up to three years in jail. The targeting of the consumer, rather than the producer, might be the most effective solution to this ever-increasing problem of fashion piracy.

PERFUME: A LICENCE TO MAKE MONEY

Arguably, Chanel No. 5, launched in 1921, is the most famous perfume in the world. It makes hundreds of millions of dollars' profit annually. Perfume is pure profit. Paul Poiret, an astute businessman, was the first to create his own scent before the First World War, naming it after his daughter Rosine. The packaging is as important to the consumer as the scent. While Poiret had his perfume bottles uniquely hand-blown from Murano glass in Italy, Chanel chose a sleek geometric art deco bottle that has never been redesigned. Interestingly, one-third of the early couture firms developed lines of perfume, whose names have far outlasted the couture houses. The houses of Patou and Lanvin no longer sell clothing, but their names have been immortalized by their perfume labels. With a 60 per cent pure profit mark-up, these sales can keep a business afloat, and often not only outstrip its couture lines, but its prêt-à-porter lines as well. What is perfume's appeal? As a status item, it is more affordable to a mass-market, and it allows a 'cheap' entry into a designer lifestyle. Perfume literally provides a touch of luxury to the mundane life of a middle-class consumer.

During the Second World War, American soldiers returning from service in Europe were known to buy the women in their lives either silk stockings or perfume, or both. In most cases, when they entered a French *parfumerie*, the only name they recognized was Chanel No. 5. Perfume sales soared for Chanel in the 1940s and 1950s; today it is still the top-selling brand, with a bottle selling every thirty seconds. It was originally created by Ernest Beaux, and it was the fifth sample Beaux asked Chanel to appraise—hence the name. By the 1960s, the three leading couture houses, Chanel, Dior and Yves Saint Laurent, were also the top-selling perfume establishments. Even though males had been wearing scents for centuries, masculine colognes—tending to have more citrus and woody notes than women's perfume—became huge marketing products in the 1970s. By the 1990s, perfume sales had reached $7.5 billion and celebrities of all kinds were marketing their own scents. However, without the networking of internationally branded names afforded by the fashion designers, the majority of the new perfume lines went out of business. Only one in five perfumes remained on the market after three years. Calvin Klein developed unisex scents, bringing out 'cK One' in 1994, and continued his success with three other lines of perfume: Obsession, reported to contain 200 ingredients; Eternity, the sales of which outstripped those of his clothing line; and Escape, which was launched at Macy's, New York's middle-class department store, in the 1990s.

FASHION AND PHILANTHROPY

In the 1980s, monster fashion shows were organized, often to benefit charities. Bruce Oldfield's show raised funds for a children's orphanage and Karl Lagerfeld's for the Cancer Appeal, while Chanel gave money to support the Metropolitan Opera. Fashion Aid was held in the late 1980s, with the proceeds used to send food to Africa. A variety of designers also participated in the prestigious Street to Couture show in the Royal Albert Hall in London.

By the early 1990s, politics had become an overt part of the fabric of fashion design. Not only did fashion respond directly to current events, but many designers incorporated philanthropy as part of their corporate profile. According to Casadio, Moschino launched Project Smile in 1993 to raise funds for HIV-positive children. An auction, 'Art in Love', took place in collaboration with Sotheby's at the opening of Moschino's New York boutique. Artists such as Julian Schnabel, George Condo, Donald Baechler, Arman and John Baldessari donated works to be sold. The profits were given to Hale House, an organization providing support for children of alcoholics and drug addicts in Harlem (Casadio, 1997: 125).

In a more blatant way, Ralph Lauren uses his Polo collection to raise funds for cancer care and prevention. This marketing technique, which uses text written across the wide display windows of his stores worldwide, is used as a sidewalk drawcard and has proved to be effective in persuading buyers to enter his shops. Most designers have adopted this philanthropic trend, as it not only supports humanitarian causes and gains goodwill, but can also be used as an effective tax deduction. Within a wider context, Hauffe argues that:

> Art and design have become dependent on sponsorship or underwriting by businesses that choose cultural sponsorship as part of their corporate identity. Even furniture companies such as the Swiss manufacturer Vitra will issue an edition of individual pieces or limited editions. The tobacco company Philip Morris offers a prize for young designers and uses the popularity and cultural recognition of design to enhance its own image—something it sorely needs in an era when the public image of smoking and tobacco products is not terribly positive, and the reputation of the firm is decaying by the minute. (1998: 172)

Figure 8.3 Ralph Lauren's Polo label window display, 2005. Photographer: author. Text on the window indicates that a percentage of the sales' monies will benefit a charitable cause.

FASHION AS INSTALLATION

Frankel (2001: 132) argues that, more than any other designer, Tom Ford will go down in history as the man responsible for dressing the final years of the twentieth century, just as Courrèges, say, dressed the 1960s, Saint Laurent the 1970s, and Armani the 1980s. Gucci was the first established fashion house to hire a new young American or European designer as the new 'image-maker'. In less than five years, Ford single-handedly transformed Gucci—seen as a tired old status label—from a $250,000 business facing bankruptcy to a $2.2 billion asset. In 2004, the *New York Times* described him as 'the ultimate *fin de siècle*' designer. Ford, who began his career on Seventh Avenue, underlined the continued importance of the interplay of commerce and culture when he explained: 'You know, I started in New York, and really if the collection you designed didn't sell, you were fired the next day.' He added: 'I don't pretend to be anything other than a commercial designer and I'm proud of that' (Frankel, 2001: 132). He was interested in the commercial as well as the design side of fashion. He became involved in advertising campaigns, store designs and the packaging of eleven merchandising lines. He has revived the 1960s, 1970s and 1980s look in his collections, of which half of the company's sales are in Asia. In 2006, he moved on to become head designer for Givenchy, displacing McQueen.

Collaborations between fashion and art shifted from low-scale displays of artwork in fashion outlets to large-scale installations in the late 1990s. Fashion designers such as Tom Ford (when at Gucci—part of the Pinault-Printemps-Redoute retail group) collaborated with the American performance artist Vanessa Beecroft to produce Show 2001 at New York's Guggenheim Museum of Art. Twenty models stood as a static display, frozen in time, on the ground floor of the museum wearing Gucci heels, thongs and tops (and some nothing at all) with fixed stares returned to the audience, who in turn became the subject of the gaze. Beecroft's photograph documenting the work comments not only on the notion of sexual fantasy, but parodies the coldness and cruelty often seen in Helmut Newton's fashion photographs. This human installation became a historically significant event in 'an evolution of supportive relationships that runs from such involvements as Schiaparelli's costuming of films by Man Ray, and Buñuel and Dalí, and her provision of mannequins for the 1938 Surrealist exhibition in Paris' (Townsend, 2002: 96–8).

A number of corporate fashion houses are funding their own museums in order to raise the public profile for their corporate identity in a way that supersedes endowments or sponsorships. Prada has established the Fondazione Prada in Milan and Cartier the Foundation Cartier pour L'Art Contemporain in Paris. This indicates the financial power and growing cultural influence that the globalized fashion industry wields. The art industry now seems to be envious of fashion's ability to be more than a rhetorical device, or a cultural object, used by artists to comment on the seduction of popular culture in our society. Perhaps designers are using fashion more effectively to communicate ideas and emotions to an audience, the majority of which has lost touch with meaning in art practice. Wearing fashion involves the audience's participation in the communicative process, an experience that the art object does not allow. Could this be the reason that presentations of fashion collections have become more like art performances, and fashion photography more like art installations?

–9–

Post-2000: Global Recession and Ideological Conflict

In difficult times fashion is always outrageous.

Elsa Schiaparelli

A SHIFT IN THE BALANCE OF POWER

The 2000s saw a change in the 'designerscape' in Paris with Christian Lacroix filing for bankruptcy, the death of Alexander McQueen, the retirement of Martin Margiela and Helmut Lang, and end-of-era retrospective shows featuring Sonia Rykiel (Plate 19), Vivienne Westwood, Yohji Yamamoto and Rei Kawakubo celebrating more than thirty years in the fashion industry. Newcomers who made their first mark on the Parisian catwalks include, amongst others, Antwerp's Veronique Branquinho and Raf Simons, who continued the tradition of classic Belgian pragmatism; the Spaniard, Nicolas Ghesquiere for Balenciaga, who maintained the technical expertise of the house using the corset as his medium in the March 2001 collection; the Los Angeles designer Rick Owens, who presented garments that looked like modern armour; Oliver Theyskens for Rochas in the March 2003 show, who reinstated 1950s French elegance and panache; and England's Gareth Pugh, whose fashion-as-performance showings exhibited forms that came close to wearable sculptures in September 2008.

It is significant that the Belgian designers, Dries Van Noten and Ann Demeulemeester, emerged as the leaders in the latter half of the decade. Van Noten, named International Designer of the Year in 2008 by the Council of Fashion Designers of America (CFDA), followed the Japanese lead in terms of consistency in his design. His work demonstrated the Belgian fastidiousness for superlative construction and cut, incorporating classical elements into contemporary design, and he aimed to create clothing that could be combined in different ways by different individuals. This pragmatic approach has been essential to his success over the past decade. Demeulemeester, in particular, seemed to capture the essence of the 'urban warrior woman' in her collections, and as leading journalists explained, her designs manifested the new generation of self-determined women who were emerging. Demeulemeester's clothes

Figure 9.1   Alexander McQueen label, floral and black printed three-piece pant suit in McQueen store window, London, 2011. Photo: author.

reflected this belief with their brutal honesty, sophistication and practicality. With the global recession impacting upon the fashion industry quite dramatically, especially in 2008, her approach to design as a form of problem solving and not just for consumption's sake seemed quite realistic. The long-term 'stayers', including Lagerfeld for Chanel, Gaultier, Kawakubo for Comme des Garcons and Westwood,[1] stood their ground to ensure that their collections had a strong commercial edge. By the close of the first decade of the new millennium, the distressed global economy had forced fashion designers not only to increase their diffusion lines but to initiate new collection ranges including menswear; to consider new methods of marketing and distribution; to reinforce their strong brand identities; to align themselves pragmatically with sports companies; to interface with biomedical research pursuing the domain of health and well-being; and to embrace emerging technologies.

Globally, other directions that emerged underlined the economic squeeze of the latter 2000s. LVMH and others who sell luxury goods have been forced to divest themselves of small and unprofitable companies originally purchased in the booming 1990s. In the 'age of rational dressing', they exchanged John Galliano for Alber Elbaz, who had previously been at Lanvin, and Hannah MacGibbon took Phoebe Philo's place at Chloe. Other 'takeover' houses like Prada bought and divested itself of Jil Sander (twice), and Helmut Lang, whose very lucrative and influential label had been renowned for his iconic flat-front pants and his low-rise denim jeans made from intricate washes coupled with T-shirts. When Prada did not invest enough in the brand, it faltered. With syndicates such as LVMH managing so many of the best known brands, the constant change of head designers made it very difficult to keep track of who was where. Interestingly, the second largest luxury company in the world (behind LVMH), Compagnie Financière Richemont, which concentrates on watches and jewellery (Cartier) rather than clothing, was the company that was making the strongest financial returns. Similarly, by 2010, the magazine *Grazia*, known for its budget outlook, had taken over the premier position in the fashion reader distribution stakes. While *Vogue* put out its biggest American issue in September 2007, advertising had dropped dramatically by 2009, and, in response, the magazine began to run a more austere format.

THE TWENTY-FIRST-CENTURY IMAGE OF MODERN WOMANHOOD

Out of this economic quagmire, the first millennium ushered in the beginning of a new era, a period when women felt stronger and thought their voices might be heard in the sociopolitical corridors of power. Initially, there had been a trend towards a masculinized form of feminism in dress, bordering on androgyny. The favourite model of 2001, Eleonora Bosé, was the daughter of a legendary Spanish bullfighter, and her strong jaw line, closely cropped hair and tattoos made her the personification of the ultimate 'warrior' woman. She was photographed by Steven Meisel and Bruce Weber for Italian *Vogue* and appeared on the covers of numerous other magazine covers, including *Dazed and Confused, Nylon* and *Pop*. Tom Ford chose her to model the Gucci range, and *Women's Wear Daily*'s caption said, 'Think Marlon Brando' and described the models in both Milan and Paris that season as 'Tough Cookies'. Interestingly, this transgender image paralleled the rise of interest in queer theory publications. Feminist theory academic Suzanna Walters commented that 'an endless commodification of difference goes on in our culture, an endless search for a variation on a theme that will sell women slightly new images of themselves' (Trebay, 2001).

According to New York fashion journalist Gina Bellafante (2004), 'the rise of corporate superbrands narrowed the range of stylistic roles a woman could play.' She explained:

> Broadly speaking, she could cast herself in the role of the Gucci woman and look like the sort of sexually hungry powerhouse who always picks up the check. Or she could become a Prada woman—efficient, coolly nostalgic and erotically aloof. Or she could shop from the world of Marc Jacobs and his countless imitators and appear detached from everything but her own worked-over image of emotional absence.

By 2006, the rest of the world caught up with Demeulemeester's concept of the new, self-assured, self-contained twenty-first-century woman (English, 2011: 144–9). Her

Figure 9.2 Ann Demeulemeester, black and white pantsuit with black deconstructed jacket, Paris Fashion Week at Couvent des Cordeliers, Autumn/Winter 2009.

consistent nonchalant styling, striking the right balance between male and female elements, offered solutions to what women felt comfortable wearing. Sarah Mower (2006) described the image that Demeulemeester has believed in for twenty years as 'a strong urban female with an elegant-barbaric wardrobe'. Significantly, Suzie Menkes (2010) commented that 'this new decade's view of the strong woman is about nobility, rather than aggression', and she acknowledged that Demeulemeester might be the designer who had created the lexicon of the twenty-first-century modern woman.

BEAUTY AND THE BEAST: FASHION NOIR

Lipovetsky (1994) in *The Empire of Fashion* initially argued that individualism was the prime focus of fashion in the twentieth century. However, he added that, 'In the late 20th century, clothing no longer arouses the interest or passion it used to illicit' (1994: 120). Similarly, Andrew Hill (2005: 67) argues that, within a postmodernist framework, 'questions of individual identity and a reflexivity about these questions have come to be fore grounded in a way not seen in earlier eras'. He reinforced the idea that anti-fashion—which initially challenged the conventions of fashion—has, in turn, been accepted as mainstream, and this 'dressing down' was the outcome of the gradual shift towards 'casual' dress or 'lifestyle' dress. By the last decade of the twentieth century, it seemed that individualism in fashion no longer denoted difference. At that time, fashion was no longer a signifying power and instead reflected disenchantment with the world. A growing number of designers believe that fashion is a legitimate communication tool for sociopolitical advocacy, and its visual potency can be used to establish aesthetic direction in design and to reflect the cultural milieu of today's society.

Central St. Martin's Caroline Evans also argued that a strong feeling of decadence and psychological trauma pervaded fashion collection showings in the 1990s and early 2000s. She explains that it was a period when experimental design and photography concentrated on the spectacle and not the essence of fashion. Just as the concept of deconstruction emerged in the 1980s with the socially challenged punks in London and the Zen antiaesthetic work of the Japanese in Paris, at the turn of the century it was the Belgians, and, in particular, the work of Martin Margiela, who continued the social, sexual and aesthetic assault on the establishment. Margiela chose abject materials for his garments and destroyed any hint of the original functionality or exclusiveness. Bill Cunningham (2010) argues that deconstruction fashion is a cultural response to the social and political unrest of the times in Europe, and this zeitgeist constituted the emergence of countercultural fashion. The critics labelled it 'Le Destroy', and Alison Gill saw 'a mirror image in these decaying garments of social stress and degradation brought by the economic recession in the early 1990s' (1998: 30). Both Evans (1998) and Gill (1998) argue that the sordid urban locations chosen for Margiela's shows—empty car parks, warehouse corridors, an unused derelict Metro station and a disused hospital—added to the deconstruction of the notion of couture as glamorous. Other prominent Belgian designers, including Dries Van Noten and Walter van Beirendonck, followed this practice by holding collection showings in the snow around coal fires and in unheated tents.

A polarity existed in the fin-de-siècle fashion trends, with Margiela and his experimental, dark and melancholic garments[2] (see Chapter 3) on the one hand and Galliano's vigorous and joyful creations that epitomized an age of luxury and excess on the other. Evans argues that both designers practiced a form of 'cultural poetics' that was 'caught up in an oscillation between novelty and decay, as cycles of consumption consign everything belonging to 'yesterday' to the scrap heap (2003: 37). Alexander McQueen seemed to be caught in the schism between these two worlds—glamorous collections expected by Gucci and his own penchant towards outrageous, irreverent and spectacular narratives (Plate 20). His hard-edged collections, unashamedly sexual and subversive, revealed nipples; contained imitation body parts as adornment; and attracted controversy with titles such as Highland Rape (1995) and La Poupee (1997), in which a black model was restrained within a metal cage and was seen by the press as representing bondage, slavery and the subordination of women. Many of these, and later, shows were inspired by the cult films of Stanley Kubrick, Pier Paolo Pasolini, Alfred Hitchcock and the dark photography of Joel-Peter Witkin.

After 11 September 2001, the world changed dramatically. A new type of *glamour noir* had emerged—one that relied on the paradox of reality and illusion contextualized by symbolic exaggeration and theatricality. Presentations became pretentious; they were a form of escapism, and fashion photography captured these images of excess, negativism and anxiety. Galliano's historical romanticism offered a form of staged escapism, while McQueen's creations, potent in their social and political meaning, spelled out the impending gloom-and-doom mind-set of the decade.

Designer fashion responded to world events—terrorism, religious wars, ethnic conflicts and global recession. Fear, uncertainty and instability created a bunker mentality, and subdued colours and foreboding silhouettes began to dominate

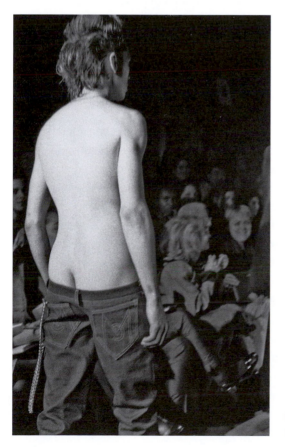

Figure 9.3 Alexander McQueen, man's bumster pants, first New York show, March 1996.

collection showings. The Web site fashionwindows.com reports that Lagerfeld commented: 'If you read the daily papers, you are not in the mood for pink and green. We have to deal now with a whole world connected.'[3] Paris fashion in 2006 reflected the sombre mood of a world in turmoil. Lagerfeld's very long, dark layered clothes, ominous in black, set the mood for other collections. Both Yohji Yamamoto and Marc Jacobs also featured a weighty look with sturdy fabrics and thick leg coverings concealing the body entirely. Fashion journalists referred to the 'Muslim-ization' of fashion—a religious influence where oversized clothes deny sexuality, and face coverings obliterate any sense of self or individuality. Suzie Menkes (2006) of the *International Herald Tribune* suggests that: 'What is hidden, secret and interior will become the new erotica.'

For a number of years, symbols of war and masculine aggression had appeared in designer collection showings. Some designers made extensive use of khaki or guerrilla warfare colours, while others relied on styling reminiscent of the 1950s motorcycle culture. A number of designers created survival coats—pocketed plastic coverings in which one's essential life possessions could be carried—while others included clothes that read like armour or uniforms (Prada's Miu Miu collection, 1 March 2006). Some designers, more directly, used text that appeared across the clothing, including Jun Takahashi for Undercover's display of antiwar T-shirts; Yamamoto's tops inscribed with the words 'Do Not Touch Me' seen in the October 2003 show; and Galliano's use of 'Dior not War' splashed on jackets and shirts. An atypical sense of sobriety dominated Watanabe's mostly black collection as early as October 2004 with clothing that looked sad and oppressive.

It became common practice for designers to cover the heads of their models with scarves, veils and other wrappings, suggesting anonymity or victims caught up in espionage. For the Fall/Winter 2006/2007 season, Takahashi's Undercover label showed models' heads completely covered, like the bags placed over prisoners' heads before execution. Vivienne Westwood also used a knitted cap that totally covered the model's face, and Viktor & Rolf's models wore pearl-and-rattan fencing masks with cocktail dresses, full-skirted suits and trenches that were a sly pastiche of 1950s French fashion. The colours varied from pebble to charcoal, with shades of grey dominating most collections. Trebay (2006) remarked that 'it's clear something ugly is going on', as the models appeared so sinister that they rivalled Robert Mapplethorpe's outrageous photographs of figures wearing bondage hoods and mummy suits. This mood of sweet melancholy apparent in fashion extended to fine art exhibitions as well. At the Neue Nationalgalarie in Berlin, the brilliantly curated exhibition 'Melancholy—Genius and Madness in Art' showed hundreds of works from the sixth century to the twentieth century that explored notions of sadness, melancholy, intellectual gravity and death (Von Hahn, 2006).

THE RISE OF MENSWEAR

One of the most positive and profitable developments to occur in fashion was the rise of menswear. Attention-grabbing collections and a sharper focus on male models have led to greater exposure of menswear on the international catwalks, in fashion photography and in magazine coverage since 2000. Jil Sander introduced her new menswear line in 1997, Galliano and McQueen in 2004, Demeulemeester in 2005, and the historic Savile Row brand Gieves was relaunched by British designer Joe Casely-Hayford in 2006. Net-a-Porter launched its dedicated designer Web site in January 2011 called Mr Porter, offering more than sixty top menswear brands and providing style advice and trend forecasts for its male customers. Not only has there been a distinct increase in the number of designers presenting menswear collections at international showings, but a pervasive element of masculinity has dominated womenswear collections as well since the turn of the twenty-first century. While androgyny-dominated collections prevailed in the first few years, 'motorcycle chic' took the lead in many designer collections between 2004 and 2007, including Lagerfeld's, Watanabe's and Kawakubo's and Gaultier's collection for Hermès, with studded and zippered black leather constructed jackets, caps and boots. While complementing the theme of the warrior woman, the trend towards nonpartisan, transgender dressing also reflected a growing recognition of both heterosexual and homosexual male standing in today's society. Undoubtedly, with a greater focus on the growing gay niche market, lucrative sales helped to sustain fashion's business status quo during the uncertain first decade of the new millennium. Alber Elbaz, director of Lanvin, used jewellery for the first time for his male models in the June 2010 collection showing, explaining, 'It's liberation for men' with necklaces of iron tusks, chains, black stones and wood, and designer Lucas Ossendrijver added, 'when women wear pants, men can wear jewellery' (*The Independent*, 28 June 2010) (Plate 21).

During a decade characterized by economic downturn, it is not surprising that exceptional technical expertise on the catwalk was showcased, markedly reinforcing the value intrinsic to bespoke tailoring as opposed to mass-manufactured garments. This message was highlighted in a novel way when A. F. Vandevorst, in the March 2001 Paris show, showcased a man's trench coat made out of brown paper rather than fabric. While, historically, the suit has been the bastion of the English Dandy, and Savile Row the mecca for status and high-end business wear, designers have capitalized on present trends to highlight their extremely sharp tailoring skills, their fine craftsmanship, their devotion to structure and fit and their use of fine fabrics over embellishment and frippery. Men's tailored clothing has changed to reflect the interest in healthy and toned bodies. Paul Smith's very successful business enterprise has been built on an 'acute awareness of British bourgeois aspirations, combining a self parodying humour'

Figure 9.4   US designer Thom Browne presents his men's Spring/Summer 2013 collection on 1 July 2012 in Paris as an outdoor installation. Photo: Francois Guillot/AFP/Getty Images.

with reference to British history, 'when gentlemen played cricket, drank pink gin, ate curry lunches, and were reliably eccentric' (Breward, 2003: n.p.). While McQueen's work reflected a preoccupation with youth and youthfulness, Galliano resurrected his poetically romantic 'gypsy' persona, Van Noten consistently relied on exclusive fabrics to create a luxurious look and Jacobs promoted the retro classics through his reference to casual 'worn-out', secondhand clothes. Until he retired in 2005, Margiela's menswear captured the essence of imperfection, personality and eccentricity.

Long-standing menswear designers including Giorgio Armani, Helmut Lang, Jean-Paul Gaultier, Vivienne Westwood, Paul Smith and Veronique Nichanian at Hermès, are joined by a bevy of twenty-first-century newcomers. These include John Cavalera (Plate 22); the much-admired Christopher Bailey of Burberry; Stefano Pilati at Yves Saint Laurent, who has built his reputation on the elegant tailoring evident in all of his clothes; Nicolas Ghesquiere at Balenciaga, whom *New York Times* journalist Cathy Horyn (2004) described as 'the most important designer of his generation'; and Hedi Slimane[4] at Dior, known for his cutting-edge, slim-line aesthetic styled for the rockers of the contemporary music scene. Legendary American labels, including Calvin Klein and Ralph Lauren, established the ultimate in men's casual lifestyle dressing.

Both John Varvatos and Rick Owens broke away from the conservative mould to introduce rock-inspired clothing, and in Owen's case, he offered the 'grunge meets glamour'[5] look in Paris. Thom Browne teamed up with Brooks Brothers in 2006 to design his very successful high-end Black Fleece range and later, in 2008, was hired by Moncler to produce the Game Bleu 2009 menswear collection. Tim Banks of style.com described Browne as 'the master showman of fashion surrealism' when his astronaut-inspired models stripped off their jumpsuits to reveal two-button jackets, Bermuda shorts and knee socks underneath (Paris, 27 June 2010). Another newcomer, Alexander Wang, offered a slouchy, rolled-out-of-bed, edgy look that appealed to the young, and Californian surfwear label, Warriors of Radness (Rick Klotz), broke through the glass ceiling with his provocative T-shirts and board shorts.

In summary, post-twentieth-century trends suggest fashion has undoubtedly become the culture of the street, a culture of conformity based on nonconformity perhaps providing a sense of belonging, a sense of security in unsettled times. Global fashion had forced the individual to become an homogenized citizen of the world during the first decade of the twenty-first century, with world events and global politics, in particular, becoming powerful influences upon Paris designer fashion. Street style fashion has mutated into a plethora of stylistic variations, and the nature of street fashion was constantly evolving (Plate 24), moving from the personal to the collective, from the regional to the global, from the social to the political.

–10–

The Changing Fashion Market in the Late Twentieth and Twenty-First Centuries

When the supply of fashion items becomes so enormous, the consumer tends to choose the leading brand, which means that others are left behind. And to establish real credibility is no simple matter.

Giorgio Armani

MARKETING AND PROMOTION

In the fashion industry, two main developments have taken place over the past ten or fifteen years that are driving profits and opportunities for expansion: e-marketing and the expanding Asian market. In global terms, by the end of the first decade of the twenty-first century, fashion made up more than 7 per cent of world exports. This suggests the prominence of fashion in the international marketplace. Interestingly, marketing surveys[1] indicate that, by 2014, China will be the largest consumer market in the world, having overtaken the Japanese and American markets. Marketing firm Galloway and Mullen forecasts that Chinese consumption is to increase to $14.6 billion by this time, with 80 per cent of the buyers aged 40 years and younger. The Chinese e-commerce market quadrupled from 2006 to 2009, and Galloway notes that 2010, in particular, 'had been a seminal year for the luxury industry' worldwide (McMahon and Morley, 2011: 74). Arguably, this is a result of the growing market in both China and India (see Chapter 12) for luxury goods, which includes fashion, electronic products and prestigious cars. To capitalize on this new Asian market, fashion designers, corporate designer labels and producers of luxury fashion brand accessories such as perfume, cosmetics, handbags (Plate 18) and shoes began to open more outlets in mainland China. For example, in June 2011, Prada, listed on the Hong Kong Stock Exchange, announced that its stores in mainland China were responsible for a 74 per cent increase in profits and that it planned to open twenty-five more stores there. Undoubtedly, this fast-growing cultural shift in the fashion industry's global marketplace will have enormous implications for future marketing strategies.

In the West, during the 1990s, retail sales enjoyed uninterrupted growth, but by the turn of the millennium, a global economic instability and downturn became apparent.

Despite the resulting downturn in sales, media personnel were still flocking to the fashion capital to capture the latest collection showings. 'The end of the 1990s saw 2,000 journalists from more than 40 counties, 100 television stations, and 400 radio stations in Paris covering the hundreds of ready-to-wear shows' (Best, 2010: n.p.). The *Los Angeles Times* (13 September 2009) reported that 'The global strategy of branding and merchandising that has dominated the luxury sector for the last decade is falling away in favour of more authentic, localised experiences. Luxury brands are borrowing ideas from the fast-fashion world—opening pop-up shops, launching limited-edition collections, even mixing it up with the mass market' (Moore, 2009). The year 2008 marked a critical point in retail selling, and new marketing and promotion strategies were employed. However, fast-fashion retailing strategies employed by mega-stores such as Zara, H&M and Uniqlo proved successful, and Jackson and Shaw's *Mastering Fashion Marketing* argued that the diversification of supermarkets into fashion, following the success of ASDA's George brand, presented a serious challenge to both clothing retailers and fashion brands. It was in the e-marketing field that there was greater evidence of increased sales, as 'more fashion brands were revisiting e-commerce as a credible distribution channel' (Jackson and Shaw, 2008: 17).

E-MARKETING AND DESIGNER WEB SITES

Interestingly e-commerce, which emerged in the late 1990s, was initially headed for a shaky start. In 2000, it suffered a dot-com crash which quickly curtailed the public's confidence in online shopping. Many online brands collapsed or limited their business activities. This was partly due to some companies not being able to fulfil the orders that they received from customers. As broadband was adopted by more customers after 2002 and online retailers such as Amazon and the auction site eBay became very successful, more retailers invested in this online method of distribution. Despite the lead taken by American consumerist marketers in the twentieth century, British, European and Japanese designers were all instrumental in recognizing the potential of the World Wide Web as a powerful communication tool that could effectively capture the immediacy of fashion (Plate 23). Major marketing surveys that followed revealed considerable competition amongst the leading luxury and designer e-tailers such as Net-a-Porter, The Outnet, Portero, Gilt Groupe/Gilt Fuse, Rue La La, online department stores and brand-owned sites and highlighted that eBay is the number one fashion retailer on the net, catering to over 85 million active users in thirty-nine countries (*The Nation*, 2008). Constance White, a former fashion editor who was the style director at eBay from 2003 to 2010, often commented that the explosion of e-commerce had significantly shifted the way people were able to shop—from restricted shop hours to 24 hours a day, 7 days a week. Her marketing promotion was based on the premise that eBay was the barometer that reflected what people were actually looking for in fashion. eBay first built its profile in fashion with auctions in vintage and preowned garments but has moved on to offer new products, including luxury brands.

The fashion industry seemed to lag behind other product promoters who immediately embraced the idea of e-commerce and recognized that new technologies were the ideal media to reach a mass market. Textile designers now use technology such as product data management to e-mail textile designs to Asian manufacturers, who then reproduce them by the thousands using advanced printing systems. Emilio Pucci, in particular, is renowned for his signature textile patterns and colours, marketed to consolidate his international corporate image. Fashion magnates such as Gianni Versace, Issey Miyake and Pucci were amongst the first to take the lead in award-winning multimedia presentations on the Web. Issey Miyake won one of the first awards for his outstanding Web site. Famous fashion photographer Nick Knight insisted that fashion shoots were performances, and the Web allowed catwalk collections to enter the global home entertainment arena. By recreating a conceptual catwalk experience, the viewer entered the world of elitist high fashion. Yet, paradoxically, the entry did not require wealth or celebrity status. Today, as has been previously asserted, designers use their haute couture collections to gain media coverage, which, in turn, supports their more profitable prêt-à-porter ranges.

Laird Borelli (2002), who wrote *Net Mode: Web Fashion Now*, a seminal text on fashion Web technology, describes designer or 'vanity sites' as 'brand building vehicles' that 'are now a necessary part of many-tentacled marketing plans' (2002: 6). Chairman and CEO of Louis Vuitton Moet Hennessy (LVMH) Bernard Arnault argues that 'The reason for being a designer . . . is to sell. Fashion is not pure art. It is creativity with the goal of having as many customers as possible wearing the product' (Gale and Kaur, 2004: 124). LVMH is one of the major shareholders of www.eLUXURY.com and uses this site to promote and sell its own prestigious product group brands such as Pucci and, until March 2011, Galliano. All of Arnault's stable of designers have their own Web sites directly linked to this key Internet address. The Galliano Girl brand site was launched by eLUXURY on 24 April 2001, months prior to Galliano's own site, www.johngalliano.com, in 2002. This seminal collection, aimed at the younger consumer, was unique because it was created specifically for the Internet and was available exclusively online, with features such as 'website' colours and fabrics and easy-fit garments to broaden the appeal to potential buyers (Borelli, 2002: 87–88).

High fashion seems particularly well suited to new media, since both are eminently image-centric (Borelli, 2002: 7). The success of online selling can be attributed to three key factors that are particular to multimedia. First, interactivity promotes an exchange of views, making the communication more personal and therefore more appealing. The consumer can send personal letters to some designers, while other designers will individually reply to customers' style queries (e.g. Max Azria at www.BCBG. com), and some Web sites offer prizes of fashion show tickets for entering their competitions. A buyer can send a fashion e-card to his or her friends displaying a garment that might appeal to them and, at the same time, seek approval of friends before making a purchase. Some Web sites allow the consumer to see the same garment pictured in different colours and fabrics. For example, the 'Dress Me Up' section of www.nylonmag.com allows the buyer to dress a virtual paper doll in different garments with varied accessories.

Second, e-commerce techniques effectively help to build a brand image that is central to the success of a designer label. Creative e-marketing allows the designer to create an image of the product which replaces the actual clothes (i.e. Benetton). In other words, the Modernist adage that 'form follows the function' has been replaced by 'the image follows the marketing'. The designer's history, accompanied by photos of family, friends or pets, creates a simulacrum of a photo album, further personalizing the site. Using Flash technology, layer upon layer of images, which constantly change and move across the computer screen, visually build the identity of the brand. This proliferation of images is often enhanced when juxtaposed images of garments from a designer's archival collection (or press clippings or sound tracks from a previous decade) are used to underline brand and emotional loyalty. Music is a powerful marketing tool when it is used as a theme for a Web site and also played in the designer's retail outlets. Advertisers recognize that both men and women find comfort in shopping in familiar stores, listening to familiar music, and wearing familiar products such as perfumes and colognes.

The third important way that multimedia play a role in the success of online selling is that the convenience of purchase is an inherent ploy of Internet marketing. It not only offers transportation-free access to products, no interference from salespeople and anonymity of personal choice of apparel, but it simplifies the shopping process of choosing appropriate garments, categorized according to department, occasion, price range and brand. Thumbnail images show the whole garment and highlight special features such as cuffs or collars. This replaces the physical act of thumbing through racks of clothes to find the desired colour or size. Often the Web sites include professional fashion editorials that convincingly argue that their ensembles are the latest trend in fashionable circles.

Clearly, Web-based shopping extends the idea of catalogue shopping, first initiated by the early department stores in the United States in the late 1800s. The famous Sears Roebuck catalogue, which provided a mail order service across the country, provided access to consumer goods to rural and remote customers that had previously been available to only department store buyers in the larger cities. In the mid-twentieth century, commercial television shopping channels promoted products that could be ordered over the telephone, and this is still used effectively on television

Figure 10.1 Net-a-Porter founder Natalie Massenet and editor-in-chief of American *Vogue*, Anna Wintour, look at a Web site, 8 September 2011. Photo: Duffy-Marie Arnoult/Getty Images for Net-a-Porter. This Web site is one of the most successful to redesign the magazine and shopping experience for the consumer.

talk shows that are often little more than sponsored advertising promotions. The style.com Web site, amongst others, helped to redefine the magazine and the shopping experience for consumers. This site is the online home of *Vogue* and *W* magazines, in association with the department store Neiman Marcus. It initially produced a duplicate print catalogue for its Autumn 2001 and Spring 2002 fashion products to ensure that it would reach both Internet and mail order clients. The Web site extends the reach of the magazines and reinterprets the 'visual vernacular' into a new technological sphere. Undoubtedly, the fashion sites have a wider net of viewers worldwide than most print magazines and therefore must project a more heterogeneous global multicultural image.

Net-a-Porter, a London-based boutique (which won the award for best fashion shop at the 2004 British Fashion Awards) and its Web site www.net-a-porter.com, sells expensive fashions at full price and markets globally. It targets the richest consumers—individuals who know their size in a particular label and who are assured that returns will be hassle-free. The site is updated weekly and promotes runway pieces and trendsetting fashions that cost an average of $800 per item. Initially, analysts were convinced that it would be impossible to sell high-end fashion on the Internet and did not anticipate consumers' acceptance of the concept and the lure and convenience of having exclusive items delivered to their door. The founder of the Web site, Natalie Massenet, a former editor of *Tatler* magazine, argues that 'the appearance of gift wrapped sturdy black boxes with grosgrain ribbon from France . . . is meant to evoke the shopping experience of a more elegant age, when uniformed porters delivered extravagantly wrapped parcels to customers' homes' (2005: 50).

In January 2011, Net-a-Porter initiated a dedicated menswear site called Mr Porter offering more than sixty top menswear brands, along with expert style advice and trend forecasts. It seems that this move responds to men's growing preference for shopping on the net (56 per cent, overtaking women).[2] Marketing surveys reveal that men, in particular, prefer to standardize their shopping, tend to repeatedly buy the same brands from the same outlets and prefer to avoid high-street shopping, thereby making their purchases quickly and efficiently. Web sites offer alternative or secondary distribution channels and often offer goods at prices lower than those in retail stores. A number of sites, such as The Outnet (launched in 2009), sell discount designer outfits from last season. The Outnet offers international express shipping and, in some cases, same-day delivery to customers in New York and London.

REINVENTING THE SHOPPING EXPERIENCE

The rise of branding escalated in the 1980s (see Chapter 8), and by the new millennium, changes become apparent (Plate 19). Many retail businesses, confronted by changing spending patterns, were becoming less brand-centric and more consumer-centric. Increasingly, marketers became aware that by 2012, an antiglobalization backlash against large corporations and their fashion brands (i.e. Levi's and Nike, in particular, despite becoming synonymous with street fashion) reflected a trend for individualism, 'self-affirmation' and niche brands (Jackson and Shaw, 2008: 20). In other words, consumers were exerting their own rights rather than following the dictates of the sellers. For example, consumers complained that the immediacy of fashion availability was compromised by the biannual fashion collection showings that promoted new styling that was not available to purchase in the retail outlets for six months after the showings. As a result, some designers began to replace the runway show with promotional events where the buyers could purchase garments on the spot. Reinventing the shopping experience and enhancing it with entertainment and technology seems to be the challenge in the second decade of the twenty-first century. For example, when Helmut Lang sent CDs and videos of his collections to international editors as early as 1998 instead of holding runway shows, it signalled a major change in the marketing of fashion. After September 11, he stayed in New York and presented his Spring 2002 collection on the Internet rather than going to Paris. Not only did he not want to travel,[3] he also believed that this would make his show internationally accessible (see The New Media: Blogs and Social Networking section).

A trend towards the mixing and matching of brand garments and accessories is becoming more prevalent on sartorial blog Web sites, and these purchases can be made at a lower cost and at any time of the day by Internet shopping. The aggregator sites allow shoppers to compare brand styles and prices from dozens of online stores at once. Cross-shopping by brand or search term (Shopstyle) allows customers to receive personalized e-mails regarding availability and sales alerts, while other Web sites find the goods that cater to a customer's measurements and style profile (MyShape) and colour and silhouette preferences (Covet). This shift in the fashion paradigm underlies the rise of 'cheap chic' and recession-regulated buying patterns and reaffirms the notion that 'customers are now spending more time each week interrogating the Internet than watching television' (Jackson and Shaw, 2008: 17).

By the end of the twentieth century, other marketing methodologies such as fashion TV, online-only fashion magazines and lifestyle selling were employed to entice customers to increase their spending. Fashion TV, for example, introduced in 1997, is the world's leading channel dedicated to following fashion. It broadcasts via satellite from all of the major fashion show presentations to millions of households in 192 countries. Other networks include QVC and Applevision, a New York service that shows fashion trends on closed-circuit TV in some New York hotels, like the Plaza, allowing guests to have their purchases such as perfumes, scarves and accessories from Chanel, Geoffrey Beene and Saks Fifth Avenue delivered directly to their rooms. As well, new modelling reality shows reflect new trends in modelling agencies, as promoted by Simon Fuller's Storm Model Management (which launched Kate Moss). Online-only fashion magazines such as *i Fashion* list the most recent stylish trends and pinpoint where customers can find the fashions online. Other online magazines, including *N.E.E.T.*, which focuses on the independent designer scene, *I Love Fake*, a more underground magazine like *i-D*, and *Runway* (led by Nole Marin from *America's Next Top Model*) have begun to dominate the market with digital copies for computers, iPhones and iPads. The Gen Y consumerist generation, in particular, expects immediate and portable access to all information systems. In comparison, printed glossy fashion publications are usually only available monthly, quarterly or biannually. Critics argue that by the time they are distributed, the clothes are already out of fashion. Finally, new retailing aims for lifestyle selling in an attempt to create a social and educational experience for the shopper by incorporating in-store events with the sales process. These might include wine and cheese tastings, football Sundays, women's parties selling lingerie, underwear and fashion and designer book and video launches. It is the *experience* rather than the product that drives demand. Retailer brand image must be constantly monitored to ensure that the lifestyle advertisements for the store were in keeping with the merchandise on the shelves. A study regarding this, undertaken by Andrew Newman and Darshika Patel (2004) of the Manchester Business School at the University of Manchester (UK), used a factor analysis of customer responses and gathered data to explain why performance levels were much lower in the Gap as opposed to Topshop, both large retail brands targeting young style-conscious UK consumers.

NEW RETAILING NETWORKS

Mega-Store Branding and Pop-Up Stores

Over the past ten years, two new retailing networks, mega-brand stores and pop-up stores, have exerted a major influence worldwide. In the first instance, the concept of branding has moved from independent designer products to collaborative liaisons between designers and mega-stores. High street stores—such as Uniqlo, founded in Hiroshima, Japan, in 1984—now provide trendy, cheap, minimalist casualwear clothing that is sold internationally. Along with other top retailers, such as Topshop, Zara, Whistles and H&M, these companies collaborate with both designers and celebrities alike (Kate Moss for Topshop, Madonna for H&M and Takahashi's Undercover for Uniqlo in 2012) to bring out designer and luxury diffusion lines that have enjoyed huge retail successes. The Gap, a US-based conglomerate, built an empire as a stylish casualwear retailer selling staple garments such as blue jeans and white T-shirts, catering mainly for the young. It advertised widely on its very efficient commercial Web site and in 2010 began a collaborative diffusion line with Valentino. As mentioned earlier, surveys evaluating business performance provide a strategic vehicle for the marketers to understand customers' perceptions of the retailer's image and whether the merchandise on the shelves reflected the lifestyles promoted in advertising.

Rei Kawakubo of Comme des Garcons is largely given credit for generating a new type of shopping venue called guerrilla stores, later dubbed pop-up stores. The ultimate in concept retailing, stores are opened for brief periods of time—maybe weeks, months or a year—in non-fashion, usually industrial parts of cities. Regardless of whether they are making a profit, they close and open again in a new location. This idea of 'finding the shop' has become part of the shopping experience and has proved to be financially very successful. With the first stores opening in Berlin in 2004 in a former bookshop (leaving the old name intact) and in Helsinki in a 1950s pharmacy, these shops were to remain unsullied by architects and designers. Other locations in Barcelona, Singapore, Stockholm, Ljubljana and Warsaw emerged spontaneously in hip, but marginalized, areas of cities. Transient distribution is a very effective

Figure 10.2   Pop-up Lyubov store, Paris, 2011. Photo: author. Pop-up stores appear, and quickly disappear, as short-term fashion budget outlets on streets in every capital city around the world. They have become a very successful distribution methodology for both high-end and low-end markets.

marketing ploy as it becomes like a treasure hunt and end-of-line clothing can be offloaded quickly at low prices.

The original idea, according to Guy Trebay (2004) of the *New York Times*, should be attributed to Nicholas Bourriaud of the Palais de Tokyo, a contemporary art museum. Bourriaud has consistently argued for 'cultural production with a built-in expiration date'. He argued that today's consumers were fickle and that obsolescence had become very marketable. The idea of the budget pop-up stores was adopted by a number of designer firms as it was cost effective, a means of direct marketing, allowed old merchandise to be recycled and avant-garde clothing to be channelled away from the catwalk.

Endorsed by the Harvard Business School, popular, middle-of-the-range retailers such as Target, Fila and Hanes followed suit. This 'provisional retailing' based on the paradigm of impermanency allows for companies to tap into new markets away from the central, high-concept flagship monoliths, pay cheap rents and have limited or no advertising costs, with the information passed by word of mouth. Stores have become reclassified as 'spaces', and this underground approach is consistent with a trend towards more direct marketing. For example, in September/October 2003, Target opened a store for Isaac Mizrahi in New York's Rockefeller Center for only six weeks and, inspired by this success, sold goods from a boat moored at the city's piers. According to Professor Nancy Koehn of the Harvard Business School, 'Accessibility has really been redefined for consumers . . . this is the wave of the future. One of the most cost-effective ways to reach a consumer is through their friends' (Horyn, 2004).

Counterfeit Chic

In a bid to economize production, many designers and design firms moved their manufacturing off-shore many decades ago to developing countries such as China and India. The factories in these countries could handle large-scale production runs for mass-produced garments. To a certain extent, this prohibited smaller firms that only wanted short production runs from accessing similar services. Off-shore production often led to problems with quality control, counterfeit/copied designs and ethical considerations, including underpaid and exploited labour, child labour and unsatisfactory working conditions, many of which could not be controlled by the designer.

Counterfeiting, or the unlawful copying or imitating goods, has become a major global problem, and lawsuits have been filed against eBay by LVMH in France, Tiffany in the United States and Hermès, amongst others, for providing a platform for sellers to traffic in fake products. The superficial image that is associated with luxury goods, designer labels and perfume brands fuels the production and sale of knock-off goods, or cheap fakes, by Asian manufacturers. An article in *Bazaar* (Thomas, 2005) argues that China continues to be the main source of counterfeiting; however, in the aftermath of negotiations by the United States–China Joint Commission on Commerce and Trade in 2004, the Chinese government announced the formation of a new counterfeiting task force to attack the problem. According to cultural anthropologist Simona Segre Reinach (2005: 49), it is estimated that of the 4,200 official Chinese shops selling Chanel cosmetics, at least one-third were fraudulent. She adds that Italy is second to China in terms of producing counterfeit goods, and China uses Italy as the standard model that it follows. Because China is a main production base for Italy, the Chinese buy Italian textile machinery and recruit retired Italian artisans to work in their factories. As well, China is a well-established manufacturer of several of the most prestigious 'Made in Italy' brands, and 'it is not uncommon for the same Chinese companies that produce the real brands to turn out fakes too . . . often as a release valve in times of recession.'[4]

Reproducing designer label goods for mass profit has been evident internationally since the turn of the century (Mah, 2006) (see Chapter 2). In 2006, Louis Vuitton—one of the most pirated brands in the world—had 40 full-time lawyers and 250 freelance

Figure 10.3   Counterfeit raid, China International Clothing and Accessories Fair, Beijing, China, 31 March 2004. Photo: Goh Chai Hin/ AFP/Getty Images. Chinese trade enforcement officers raid a display stand where fake Italian Pierre Cardin leather jackets hang on the wall in the background.

investigators, and spent €15 million to fight counterfeiting. In the same year, LVMH, Prada Holding, the Burberry Group and Pinault–Printemps–Redoute's Gucci label successfully sued a Silk Alley landlord in Beijing, China, for copyright infringement. Despite the court ruling, newspaper journalists rationalized that it would not increase the sale of the authentic luxury goods, because buyers in that market usually could not afford 'the real thing' anyway. Indicam, an Italy-based anti-counterfeiting coalition, reported that worldwide production of counterfeit goods reportedly jumped 1,700 per cent between 1993 and 2005, and the number of fakes seized in the European Union increased tenfold between 2000 and 2005 (Anti-Counterfeiting Group, 2005). In the United States, law authorities (in a report to the US Congressional House Committee on International Relations, 2003) argue that they are now recognizing the connection between terrorist financing and intellectual property crime. Undoubtedly, one main concern relates to the negative financial impact this is having on legitimate businesses.[5] In France, where anyone found guilty of producing, importing or exporting fakes as part of an organized gang can receive up to five years in prison and a fine of €500,000 Even tourists passing through France with counterfeit goods bought elsewhere risk a maximum fine of €360,000 and up to three years in jail. Similar fines exist in Italy as well.[6] The targeting of the consumer, rather than the producer, might be the most effective solution to this ever-increasing problem of fashion piracy. Michael Kaplinger of the World International Intellectual Property Organisation adds that 'While digital technologies have revolutionized the way in which we create and do business, those same technologies have fuelled a dramatic escalation in IP-crime' (Kaplinger, 2008: 2).

LUXURY HERITAGE BRANDING

Syndicates of multibrand groups such as the leading LVMH, Compagnie Financiere Richemont and Gucci created empires built on the acquisition of labels, particularly in the 1990s. In the 2000s, they were divesting themselves of some poor performers and investing more in their core brands. A trend emerged over the first decade of the twenty-first century where more profits were being made in luxury goods such as watches, jewellery and perfume than in designer clothing. Luxury heritage brands such as Chanel, Dior and Givenchy have relied on their appeal as labels exemplifying status and prestige, based on a classic timelessness—in historical as well as emotional terms (Plate 24). According to McMahon and Morley (2011: 69), the success of these brands in the twenty-first-century market is determined by 'their ability to develop new design and branding strategies in response to consumer feedback, while retaining the emotional core values of their heritage.' For instance, Karl Lagerfeld's success designing for the Chanel label underlines McMahon and Morley's observation that 'new designers need to create product that identifies and continues to express and repeat elements of the original creator's signature style while imbuing creations with their own creative identity to make the product relevant in the present' (McMahon and Morley, 2011: 72) (Plate 25).

Luxury heritage brand labels such as Gucci (revived by Tom Ford in just a few years) and Cartier have a familiar built-in brand stature and 'authentic' strength that immediately attract consumer respect. Consumers can develop a psychological connection with these products as they enhance their own sense of self-esteem, self-concept and self-worth. Kapferer and Bastien (2009) argue that to desire luxury is to desire becoming part of an elevated class. In the contemporary market, as iconic brand 'signatures' rely on this essence of exclusivity or rarity (not offered by counterfeit copies), they must protect the distribution networks by limiting accessibility (i.e. De Beers

Figure 10.4 Prada headquarters, Tokyo, Japan, 2011. Photo: author. Designed in 2003 by Herzog and De Meuron, the unconventional contemporary building celebrates and reinforces the fashion brand's success in the international industry.

diamonds). Limited edition production, characterized by craftsmanship and more valuable materials, is an alternate marketing strategy used to protect product integrity.

Luxury brand marketing in the fashion sector has recently become inherently linked to the flagship store experience. The brand headquarter store must be architecturally unique and designed by one of the most famous postmodernist architects of the twenty-first century. The prestige and status associated with the architectural brilliance is transferred to the products and to the customers themselves. As the Japanese are among the world's biggest luxury consumers, Tokyo is a key location and Prada is one of the leading firms represented by cutting-edge architectural design there. In Aoyama, Tokyo, its flagship store, designed in 2003 by Herzog and de Meuron, is a strikingly unconventional, five-sided, six-storey glass crystal with signature diamond-shaped glass panes that resemble bubbles from the outside of the building. The Maison Hermès in the Ginza district of Tokyo designed in 2001 by Renzo Piano uses extensive areas of glass square cubes, inspired by traditional Japanese lanterns, as a curtain-walling. The density of the glass sound-proofs the interior, and at night the entire building glows from within. The Tokyo Comme des Garcons headquarters designed by Spiral 0407 has pixilated windows of blue dots that make the people inside appear as if they are on a television screen. Christian Dior's Tokyo store designed by architects Kazuyo Sejima and Ryue Nishizawa has floors of different heights, and Puma House designed in 2011 by NENDO is made up of multiple staircases used as display stands throughout the interior of the building. It symbolizes movement and the relationship between fashion and sport. Rem Koolhaas designed Prada's New York flagship store and also its 'transformer' shape-shifting building in Seoul, which was designed as a unique temporary structure that could be picked up by cranes and rotated to accommodate a variety of cultural events. Other outstanding flagship stores include Fendi in Beverly Hills designed by Peter Marino and Alexander McQueen in Los Angeles designed by Pentagram.

In the twentieth and twenty-first centuries, marketing strategies have been reinvented, changed, modified or consolidated. Franchising, licensed copying, diffusion lines and the process of branding were initiated well before the twenty-first century. Bridging the gap between the expensive, high-fashion garment and affordable mass production lines relied on the media landscape, and its role was critical to the fashion system. The 'signature label', inherent to the two-tiered system of couture and ready-to-wear, had been exploited by a succession of designers since the early 1900s, but became even more important in the twenty-first century to reinforce quality and authenticity and to develop brand loyalty. To summarize, Power and Hauge outline the five key operational rationales adopted by most successful firms, which include the use of brand building: first, as a strategy to differentiate your product from your competitors; second, as an umbrella that focuses on the firm/syndicate and its image rather than on individual products; third, as a means for firms to diversify into product and service provider areas outside the core business; fourth, as a vehicle to allow for flexibility or change in managerial or designer structures; and, finally, as a platform for co-branding or linking brands together (Power and Hauge, 2006: 8–10).

INTERNATIONALIZING FASHION

Over the past twenty years, the growth and nature of fashion weeks and blockbuster exhibitions of fashion in museums around the world signifies their importance as key marketing strategies to increase revenue in the fashion and associated industries. Promoted as cultural events, they broaden the perception of what fashion is, and what it can be.

Fashion Weeks

Initially, the Chambre Syndicale de la Couture Parisienne was established in 1868 as a type of trade union for haute couturiers. It initiated and organized fashion *maisons* to present their haute couture collections in a central location in Paris and at a time of the year that would maximize potential sales to overseas buyers. In 1973, the syndicate established the Chambre Syndicale du Prêt-à-Porter des Couturiers et des Créateurs de Mode (Trade union of [women's] ready-to-wear of couturiers and fashion designers), which organized the ready-to-wear or prêt-a-porter collection showings in Paris. Fashion weeks, usually lasting seven days, are appearing in a greater number of major cities around the world. In an attempt to draw attention to a country's emerging fashion talents, they promote local and national industries and increase export market possibilities. Fashion weeks are now advertised in countries outside of western Europe, Britain and the United States, such as Australia and New Zealand, Africa, Canada, China, Croatia, India, Indonesia, Malaysia (Singapore), Mexico and Russia, amongst others.

Fashion weeks are semiannual events allowing time for retailers to arrange to purchase or incorporate designers' work into their retail marketing. Today, the four premier international fashion centres include Paris, renowned as the central venue with the top credentials; New York[7] for its slick production and marketing expertise; Milan for its economic/business caché; and London for its fresh, cutting-edge vitality. These cities hold two fashion weeks per year, with Paris adding another two haute couture weeks. In March/April, designers present their collections for the Autumn/Winter season, and in September/October, they parade the Spring/Summer lines. This is reflected in fashion magazine spreads as well, and, for the buyers, this means forward-thinking and planning. In recent years, and in an attempt to counteract the global downturn, more designers were showing their commercial interseasonal collections between the traditional seasons to shorten customers' wait for the new season's clothes. The interseasonal collections are resort/cruise (before Spring/Summer) and pre-fall (before Autumn/Winter). Genre-specific showings, such as swimwear, have been the theme of both Miami and Rio Fashion Weeks. New and unusual venues have also been used by designers, including Karl Lagerfeld, who held his resort and pre-fall collections for Chanel in cities such as Moscow, Los Angeles and Monte Carlo instead of Paris. For the first time, a womenswear haute couture collection showing was held outside of Paris in Singapore in October 2011.

The success of a fashion week is determined by the number of leading models, celebrities, big-name designers and prestigious clientele and corporate buyers that it attracts, not to mention the international press coverage that it draws. In 2009, London's 25th Anniversary Fashion Week was held in the historic palladium of Somerset House and wooed designer firms such as Burberry, Jonathan Saunders, Pringle and Matthew Williamson away from Paris. In the same year, having suffered a major economic setback in 2008, the New York Fashion Week, where 250 designers presented their collections in tents in Byrant Park, in Lower Manhattan, showed signs of enforced economies (Schwartz, 2009): models halved their catwalk fees, and a number of designers scaled back their presentations. Marc Jacobs cut his guest list from 2,000 to 500 and did not hold his traditional after-party. The event signalled a new trend towards a more conscious consumerism.

Museum Exhibitions of Fashion

In 2011, thirty-seven major fashion exhibitions were held worldwide. According to the Fashion Institute of Technology's Valerie Steele (2011), when the Metropolitan Museum of Art in New York first held a retrospective show of the work of a living designer—Yves Saint Laurent in 1983[8]—it was the first time this type of exhibition had been held. The ensuing controversy created amongst the museum trustees led to a decision that all future solo retrospective exhibitions had to represent the work of deceased designers only. Ironically, this dictum did not apply to fine artists.

Today, fashion exhibitions attract a large audience and have become major block-buster shows for museums around the world. Finally breaching the gap between commerce and culture, progressive museum directors and curators now appreciate that the methodologies employed in display and presentation both in the (department) store and the museum share a common objective: that of creating a spectacle. Acknowledging that the fashion industry and the art museum rely on this centrality of display, other links between fashion and art can be assessed. Distinctive fashion garments, designed by both the masters of haute couture and ready-to-wear collections, are now conceived as being both cultural and commercial treasures and command respect in national museum holdings.

Curatorial rationales for fashion exhibitions often reference themes that contextualize fashion within a changing cultural arena, such as 'Radical Fashion' at the Victoria and Albert Museum in 2001–2002, which considered the concept of the avant-garde in postmodernist fashion; 'Superheroes: Fashion and Fantasy' at the Costume Institute of the Metropolitan Museum of Art in New York in 2008, which created a vision of fashion superheroes as the ultimate fashion icons; and 'Art and Fashion: Between Skin and Clothing' at the Kuntsmuseum in Wolfsburg, Germany, in 2011, which considered fashion as a legitimate art form. Recent retrospective designer exhibitions that reveal the aesthetic development and historical narrative of the oeuvre have attracted unprecedented attendances in museums worldwide. The proliferation of retrospective block-buster shows suggests that we are marking the end of an era for some of the twentieth and twenty-first centuries' greatest designers. For the Metropolitan Museum in New York, the Costume Institute's 2010 Alexander McQueen exhibition, 'Savage Beauty', curated by Andrew Bolton, drew more than 660,000 visitors—one of the largest recorded audiences in the museum's history. In 2010, the Petit Palais in Paris held the first retrospective show of Yves Saint Laurent since his death in 2008. Christian Dior's work was celebrated at the State Pushkin Museum of Fine Arts in Moscow in 2011.

In the same year, Jean-Paul Gaultier's travelling exhibition was first displayed at the Montreal Museum of Fine Arts and Yohji Yamamoto's thirtieth anniversary show was feted at the Victoria and Albert Museum in London.[9]

THE NEW MEDIA: BLOGS AND SOCIAL NETWORKING

Blogs

The Sartorialist blog site (www.thesartorialist.com), created in 2005, very quickly attracted a huge international audience and responded to an upmarket street style interest in fashion. The founder, Scott Shuman, who is well versed in fashion trends, provides an informed yet somewhat elitist view of what people are wearing on the street. His profile has reached epic heights, and he is invited to attend high fashion collection showings. He selectively posts photographs online of stylish individuals, usually impeccably dressed, whom he had photographed in a number of urban centres around the world. He provides descriptions of the fashion and cityscapes and solicits

Figure 10.5 *New York Times* photographer Bill Cunningham outside the Ralph Lauren showing, Skylight Studios, for New York Spring Fashion Week 2012, New York, September 2011. Photo: Monica McKlinski/Getty Images. A well-known figure on the streets of New York, Cunningham became the seminal sartorialist.

comments from the e-audience as to their preferences. Interestingly, this blog site was documented by *Time* magazine as one of 100 top design influences in 2007. This audience interaction has become an important marketing strategy that underlies various media formatting in general. The popularity of similar fashion blog sites[10] is reinforced by Anna Wintour of *Vogue*, who references the bloggers' comments in the publications alongside those of the international fashion journalists. Other bloggers such as Gala Darling, Tavi and Garance Dore have participated in fashion design collection collaborations and received front-row, international fashion week seats next to some of the most notable figures in the couture world. A 2009 *Financial Times* article (Copping, 2009) notes that being a style blogger is a perfectly respectable career for someone in the fashion industry.

It is significant that Bill Cunningham of the *New York Times* preempted this type of blogging by taking photographs of individuals in the street and at high-street functions in New York and Paris for over fifty years and publishing them with his column in the *Times* since 1978. Cunningham was 'looking for', what Harold Koda, chief curator at the Costume Institute at the Metropolitan Museum of Art, describes as 'ordinary people going about their lives, dressed in fascinating ways' (Cunningham, 2010). In Cunningham's *New York Times* social column entitled 'On the Street', he does not provide commentary but visually records people wearing original designer garments, or imitations of original garments, in everyday life. His column became the litmus test pointing out which specific designer garments had the greatest impact on what society wanted to wear.

Blog sites and social forum sites allow individuals to discuss new trends in fashion and disseminate information about resources and access. They provide a network for people of all ages to provide opinions, receive feedback and share knowledge without having to leave the security of their own homes. Interestingly, numerous researchers, including Okonkwo (2010) and Christodoulides (2009), have found that luxury fashion consumers find blogs as a more honest, reliable and authentic source of information than the brand Web sites.

Social Networking

Social networking and the use of technologies such as mobile devices and smart phone applications allow for shopping anywhere. This media has become the new platform for presenting fashion that encompasses millions of people around the world. Cybershopping allows a buyer to view many different sites within a relatively short time, share images of products with friends and upload the images on social networking sites such as Facebook, Twitter or YouTube for other people to make comments. As well, BlackBerry now enables users to link their video of a catwalk show directly to a social network. It is estimated that in January 2012, there

Figure 10.6   Blogger Susie Bubble wearing Emma Cook and Christopher Cane, Manhattan, New York, during Spring Fashion Week, September 2011. Photo: Ben Hider/Getty Images. Bloggers have gained a reputation as the unofficial fashion journalists of the street.

were 800 million users on Facebook[11] and 119 million on Twitter.[12] Tweeting opens up a dialogue between the designers, bloggers and social media gurus as well as anyone interested in fashion.

Immediacy of access is the main appeal, as bloggers argue that by the time the September issue of a fashion magazine appears, the fashion trends are already stale. For fashion firms, social networking provides: a way to monitor consumer sentiment; a way to launch new products, keeping costs low in a tough economy for luxury products; a means to publicize their last runway collection; and, through a GPS app (location-based mobile marketing), directions to local fashion shops carrying the brand merchandise that the user is interested in. By using apps, businesses can also house a large online retail catalogue of brand-name clothing and extend their online presence and widen distribution channels. Location-based networks such as Gowalla and Foursquare have massive potential for promotions and will likely be a focus for mobile fashion marketers. Chanel shows its runway collections via iPhone app, and the Gilt Groupe app allows users to shop sample sales and receive alerts about when sales are starting.

User-generated content, including photo competitions and product reviews, are all key to social media and fashion. While the mega-store Topshop was one of the first to engage with the network, more upmarket firms like Burberry launched its 'Art of the Trenchcoat' campaign to encourage user-generated content in this niche network. Users are encouraged to upload images of themselves wearing, for example, Burberry's signature item—the trench coat. Other incentives to increase fan contributions include: social media campaigns to find 'reporters' to attend the brand's fashion show at upcoming fashion weeks; a brand offering weekly trivia contests with giveaway prizes; T-shirt design contests where the winner will have his or her design produced and sold online with a fashion-filled trip to New York City thrown in; and 'style assignments' given to fans where they send photos to the brand's Facebook page or other network wall. Luxury brands Louis Vuitton, Dolce & Gabbana, Chanel and Burberry have launched their own social networks or added social components to their existing Web sites. Now that some fashion brands have learned to navigate social media, many are experimenting with development of their own social networks or even invitation-only communities.

With the rise of streaming and mobile broadcasts of runway shows, these major events become more financially viable for the design firms and increase the viewing audience considerably, from 700 invited to the collection showing to millions. *Time* magazine's 2009 article 'Will Fashion's Biggest Names Kiss the Runway Goodbye' reported that:

> 'The cost of a fashion show has become prohibitive,' says David Lauren, Polo Ralph Lauren's marketing chief. 'And because of the economy, fewer members of the press and buyers are making the trip to New York to see the show.' The result is that many designer-initiated brands—including the less-expensive lines, like Donna Karan's DKNY, that are presented during New York Fashion Week—are rethinking the traditional fashion show. This fall the British designer Alexander McQueen made a splash by live-streaming his Paris show on his website. The season before, Louis Vuitton 'live-streamed' its show on Facebook. Lauren is the mastermind behind a new initiative to present his company's brands in virtual fashion shows as opposed to have-to-be-there runway extravaganzas. (Betts, 2009)

Despite the success of this technological feat, viewers are just as interested in the celebrities who attend the showings as they are in the garments themselves. It is all part of the spectacle that fashion showings present, which, arguably, will continue to be an inherent part of the fashion system.

–11–

Eco-Fashion, Sustainability and Ethics

Our personal consumer choices have ecological, social, and spiritual consequences. It is time to re-examine some of our deeply held notions that underlie our lifestyles.

David Suzuki

GREEN AS THE NEW BLACK

While the 'Green Designer' exhibition was held as early as 1986 at the Design Centre in London and the label Esprit led the way with its inaugural Ecollection in November 1991, 'fashion as a design discipline has been late to investigate the theoretical greening of the design production loop, lagging behind industrial design and architecture' (Thomas, 2008: 526). Yet, interestingly, consumer activist group campaigns have tended to target fashion events more than other disciplines. Marketing strategists realize that, in the postmodernist age, when social and political commentary has become associated with both art and sartorial design, consumers now demand accurate and truthful labelling (provenance) and information relating to fair payment and healthy working conditions (fair trade) in order to make informed and conscientious decisions regarding their choice of clothing. For some, shopping has become an ethical minefield.[1] According to Thomas, 'potentially, there is an ideological connection between ethical trading and ethical fashion, thus conferring on both an altruistic intent and political stance' (2008: 532).

The dichotomy still remains that fashion, throughout history, has been driven by a desire to establish social class differentiation and status within a group through conspicuous consumption, but the desire to ally oneself voluntarily with an ideology has proved to be a stronger incentive in the twentieth and twenty-first centuries. In the 1970s, in particular, environmental concerns, including the energy crisis and the inhumane treatment of animals, led to major changes in the textile, fur and cosmetic industries. Subsequently, it became very fashionable to wear multilayered natural materials, such as wool, cotton and hemp, fake fur coats and to don natural complexions. Quentin Bell argued that one's degree of commitment to a cause became visibly evident in one's dress and that 'it is as though the fabric were indeed a natural extension of the body, or even of the soul' (1992: 19). Mixing art and politics, artist Kathleen Hamnett initially exhibited her 'environmental' T-shirts (Chapter 5) in the 1980s and has continued with garments donning activist slogans such as 'Make Trade Fair' and 'No More Fashion Victims'. She then turned to fashion design and today creates 'fashionable' clothing, adhering strictly to environmental and ethical guidelines. Quite rightly, Kate Fletcher (2007), in her essay 'Clothes That Connect', also argues that, in order for eco-fashion to be sustainable, its clothing must now be fashionably stylish as well as environmentally correct. American academic Theresa Winge postulates that eco-fashion has now become depoliticized (no longer associated with anti-war campaigns and anti-mainstream activities as it was in the 1960s and 1970s) and less stereotyped as a commodity fetish by celebrities, including actors George Clooney and Julia Roberts and photographer Annie Leibovitz, who promote sustainable fashion as an aesthetic life choice 'on the red carpets and in the pages of magazines' (2008: 513).

This chapter will deal mainly with environmental, design sustainability and ethical issues that relate to the choice and production of materials used for clothing, textiles and footwear. It will attempt to respond to a question posed by fashion writer David Lipke in *Women's Wear Daily* (31 March 2008), which asked, 'Is Green Fashion an Oxymoron?' How is it that 'an industry driven by disposable trends and aesthetic whims can reconcile itself to an era of conservation'? By briefly charting past and existing practices, this chapter will consider new strategies introduced and developed in the twenty-first century to foster sustainable textile production that could impact upon both developed and developing countries. By outlining the social, economic and environmental effects of current practices, including reference to fabric wastage, recycling and reusing materials, it will reinforce the need for a symbiotic liaison between the designer, the patternmaker and the manufacturer. It will consider new emphasis on the use of chemical-free organic fibers and textiles, the use of nontoxic dyes as well as methods of construction and deconstruction informed by environmental concerns. It will outline revived historical methodologies, including examples of fully fashioned and seamless knitwear, draped garments made from uncut, rectangular lengths of fabric and one-size-fits-all styling as well as current eco-fashion practices evident in the work of leading fashion, textile and footwear designers.

MORE THAN JUST A MARKETING STRATEGY?

Since 2006, eco-fashion has attracted a much wider audience. It was a popular theme targeted by magazines, journals, Web sites, special events, educational institutions and corporate and commercial bodies. For example, at that time, *Vanity Fair* magazine brought out its 'Green Issue' outlining the designers[2] who had presented eco-fashion on the runway. Other niche magazine publications endorsing eco-fashion include the *New Consumer, The Ethical Consumer* and *Ecology* (United Kingdom), *Organic Style* (United States), *Green* and *GreenPages* (Australia) plus other mainstream magazines that contain photographs and articles featuring celebrity activists with environmental issues such as *Elle, Glamour* and *Marie Claire*. Numerous academic book publications and journal articles have proliferated, including the international journal *Fashion Theory* (Bloomsbury), which in 2008 dedicated a special issue to eco-fashion with writings from scholars around the world discussing the complexity of sustainability issues in fashion. More recently, a new ethical and sustainable magazine called *SIX* was launched in 2011 to celebrate the designers, individuals, independent brands and companies that are creating a more ethical and sustainable future for the fashion industry. Online sites have flourished, including the Ethical Fashion forum (www.ethicalfashionforum. com), which outlines how to combine sustainable practice with commercial success in fashion, and fashion-conscience.com, which operates vending portals that offer different 'interpretations' of ethical fashion. Exhibitions, trade fairs, global forums and eco-friendly design competitions and awards have attracted considerable local, national and international interest. Amongst many others,[3] more recent events include the Shanghai International Fashion Culture Festival in 2009, which included the 'Green Fashion' International Clothing and Textile Expo (covering a vast area of 50,000 square metres in its International Expo Centre), and exhibitions such as 'Eco-fashion: Going Green' at the Fashion Institute of Technology, New York, in 2010, which considered ecological practices, both good and bad, over the past 250 years. In terms of education, one UK MBA business degree, in conjunction with the conservation charity World Wildlife Fund, has incorporated sustainability at its core, entitled the 'One Planet MBA' at the University of Exeter (Morgan, 2011).[4] Corporate social responsibility has influenced many fashion distributers and corporate retailers, including the Arcadia Group and Marks & Spencer, whose marketing campaign 'Look behind the label' highlighted its use of fair trade cotton and food products, becoming 'its most successful consumer campaign ever (Attwood, 2007, in Beard, 2008: 452), and the company aims to be carbon neutral by 2012. Walmart, the largest retailer in the world, became the biggest US producer of organic cotton in 2009. As well, in 2011, H&M launched its first eco-collection called Conscious made from recycled polyester, organic cotton and Tencel®, a natural manmade fiber; H&M caused a buzz when it partnered with the French fashion house Lanvin for its Waste collection, but seemingly, 'the line of dresses and bags were at too high a price point for many of its customers' (Kaye, 2011; Leon Kaye is the founder and editor of GreenGoPost.com); individual designer houses such as YSL adopted the strategy of upcycling preconsumer waste; and Issey Miyake opened his newest concept shop Elttob Tep (Pet Bottle spelled backwards) in Ginza selling innovative fabrics created from recycled plastics.

THE ENVIRONMENTAL FOOTPRINT

Sourcing Environmentally-Friendly Textiles

The fashion industry has relied on the production of textiles made from raw fibres that are cultivated in fields where considerable amounts of water are needed and chemicals used despite the fact that insecticides pollute both the air and water. The World Wildlife Fund has estimated that it takes 8,500 litres (2,245 gallons) of water to raise 1 kilogram (2.2 pounds) of cotton lint—enough to make one pair of blue jeans (Kaye, 2011)! Energy is expended in the spinning, weaving and knitting processes, and, along with the transportation and distribution of the raw and finished products, this increases greenhouse gas emissions. The production of synthetic fabrics depletes finite resources such as petroleum (that are nonrenewable and incapable of being fully biodegradable), and most textiles today are treated with various finishing chemicals, further polluting the environment and considered a health risk to humans. Whereas in the nineteenth century, dyes contained highly toxic chemicals and pesticides such as arsenic, in the twentieth century, one of the most polluting fibres to manufacture was viscose rayon. In Africa, mountains of plastic and polyester/synthetic throwaway apparel are being used for landfill, which will never break down. While there has been a resurgence in recent years of the rediscovered art of hand dyeing and fabric printing using natural vegetable dyes or azo-free dyeing, these craft-based techniques are too labour intensive and expensive to offer a solution to the global industry. According to Scaturro (2008: 469–88), textile conservator at the Cooper-Hewitt National Design Museum, Smithsonian Institution, New York, technology plays an ambivalent role in the environmental debate, as it acts as both a destructive and enabling force. Scaturro argues that it heralded the built-in system of redundancy through efficient 'fast fashion' products, which led to 'a profusion of detrimental textile manufacturing by-products and waste entering the ecosystem' as well as 'a vast amount of energy needed to make and take care of all the clothing produced'. As a more positive facilitator, she believes that, in the future, technology can serve to improve methods of clothing creation, consumption and disposal. 'This tension between technology, as a positive or negative factor in the sustainable reality of a culture's resources, is at the core of any discussion on technology and environmentalism' (Scaturro, 2008: 474). It seems that there are no easy solutions. For example, she points out that while the organic fiber advocate organisation Organic Exchange is committed to increasing the production of organic cotton by 50 per cent a year in the United States, the reality is that organic cotton does not produce the same yield or volume that conventional cotton can, making it more costly, and there is virtually no reduction in the harm that occurs during the subsequent dyeing and manufacturing process. It would seem that a national standard is required that oversees the entire production cycle not only of cotton yarns[5] but fabrics generated from renewable sources such as bamboo, seaweed, corn, soy, eucalyptus, milk and beechwood in the creation of polymers. For a successful outcome to occur, 'technology must be precisely applied to limit pollution and energy expenditures' (Scaturro, 2008: 480).

Experimental interdisciplinary research projects that investigate the possible interface between textiles, clothing, biological science and health are increasing. This collaborative work, based on nanotechnology, has created 'smart' fabrics, 'interactive textiles' and thermal shape memory fabrics, which can change colour through light and heat applications, control body temperature through microfibres, absorb odours and create scents that enhance well-being, protect skin tear and block out ultraviolet rays. Since the 1990s, wearable technology incorporating hybrid textiles and garments has been an expanding field requiring the expertise of scientists, computer analysts, electrochemistry and electronics specialists as well as textile and fibre engineers and, of course, fashion designers. Recent innovations have been developed by design professor Helen Storey of the London School of Fashion in collaboration with scientist Tony Ryan in dissolving fabrics, producing catalytic clothing that is both futuristic and life-changing. Their catalytic clothing (Dezeen, 2011) is a radical project in which photocatalysts, washed into the fabric, bind to the textile, creating an anti-pollutant surface that purifies the surrounding air. The photocatalyst gains its energy from light and breaks down pollutants in the air and turns them into non-harmful chemicals. This clothing technology has the power to change the way we live by making our lives greener and more sustainable.

Pattern Making—Fabric Wastage

Fabric in particular and fashion in general, by their very nature, are vehicles of built-in obsolescence—it's about waste. Pattern making is integral to the design process as technical and aesthetic considerations must be considered simultaneously. In today's fashion production, fabric (preconsumer) wastage equates to 15 to 20 per cent in traditional cut-and-sew methodologies. When methods are informed by environmental concerns, designers look back to historical precedents, including fully fashioned knitted garments that have no cutting, tube-knitted seamless garments informed by advanced technology (Miyake's APOC) or one-size-fits-all made from uncut rectangular lengths of fabric. When there are fabric off-cuts, this material must be able to be recycled, and this could include using it for quilts, as fibre, or as rags to make rugs, blankets, stuffing or other small craft items. This would allow all off-cuts to be made into new fabrics. Chemical companies like Wellman USA, an early leader in synthetic fiber recycling, and Japan's Teijin, which introduced Eco-Circle, have established successful polyester-recycling technology schemes.

In general terms, waste reduction is preferable to recycling or disposal, because 'recycling can impact negatively on the environment through transportation (fuel, emissions) and reprocessing (in particular, water, energy and chemical consumption)' (Gertsakis and Lewis in Rissanen, 2005: 3). Historical precedents established in fashion history present more sustainable constructive methods than are used today. These included ancient traditional and national costumes such as the Greek peplos made from two large rectangular pieces of fabric pinned at each shoulder, the Japanese kimono, which was made from eight rectangular pieces of fabric sewn together, and the Indian sari, which wraps around the body. Madeleine Vionnet and Madame Grès (Plate 26), renowned as masters of drape in the early decades of the twentieth century, were admired for their genius in manipulating cloth rather than cutting it; Zandra Rhodes's textile designs determined the shape and form of her garments in the 1970s and 1980s; Hishinuma's experimental use of triangles in the 1980s fitted together to form a modular unit as a means of preserving fabric; Miyake's APOC vision introduced in the 1990s used a tubular knitting system as a means of revolutionizing and simplifying garment construction; and the label MATERIALBYPRODUCT was created by Australian co-designers who developed a new system of pattern-making in the 2000s where the off-cuts are used as a decoration or extension of the main garment.[6]

Figure 11.1 MATERIALBYPRODUCT (MBP), Susan Dimasi and Chantal Kirby (collaboration 2005–11), brown digitally printed wood grain silk satin dress with tapes revealed, Melbourne, Australia, 2008. Photo: Sue Grdunc. Courtesy of MATERIALBYPRODUCT.

Recycling and Vintage Clothing

Historically, recycling has been embedded in the fabric of society. Throughout the ages, garments were passed from mother to daughter, father to son or to other family members or friends. Worn parts were eliminated, clothing was resized and, in some cases, stylistically modified or redesigned. The 1970s back-to-nature era saw the mushrooming of secondhand clothing or charity stores opening in towns and cities across the Western world. Driven by a global energy crisis, these outlets allowed buyers, often of limited means, an opportunity to be seen as environmentally conscious. Many of these clothes that were recycled or 'upcycled' were originally made from 'good' materials as the integrity of the fabric prolonged the life of the garment, and their construction was based on quality craftsmanship. Garments originating in the 1920s and 1930s, for example, were valued for their uniqueness, their hand-beading and embroidery and for their ability to be easily transformed into contemporary pieces. It was a nostalgic decade, very much in keeping with postmodernist trends, which appropriated not only fashions from the past (Plate 26), but classic films and furniture also became popular modes of consumption as well. In humanistic terms, this heralded the reemergence of emotional connectivity—of acknowledging that clothing with links to the past can have an in-built memory. This tenet is now widely accepted and has proved to be an incentive for contemporary designers such as Yohji Yamamoto and Martin Margiela. Yamamoto's famous quote that he liked clothes that were old and worn and that throwing out an old coat was like throwing away an old friend (see Chapter 7) is testament to this statement. Margiela experimented with the concept of degeneration and 'the effect of decay on the material structure of fabric', a theme 'that has been central to the work of many contemporary artists' (English, 2011: 138).

According to Kaye (2011), the stark reality of today's recycling dilemma is that in the United States alone, almost 11 million tonnes of textiles ends up in landfill. In Britain, 1 million tonnes of discarded apparel needs to be recycled annually. He points out that some of this post-consumer waste is used creatively: denim is making a comeback as a building insulator, and Walmart is working with vendors to increase the recycling of polyester and nylon for industrial use. Some clothing manufacturers are moving towards a closed-loop system: Patagonia, for example, allows consumers to drop off unwanted clothing bearing its label at company stores and allows consumers to post unwanted clothes back to its Nevada (US) service centre. In a recycling centre, 70 per cent is sent to be used as fibre, and 'items of higher quality end up in Eastern Europe or China where there is a market for used clothes that will not sell in "vintage" shops'.

According to Alexandra Palmer in *Old Clothes: New Looks*, second-hand clothing can adopt a form of exchange value, especially if the unwanted garments are high-end designer labels. Websites such as vintagecouture.com, established by Linda Lattner in 1999, have become lucrative businesses as the old garments are seen as a unique sign of individuality and connoisseurship. As in the art world, when the original designer becomes deceased, the clothing becomes more valuable. Vintage shopping can be viewed as a continuation of discount culture, while simultaneously achieving an individual identity and exclusivity that the brand names have lost (Palmer and Clark, 2005: 199). Designers such as John Galliano often draw inspiration from vintage clothing (Plate 27).

As the repurposing of textiles and the recycling of clothing has become the most responsible practice in eco-fashion in the twenty-first century, it is not surprising that the Internet now plays an important part in disseminating and sharing information, through commercial sites, online editorial magazines and blogs and social networks about ideas associated with reconstructive sewing methods and distribution outlets or Web sites such as eBay for preowned merchandise. Some vendors will operate smaller stores within these sites, reselling items sourced from local outlets. These online vending options, facilitating the global distribution of old clothing, are the antithesis of today's 'fast fashion' where newness and expendability have been canonized and ideals of novelty and profit firmly embedded in the industry's agenda. Fashion's inherent consumerism has increased exponentially since the Second World War, fuelled by the media, but is now being questioned following tragic world events and the global economic downturn experienced since 2000. Have these events forced some sectors in society to reevaluate their ethical standards, value systems and environmental concerns? Is the world developing a growing social consciousness?

According to Alexandra Palmer, the revival of second-hand clothing, in most cases, has little to do with environmental concerns. She argues that few 'vintage whores' (Palmer and Clark, 2005: 197) are motivated solely by altruistic motives, such as a concern for sustainable fashion, and are drawn, in part, to the aura of the clothing in its past life, its history concealed beneath the surface of the garment. Vintage wear also appeals to the younger generation for financial or economic reasons because it allows for a fast turnover of clothes in one's wardrobe. Historically, clothing was often used as barter, exchanged for cooking utensils for example, and this practice has been reinstated in modern society. This act of bartering, where one item is exchanged for another, has long been an inherent part of everyday life in the markets of Zambia and other parts of Africa, amongst other cultures, where nothing is wasted and the concept of reusing and modifying is indicative of the cultural ethos.

ECO-DESIGNERS

In today's society, individual designers have responded to this global issue by adopting a more responsible design methodology that can be formulated within existing

technology. By using more holistic approaches, their work reflects sustainable practice in terms of textile development, minimizing fabric waste, manufacturing methods, and aftercare and disposal with an emphasis on innovative research to develop
new products. Large footwear corporations, amongst others, in order to build a successful brand identity, have embraced eco-design as an effective marketing strategy.
Nike, for example, recycles used rubber trainers for playground surfaces (Delong,
2009: 109).

While some designers recycle old products or use only organic materials, others are
concerned more with design integrity, insisting on the evolution of an idea rather than
responding to consumerist demands. Eco-consciousness is fundamental in the work
and philosophy of both established and emerging international designers in their quest
to reduce the fashion industry's environmental footprint. They include, amongst others, British designer Jessica Ogden and her use of secondhand fabrics; Russell Sage
(Plate 28), who revamped trademark fabrics like Burberry; Katherine Hamnett's use
of organic cotton and eco-awareness statements printed on her T-shirts; Americans

Figure 11.2 Jessica Ogden, brightly coloured
checked sleeveless cotton summer dress, London
Fashion Week, Spring/Summer 2006. Photo: J.
Tregidgo/WireImage.

Susan Cianciola, who used vintage fabrics for one-off garments, and Miguel Adrover, who presented a 'garbage collection' using unusual recycled products; and Yeohlee Teng, who produces one-size-fits-all garments and fights to preserve local rather than overseas production by producing nearly every garment she sells right in the Garment District in New York City. Luxury eco-brands are limited, with the exception of Stella McCartney and Ciel in the United Kingdom, Noir in Denmark, Fin in Norway and Linda Loudermilk in the United States.

Sustainability of craft, or the incorporation of hand-worked techniques, now referred to as 'slow design' has become central to the philosophy of eco-conscious designers. Brown's *Eco Fashion* (2010: 13) states that 'these traditional craft skills have become more valued and used, and eventually incorporated into the fashion industry through partnership with high-end designers'. Brown cites examples of fair trade, community-based liaisons that have produced 'Indian embroidered sundresses, African beaded jewellery and Peruvian knitted sweaters'. With the eradication of traditional craft talent in the developed nations of North America and Western Europe, she argues, a greater appreciation has developed for the indigenous and inherited craft expertise in communities around the world. She provides specific examples of this practice:

Figure 11.3 Linda Loudermilk, full-skirted dress with short jacket, Spring collection 2005. Photo: J. Sciulli/WireImage for Linda Loudermilk.

Noir in Denmark is in partnership with Ugandan farmers and supports their development and production of organic long-staple cotton. Carla Fernandez of Taller Flora works with Mexican artisans, reinterpreting their techniques into highly sophisticated designs while learning from their knowledge: a truly collaborative process. With every design and every stitch, Alabama Chanin honours the women of the south of the USA, their history, their struggles and their everyday skills sets. Her work is a labour of love. (Brown, 2010: 13)

African designer Lamine Kouyate, with his label XULY.Bët, deconstructs and reconstructs recycled clothing 'by applying stitches on the outside of his garments to focus attention on the (frayed) edges where threads hold garments together' (Rovine, 2005: 215). According to Rovine, 'The garments incorporate visible seams, like healed wounds that have left their mark (by using red thread), the past lives of clothes that have been re-shaped into new forms' (2005: 219). Kouyate incorporates torn pockets and discoloured collars along with the old collar labels of used shirts and pant waistbands to visibly exaggerate the links with the garments' past lives and as a way to 'document the changing identities of these garments . . . and their attraction lies in the imaginative potential of their former life' (Rovine, 2005: 221).

Rebecca Earley from the Chelsea College of Art, London, transforms and reinvents discarded blouses from charity shops. She employs upcycling techniques, using heat photograms and overprinting the surface of the reshaped garments. Stains are covered with the reactive overlaid dyes, and when it completes its second life, the garment can be transformed a third time into a quilted waistcoat. A Textile Environmental Design student, Kate Goldsworthy, who works with Earley, has developed a method of bonding a lining made of recycled polyester fleece to the original textile without the use of adhesives or bonding agents to produce the textile for the waistcoat. Laser etching creates a delicate lacelike effect, with melted transparent materials digitally controlled to facilitate the process of fusing (Brown, 2010: 164).

ETHICAL CONCERNS

Exploitation and Reflective Practice

Fashion, in the second decade of the twenty-first century, has finally found its consciousness, and its designers, models and business entrepreneurs alike have joined global musicians to attempt to make the world a better place (Plate 29). It began in the 1970s and 1980s—a time when unethical practices were publicly highlighted in the fashion and associated industries with attention on the wearing of fur, feathers and animal skins and the inhumane and barbarous treatment of animals as well as their use in the research and development units of cosmetic companies.

Figure 11.4 Protesters rally against the use of fur by designers outside the Dior fashion show at Paris Fashion Week Spring/Summer 2005, 5 October 2004. Photo: Michael Dufour/Getty Images.

Ethical practice relates to the culture of advertising and, in particular, the exploitation of child models to promote a prepubescent sexuality in fashion advertising, which fulfils a cosmetic function, distorting social values and attitudes. Over the past few decades, socially responsible practices drew attention to the rise of racial discrimination in modelling and the very limited number of African and Asian models used. While projecting an image of multiculturalism, American *Vogue* included only a handful of black celebrity faces on its covers between 2002 and 2009.[7] Fashion photographer Nick Knight made particular reference to this commercially driven racial favouritism in his film *Untitled* (2008) featuring Naomi Campbell. As well, the promotion of a poor body image—a trend impacting greatly upon young men and women worldwide—has led to a disturbing increase in anorexia and bulimia in today's society. A number of designers have attempted to counteract stereotypical and idealized gender and body images through their styling. In Italy in 2006, fashion agents signed agreements not to use underage or underweight models for runway shows.

Greenwashing is a term (like whitewashing) that has been adopted recently to describe a cover-up marketing ploy often used by individuals, companies and organizations to downplay the unethical practices that proliferate in the fashion industry, including the use of child labour. Labelling inconsistencies and misleading classifications confuse the buyer and often compromise provenance. Sandy Black, in *Eco-Chic: The Fashion Paradox* (2007), reports that those buying fair trade cotton may not necessarily have an organic product, and some companies blur the component content of blended fabrics. Workers' wages in Third World countries are difficult to contextualize, and Western designers are often misled into believing that workers are being paid a reasonable sum for their production practices. Australian journalist Elisabeth Wynhausen (2008: 28) tried to map the supply chain or trail of a designer garment. She found that manufacture took place in China if more than 300 garments in one style were required (otherwise a surcharge was imposed), as US orders of one style were often in the tens of thousands. The garment designs (often samples made from photographs of garments seen in New York shop windows) were handed to the trading houses in Hong Kong (or existing product was purchased there), which acted as the intermediaries between foreign buyers and Chinese factories. A shirt could be made and delivered to any major city worldwide for approximately one-half of the cost of making it on-shore. For smaller orders, local factories with in-house machinists were used, but a certain amount of outsourcing or subcontracting to sweatshops was also used, where migrant workers were unlawfully paid below minimum wage, contrary to restrictions imposed by the Australian government. A number of unscrupulous employers get work done outside their factories without registering with the Australian Industrial Registry, a requirement under the federal clothing trade's award. While unsustainable levels of clothing production and consumption may exist in the developed world, a more far-reaching problem is 'the negative economic, social and environmental effects (that) tend to fall upon developing countries where an ever-increasing proportion of clothing is produced' (Rissanen, 2005: 7). With an estimated 30 to 50 per cent of British, European and American fashion manufactured goods now being produced off-shore, the subsequent exploitation of local and national factory and industry workers in terms of health and working conditions has led to concerns about the treatment of garment factory workers in locations such as the Pearl River Delta in China and the ghettos in India. This exploitation includes the use of very poorly paid sweatshop labour, using dangerous chemicals to produce textiles and clothing and the use of limited fossil fuels (already exhausted) to sustain the supply chains, leading to the gradual degradation of the environment.

It seems that there is 'no single organization or government body to regulate any specific "code of conduct" for the fashion industry although there are several trade associations with schemes set up to monitor and encourage ethical practices amongst commercial firms such as Ethical Trading Initiative in the UK, Solidaridad and the Clean Clothes Campaign in the Netherlands, Fair West in Australia or the Fair Labour Association in the USA' (Beard, 2008: 450). Regarding other problems such as 'counterfeit chic' (see Chapter 10) and the theft of creative intellectual property, some fashion industries are attempting to establish both formal and informal ethical codes. For example, in New York, Diane Von Furstenberg, as president of the Council of Fashion Designers of America, has been seeking greater government regulation of intellectual property design and fair trade policies. Despite highly globalized consumer markets, individual designers have fought to retain financial independence, allowing them to maintain a moral responsibility towards worker exploitation and providing protection for their own intellectual property. However, due to the limited supply of eco-friendly material, products often display an inflated exchange rate. For the limited, yet expanding, eco-conscious consumer base to become part of the mainstream or dominant culture will take time and money. Luxury sustainable goods offered by leading style labels help to reinforce the notion that eco-fashion of the twenty-first century represents a commodity that has an appeal to a much broader consumer market than its counterpart of the past. It also underlines the fact that guilt doesn't sell fashion, desire does.

–12–

Looking Ahead: The Emergence of Asian and Indian Fashion Design Industries

> For emerging Chinese designers—'Without regrets or nostalgia, it is important to cherish the past, but it is also inspiring to look forward.'
>
> Franca Sozzani, Editor, Italian *Vogue*[1]

This chapter will discuss the major changes that have occurred in both China and India, the main source of textile production and mass-produced clothing for the Western world. A decade ago, experts agreed that the rise of China and India heralded 'a transformation of the global economic and political order as significant as that brought about by the industrial revolution' (*Financial Times*, 2003: 10). The world has witnessed the rise of India's and China's own fashion design, manufacture and distribution as fashion weeks have been presented in Hong Kong, Beijing, Shanghai, New Delhi and Mumbai.

CHINA: BUILDING AN INFRASTRUCTURE

According to Xiao Yan, deputy editorial director of fashion magazine *Elle China*, the international fashion industry is paying more attention to China's design talent. However, she qualifies this statement by adding that, in international terms, 'Chinese designers are still in the very early stage' (Yee and Qin, 2006). Influenced mainly by Western styling, there is pressure for designers to simply copy from other brands, and 'for grassroots designers, the fashion landscape is still largely difficult' (Farrar, 2011). It is significant to point out that it was not until the mid-1980s that Chinese reformist fashion withdrew from the dictatorship of dress as sociopolitical ideology. Without a background history in the industry, no foundation existed upon which to build a future. Fashion historian Juanjuan Wu argues that 'China's fashion designers have been ignored or have functioned only as "ghosts" designers for fashion brands produced in China' (2009a: 127). As the world's leading global apparel manufacturing industry, China has been attempting to position itself as a major force in *both* design and manufacture, particularly over the past ten years. The two main ways that China aims to achieve these goals are through education by promoting young, emerging designers and through the development of economic strength in both domestic and international markets by instituting effective and collaborative marketing strategies.

Fashion Education

An educational infrastructure has been established to support the design industry with fashion design courses proliferating in Chinese universities. The Chinese are fostering liaisons with leading international fashion design institutions and with the international fashion industry. According to Wang Qing, head of the China Fashion Designers Association, this includes private institutions, including those run by Singapore's Raffles Education Corp., which opened its first design school in Shanghai in 1994. One of the latest schools to add a fashion degree major is Beijing's prestigious Central Academy of Fine Arts, or CAFA, which graduated its first fashion design class in 2006. Dr Zang Yingchun, director of international fashion and textile design education at Beijing's Tsinghua University, explained that the university first established a fashion program in 1958 and now attempts to encourage experimental and innovative practice in its program (English, 2011) rather than following an exclusively

Figure 12.1 Garywat QuTingnan, rectangular fabric-linked dress, Mercedes-Benz China Fashion Week, Beijing, Spring/Svummer collection 2011. Photo: STR/AFP/Getty Images.

commercial line. Donghua University in Shanghai, amongst others, has invited over the years many guest and advisory professors from abroad as well as visiting designers, including Ungaro, Rykiel, Lapidus, Ferre and Missoni, to contribute to their programs. More recently, a number of young Chinese people who have enrolled in leading London or New York fashion institutions plan to take their global skills back to China. The Chinese government offers scholarships to outstanding students to attend overseas institutions such as the London School of Fashion and Central St Martin's Art School in Britain (where other art school–trained fashion designers, like Vivienne Westwood, John Galliano and Alexander McQueen studied). These schools have become a major draw card as they encourage a type of fashion design thinking that extends beyond European haute couture or high-end fashion, encouraging a more creative noncon-formist outcome often influenced by youth subcultures or street style directions. While some of these students attempt to establish individual labels, most of them return to China to work for 'brand companies'.

Marketing and Promotion; Fashion Magazines

The initial production of Chinese-based international glossy fashion magazines[2] in-cluded *Elle China* in 1988, *Esquire China* in 1996, *Harper's Bazaar* in 2001, *Marie Claire* in 2002 and *China Vogue* in 2005. The magazines slowly evolved from the use of coarse paper with colour inserts and clothing patterns in the early years to a more visually oriented, marketing-savvy, contemporary format. In terms of sales and wider distribution, it took seven years for *Elle* to show a profit in 1995, and yet, a year later, the magazine had a circulation of 180,000 copies. According to the *New York Times* (1996), Condé Nast tried unsuccessfully for nine years to convince the Chinese authorities to allow the company to publish *Vogue*. When permission was finally granted, *China Vogue* quickly established itself as the leading contender not only by of-fering gifts to readers but by repeatedly underlining its powerful position in the media. *Vogue*'s launch issue in September 2005 featured a lineup of six models on the cover styled by the editor of *Vogue Paris*, Carine Roitfeld, and photographed by leading inter-national photographer Patrick Demarchelier. Zhang Wenhe, editor of the Beijing journal *Art and Design*, lamented that 'there is currently no fashion industry in our country; even the embryo hasn't been formed, and fashion magazines in China are no more than a clothes horse for the international fashion industry' (cited in Finnane, 2007: 279). While this may be true, the magazines also offer a benchmark by which to measure domestic directions. Fashion houses use magazines as a way to construct brand images that are purchased along with the products. The photographic images in-cluded in the magazines were deliberately conservative, as fashion, especially amongst middle-aged Chinese women, had a history of collectivist rather than individual styling.

It would take time for clothing to break away from the pre-1980s mode of being conformist or symbolic of the political ideology of the day. The magazines instead highlighted fabrics and luxury items as a purveyor of success in modern-day China. According to Hartley and Montgomery,

> *Vogue* offers an image (in Elizabeth Wilson's sense) of the complete woman; its fashion pages are 'portraits of a woman', not a catalogue of clothing; its information, travel and style sections are all variations on the theme of 'good living'. In short, *Vogue* speaks to 'honorific' rather than to 'utilitarian' values. (2009: 71)

Mary Yan Yan Chan, Hong Kong-based founder and director of Style Central Ltd. and an exclusive agent of trend forecaster Peclers Paris, believes that, essentially, the lack of marketing expertise is holding the Chinese designers back. In China, fashion ads often show a white person posing in the wares of a local brand, implying that the clothes are good enough for Westerners, she says. 'That's very old-school thinking and that's been the traditional type of advertising' (Yee and Qin, 2006). However, this perception still exists, and the Chinese market looks constantly for Western confirmation before being ready to buy. Improving marketing savvy relies on two options for improvement: first, to team up with a Western firm and, second, to increase the links between industry and academia. For example, Hong Kong lifestyle brand Shanghai Tang is an international clothing chain company founded in 1994 that pursued such a tie by sponsoring the graduation runway show of CAFA's first fashion class in Beijing and by offering to present two graduates' creations—contemporary cheongsams—in its own ready-to-wear collection.

While the more conservative city of Beijing has long been seen as the political and cultural capital of China, Shanghai's port has been the centre of international finance and trade for centuries, and this city, called the 'Paris of the East', exudes a certain cosmopolitanism that extends to its role as a key fashion hub. Yet both cities vie for sartorial supremacy; Shanghai established its grand spring fashion event in 1995 called the Shanghai International Fashion Culture Festival, and Beijing established the China's Fashion Designers' Association in 1993, with an outstanding design award known as the Golden Peak instituted in 1997. China has also established national design and research competitions and fashion forecast runway shows and encouraged the publication of major fashion journals, including the top-selling *Shanghai Style, Fashion* (Shanghai) and *China Garment* (Beijing) in 1985. In 2009, the international modelling competitions in Shanghai 'attracted contestants from over 20 countries and territories and early winners of this contest include Ma Yangli, Jiang Peilin and Xie Dongna [who] became China's first generation of supermodels' (Wu, 2009a: 261). Clearly, China is attempting to build foundations for the future of the industry.

Luxury Goods: Consumption and the Rise of the New Middle Class

Chinese fashion is showcased in Beijing, Shanghai and Hong Kong biannually in March and October. 'Huge changes have taken place on the product marketing front with the new policy of *branding* by Chinese companies, for both the domestic and international market' (Reinach, 2005: 45–46). It seems that the Chinese consumer is becoming a leading force in the global marketplace. According to a HSBC survey in 2010, main-land Chinese are getting richer at a younger age (average age of 36 years) compared to other Asian countries, and this growing class of young, rich Chinese has a taste for luxury labels, suggesting that there is longevity for luxury brand sales in China (Red Luxury, 2010a). A 2009 survey in *Women of China* magazine indicated that women in China's major cities spent 63 per cent of their income on consumer goods ranging from clothes to cosmetics, and the Chinese Ministry of Commerce announced that total retail sales were up 16 per cent in the same year (Red Luxury, 2010). All of these data indicate that if China were able to establish its own fashion design empire and persuade Chinese consumers of its international viability in terms of styling, qual-ity of material and workmanship, then it would have no need to woo an international audience.

With Chinese millionaires set to hold half of Asia's wealth by 2015 (Red Luxury, 2010b), it is not surprising that European and American luxury goods companies opened more than eighty new outlets in China in 2011 alone, with the most popu-lar high-end brands being Louis Vuitton, Chanel, Gucci, Armani, Christian Dior, Rolex, Cartier and Hermès. Cosmetic companies, including Estee Lauder, Procter & Gamble and L'Oreal, plan to launch more shops, e-channels and production factories in China in the coming years (Red Luxury, 2010b). ABC documentary producer Yue-Sai Kan, a Chinese American, launched one of the major cosmetic companies in China after being asked by the Chinese government to establish a business in China that would strengthen foreign investment. In 1992, she founded Yue-Sai Kan Cosmetics Ltd, and by 2003, the business was generating annual revenue of $50 million. It was later sold to L'Oreal, the world's largest cosmetic company. Not surprisingly, more international brands are setting up design studios in China, including Burberry and Hermès (which produces a specific Chinese label called Shang Xia), to take advantage of the proxim-ity to their manufacturing operations; to reinforce their product in China; and to foster the growth of a potential new consumerist audience there. Other Western designers recognized the potential growth in the Chinese market in the late 1980s[3] and more recently have linked their names with blockbuster events in China.[4]

This trend towards macro development has been embraced by numerous local Chinese governments as it is seen as a means to bring wealth and prestige to the area. China's Ministry of Commerce announced a plan in June 2011 to lower import tar-iffs, including duty on middle- and high-priced products to further increase domestic

Plate 17 Kosuke Tsumura for Final Home, transparent nylon coat with hood and multi-pockets, Japan, 2005. Collection: Powerhouse Museum, Sydney. Photographer: Marinco Kojdanovski. This survival coat is composed of pockets used to hold the necessities of life.

Plate 18 Dior cruise fashion show opening in Shanghai on 14 May 2010, Dior designer John Galliano with LVMH chairman Bernard Arnault and his wife, Helene Arnault. Photographer: Seppe Van Grieken/Stringer/Getty Images.

Plate 19 In honour of the House of Rykiel's fortieth anniversary, individual designers (top left Jean Charles de Castelbajac, top right Christian Lacroix, lower left Martin Margiela, and lower right Jean Paul Gaultier) have fun creating visual images of Sonia Rykiel in their garments, which were paraded after her Spring/Summer 2009 ready-to-wear collection show in Paris, 1 October 2008. Photographer: Pierre Verdy/AFP/Getty Images.

Plate 20   Model drenched in rain shower at Alexander McQueen's 'Black' fashion show, London, June 2004. Photographer: Nicolas Asfouri/AFP/Getty Images.

Plate 21 Alber Elbaz, Lanvin, menswear Spring/Summer 2011, Paris Fashion Week, June 2010. Alber Elbaz adorned his menswear with jewellery for the first time. Photographer: Kristy Sparrow/Getty Images.

Plate 22 John Cavalera, men's white suit with blue and red designs, Sao Paulo Fashion Week, Brazil, Summer 2012. Photographer: Fernanda Calfat Studio/LatinContent/Getty Images.

Plate 23 Customer scans and orders goods online using a mobile phone/tablet in eBay's first UK High Street store, central London, 1 December 2011. Photo: Dan Kitwood/Getty Images.

Plate 24   Hand beading and embroidery applied to Dior's garments in House of Dior's fine finishing workroom, January 2001. Photo: Jean-Pierre Muller/AFP/Getty Images. Long hours of craft-based handwork continue the tradition of haute couture workmanship.

Plate 25 Chanel window display, Ginza, Tokyo, November 2007. Photographer: author. This display exaggerates Chanel's accessories but at the same time, perhaps inadvertently, comments on the growth of object-obsessed consumerism.

Plate 26 Madame Grès, white Grecian-inspired gowns, Mme Grès exhibition, Bourdelle Museum, Paris, June 2011. Photo: author.

Plate 27   John Galliano, vintage-inspired ensemble with parasol, Paris, Spring/Summer, January 2000. Galliano often frequented second-hand shops for inspiration for his designs. Photographer: Antonio de Moraes Barros Filho/ WireImage.

Plate 28 Russell Sage, dress designed from Zoffany curtains, Chelsea Flower Show, May 2004. Photographer: Jon Furniss/WireImage.

Plate 29 British supermodels Naomi Campbell, Kate Moss and Annabelle Neilson pose for Fashion For Relief Haiti poster, advertising fashion show at Somerset House, London on 18 February 2010, organized by Naomi Campbell as a tribute to the deceased fashion designer Alexander McQueen. Photographer: Ben Stansall/AFP/Getty Images

Plate 30   Chinese label NE TIGER, long red evening gown with emperor sleeves, Mercedes-Benz China Fashion Week, Beijing, October 2011. Photographer: Linglin Zhu.

Plate 31 Indian designer Tarun Tahiliani, short garment with full sleeves and skirt embellished with a border decoration. Photo: Paolo Cocco/AFP/Getty Images. Considered a pioneer in the Indian fashion industry, Tahiliani borrows heavily from traditional styling, fabrics and embroidery.

Plate 32   Manish Arora, long, full-skirted dress with bold, graphic textile design, London Fashion Week, September 2006. Photographer: John D McHugh/AFP/Getty Images.

spending on luxury consumer goods (Yan, 2011). Up until 2011, consumers paid up to 50 per cent more for luxury products in China, as compared with their European counterparts. According to Hung Huang, CEO of China Interactive Media Group, there is a growing trend towards celebrating Chinese design brands instead of the ubiquitous foreign luxury goods and their counterfeit reproductions over the past few years. She runs the *iLook* fashion magazine, frequently appears on television as a cultural critic and writes one of China's most widely read blogs. She runs a retail outlet called Brand New China in Beijing's Sanlitun area to encourage high-quality, independent Chinese fashion (Business of Fashion, 2011). While the store carries mainly global brands like Balmain, Balenciaga, Lanvin and Comme des Garcons, some Chinese fashion, accessories, and lifestyle products are sold on consignment. Tali Wu, a Shanghai-based designer of the leather goods brand Flying Scissors, is looking to design and manufacture her goods, especially handbags, in China as she feels that there is a growing sense of nationalism especially amongst the younger clientele (Red Luxury, 2011). Self-sufficiency has always been the mainstay of Chinese industry. In industrial terms, the nation has a long history of appropriating knowledge and skill by importing goods from other countries and then establishing its own industry. In terms of fashion design, this is clearly a major strategy. Once a culture develops an appetite

Figure 12.2 Chinese label NE Tiger, royal blue evening gown with gold brocade embroidery. Mercedes-Benz China Fashion Week, Beijing, October 2011. Photo: Linglin Zhu. This label is known for its combination of traditional and contemporary features.

for luxury goods, which is in keeping with higher wages being paid to workers in China, the emerging middle-class consumer can be tempted to buy cheaper Chinese luxury goods instead.

China has established a reputation for being 'the Asian country that produces the majority of copies, fake brands, and imitation goods on the whole, and in the textile sector in particular' (Reinach, 2005: 48). Surprisingly, China followed the model established by the second-ranked country, Italy. China's unprecedented speed in copying cannot be surpassed, but so far it is not able to set the trends. Other fast-fashion outlets that copy and simplify parts of the ranges shown on the prêt-à-porter catwalks (some which use digital imaging to advertise the goods on the Internet very quickly) range from the Spanish Zara and Mango, both partially produced in China, to Scandinavia's H&M. Reinach postulates that, 'Of the 4200 official Chinese shops selling Chanel cosmetics it is estimated that at least one-third are fraudulent . . . and it is not uncommon for the same Chinese companies that produce the real brands to turn out fakes as well' (Reinach, 2005: 49).[5] This offers Chinese consumers a three-tiered market: the lowest-priced goods are the counterfeit; the middle-level goods are authentic Chinese-designed goods; and the top level offers the more expensive luxury heritage range.

Leading Designers

In domestic terms, while apparel sales increased threefold in urban department stores in China between 2000 and 2005, cutting-edge fashion is not embraced on a large scale, and, subsequently, young designers must look to the international marketplace. Xie Feng (Frankie Xie) became the first Chinese designer to open Paris Fashion Week in 2006, where he presented his label Jefen. The well-known Chinese American designer Vivienne Tam grew up in Hong Kong but built her very successful business in New York. Despite the lack of radical design, which catapulted the Japanese designers into recognition, emerging Chinese designers, including Mary Ma, Ma Ke and Uma Wang, all women in their late thirties or forties, have initially attempted to create innovative trademark fashion relying on more conservative, luxury-driven design to ensure commercial success. Designer Mary Ma concentrates on the local market in her couture house in Beijing by creating opulent gowns for Chinese socialites and actresses under the Maryma label. In 2007 she designed a line of dresses for a Montblanc jewellery show in Geneva. In the southern city of Guangzhou, Ma Ke, who has twenty-nine stores from Harbin to Zhuhai, is the creative force behind Exception de Mixmind, a leading casual wear brand known for its urban and slightly earthy aesthetic. She was invited by the Haute Couture Syndicale de Paris to show her work at the collection showings in February 2007. She presented a collection called Wuyong (useless), based on promoting ecological sustainability and freedom of artistic expression. In-spired by Martin Margiela and Rei Kawakubo, her work referenced Chinese history and resonated a feeling of oppression, complexity, and ritual. Heavy drapery of natural, handwoven fibres created a metaphoric image of a hard journey or struggle in life. The work was exhibited in the Victoria and Albert Museum, and when asked about whether she saw the work as art or commodity, Ma Ke replied that the difference lay 'in the reasons *why* they are created—meaning their origination. Those created for faith and joy are art; for fame and benefits (they) are commodity' (Tsui, 2009: 186).

The work of a number of Chinese designers was celebrated in the 'China Design Now' exhibition held at the Victoria and Albert Museum in London in 2008, including the prominent Ma Ke and lesser-known designers Ji Ji, Wang Yi-Yuan, Lu Kun, Han Feung and Zhang Da. According to Christine Tsui in her book *China Fashion: Conversations with Designers*, Ji Wen-Bo, one of the most prominent menswear designers in China, presented the brand Li Lang in the Tokyo Fashion Week in September 2008, and Luo Zhen presented her brand of Omnialuo in New York Fashion Week in September 2008 (2009: 215). Franca Sozzani, editor of Italian *Vogue*, also cites Luo Zheng as one of the first Chinese designers to bring a Chinese dress to New York Fashion Week in the 2009 Spring/Summer collection showing, and Richard Wu debuted the VLOV menswear brand there in September 2011. Another influential figure in Chinese fashion has been Liang Zi, founder and director of the 1995 label Tangy, who received the prestigious Golden Peak Award in 2007 at China's Fashion Week for her ecologically friendly use of precious tangy silk. She paid tribute to her Chinese heritage through rediscovering the traditional method of creating this luxurious cloth that dates back to the fifteenth-century Ming Dynasty. It is called *lingchou* and becomes two-toned as a result of the natural dyeing methods employed. Educated in both France and America, she combined her gambiered silk and silver ethnic decoration with the Zen theme of calm 'nothingness' in her 2008 collection. She believes that her label appeals to those who are looking for the 'oriental' in their clothes.

From a base in Shanghai, Uma Wang, a fashion graduate of St Martin's College of Art and Design in London, has added boutiques in Germany and the Netherlands to those in the United Kingdom that stock her collection of high-end cashmere knits. After designing for labels in China for eight years, she established her namesake line and presented her first ready-to-wear collection at PURE in London. More international and universal in scope, her design work seems 'to reference the more avant-garde styling pioneered by Comme des Garcons and others' that flattered both Asian and Western women (Daily, 2011). Similarly, Chen Ping, a graduate of Tianjin Polytech University, has designed classic-styled clothing for ten years and most recently showed her brand Pari Chen at Shanghai Fashion Week in 2011. Other newcomers such as Jenny Ji appropriate historical cues from 'Old Shanghai', and her 2010 Blue Tiger Porcelain collection blended both Eastern and Western motifs and techniques.

While the proliferation of fashion magazines provided an impetus to advertise the new national talents, few new emerging designers had a solid financial base upon which to build a long-term career. This proved to be a further deterrent for individual designers to establish a large-scale business on their own. There is a plethora of designers' names highlighted on Web sites listed amongst the 'top ten', but, with each subsequent collection showings, these names disappear—being replaced by a new list. This lack of designer sustainability prevails unless the designer has a substantial financial backer or is supported by the state. While Qui Hao, who studied on the Central St Martin's MA womenswear course, won the £100,000 Woolmark prize in 2008—the same famous prize that anointed both Karl Lagerfeld and Yves Saint Laurent in 1954—his atelier collections are expensive to produce and the subsequent garments so costly that they are out of reach for mainstream consumers. Wang Wei, who established studios in both London and Shanghai in 2005, was introduced to London fashion by Vivienne Westwood in 2006 and participated in the Vendome Luxury Salon in Paris in 2007. Having worked for the fashion brand S.B.Polo in Hong Kong, he felt that he had some insight into international business operations, where a good mix of creativity and commercial success was needed. Many domestic designers, including Wang Wei, 'all agreed that Chinese brands should target the mid-range market

Figure 12.3 Simon Wang, short yellow draped Nirvana fashion dress, Shanghai Fashion Week, Autumn/Winter collection, April 2009. Photo: ChinaFotoPress. This Mongolian-born designer debuted his work at the London Fashion Week forum in 2004 and began to sell a small collection at Topshop in London in 2005.

niche' . . . as 'it has taken decades for luxury brands to establish their global fame, and Chinese brands all lack a history, an essential ingredient of a luxury brand' (Wu, 2009a: 179). Long-term success has been achieved by the brand companies Toray, NE TIGER (Plate 30) and White Collar. Cabeen Chic participated in fashion weeks for ten years before the designer's name and label became well known.

Fashion as a Cultural Industry

Historically, designers worked for state-owned clothing and textile manufacturing cen-tres (Silk Corporation and Silk Parks) and were not acknowledged for their individual contributions. With their creativity somewhat stifled, it is not surprising that 'the Chinese Fashion Industry as a whole has never been innovation-driven and innovations on a large scale are still to be realised' (Wu, 2009a: 127). Wu, in her comprehensive book *Chinese Fashion: From Mao to Now* (2009a), explains in detail how the industry emerged over the past thirty years and states that, in the post-Mao era, 'dress mirrored the drastic changes taking place in Chinese society' (2009a: 10). In this relatively short time, society had moved from viewing blue jeans, men's long hair and bell-bottom pants as both an immoral and criminal activity, punishable by death (for young men accused of immoral sexual promiscuity), in 1983 to one that tolerated most of the bizarre looks of Western culture. When the restrictions imposed by the state-owned garment factories lifted in the 1980s, fashion trends were directly copied from the world of stage art, TV entertainment shows and extravagant costumes seen in Western films. With more private clothing merchants emerging, the influence of international fashion became more evident. By the 1990s, 'rapidly increasing levels of trade between China and Japan and China and Korea facilitated and stimulated cross-cultural communications, including the exchange of fashion ideas' (Wu, 2009a: 97). The impact of popular culture, including music, anime, books and the Internet, promoted a street style that was quickly imitated by Chinese youth, transforming their everyday dress. In terms of fashion journalism, the 1990s saw the influx of hybrid domestic and foreign fashion magazine titles flooding the market, which connected the fashion industry to the international world. Foreign funding smoothed the way towards an increased tolerance for body exposure and 'odd' design, image-based rather than text-based design and the introduction of seamless airbrushing techniques to enhance the brand image. Subsequently, rapid increases in consumerism resulted in a growing interest in luxury goods.

Guy Debord, the French Marxist theorist, prophesied that by the end of the twentieth century, culture would become the driving force in the development of the economy, and that cultural industries would drive the economy of our information technology society. Fashion as a cultural commodity has been embraced in the Western world and is now influencing directions in non-Western societies, including China. Angela McRobbie discusses how New Labour's cultural policies in Britain in the late twentieth century 'attempted to put the arts in the service of social goals and political aims' and implies that this implicitly Foucauldian approach marked 'a new modality of power' (McRobbie, 2000: 255), in which the government promotes a 'vision of culture as a participative, non-elitist . . . field to which more people must have access' (Frith, 2000: 255). Interestingly, this has led to the creation in both Britain and China of fashion and art spaces to encourage lesser-known or emerging artists and designers to work in an experimental space. In Beijing, for example, Space 798 has been established as an artists' quarter where studios, shops, exhibition spaces and galleries merge as a means to publicly promote cutting-edge cultural activities. In Britain, McRobbie refers to this kind of community phenomena as a source for moral and spiritual regeneration and also for creating better citizens (2000: 256). For China, with the rising lucrative profits in the luxury fashion markets, the fashion industry becomes both a financially and culturally beneficial enterprise.

INDIA: THE OLD AND THE NEW

Like China, India is in the preliminary stages of transforming its fashion industry from being a global textile producer to a designer-based innovative manufacturer. Emerging Indian designers are integrating ancient traditions of Indian craftsmanship with both national dress and contemporary fashion. In terms of popular culture, since the 1960s, ethnic dress and world fashion have been interrelated as a form of identification or group affiliation, especially amongst fashion's subcultures. An eclectic mix of cultural elements became more evident in 1990s high fashion, and this offered greater opportunities for non-Western designers to establish a foothold in the Parisian fashion sphere. India is a culturally diverse nation, and yet the draped sari is retained as the mainstay of its national wardrobe. The traditional *salwar kamiz* or sari is coupled with other indigenous garments such as the *churidars* and *kurtis* (other items of regional wear) to create innovative and unique garments in India's fashion industry. Reinforcing independent nationalism in the postcolonial era, it was important for India to reassert its own identity found in traditional handspun and handwoven cloth (*khadi*), mirror work and *zardozi* (embroidery with gold thread and sequins), and resist-dye prints. High-profile public figures, including Indira Gandhi, purposely wore traditional textiles to reinforce the cultural and economic significance of one of the nation's primary industries. This led to a resurgence of classic weaving, printing, embroidery, tie-dye and patchwork techniques. Young designers began to work with traditional craftspeople as a means to revitalize and redesign patterns and motifs within a contemporary context.

Historically, with the increasing industrialization, hand-loomed textiles gave way to much cheaper power-loom methods of production, which not only reduced the price of clothing but increased the volume and range of clothing available to consumers. While cotton and silk were the predominant fibres produced in India, shiny, long-lasting nylons and synthetics, boldly patterned in bright colours, developed a popular appeal in the 1980s in the domestic market, particularly in rural areas. Imported goods such as Levi's jeans became cult clothing worn with a tie-dyed T-shirt or a hand-embroidered bustier top and a *jhola* cloth shoulder bag, and men shifted to trousers and shirts for office wear. Fashion historian Laila Tyabji (2010), in 'Fashion in Post-Independence India', argues that it was this eclectic array of mixed styling that reinforced India's diversity rather than establishing recognizable trends. She documents that, by the first decade of the twenty-first century, India had become the second largest producer (next to China) of international fashion brands. Resulting from an influx of foreign brands, satellite television with Western programs and the repercussions of globalism, 'the sheer range, diversity, and eclecticism of clothing products [were] unprecedented' (Tyabji, 2010: n.p.). This multiplicity in fashion styling became the common denominator in India's global profile. Arguably, the infiltration of international fashion magazines

Figure 12.4 Indian designer Ritu Beri with model, Summer collection, New Delhi, April 2005. Photo: Prakesh Singh/AFP/Getty Images. Beri was the first Indian designer to present fashion in Paris, then the United States and London.

helped to Westernize Indian consumers, as it had in China as well. *Elle* magazine was one of the first to appear in 1996, followed by *Vogue* India's inaugural issue in October 2007 and *Harper's Bazaar* in March 2009. *Vogue* followed a similar format to the inaugural China edition by using a Western model flanked by two Indian models for the cover design.

Seemingly, the emerging fashion industries in both China and India are following a parallel path. India is now considered an attractive market for luxury brands; about fifty premium and luxury brands, including Jimmy Choo, Gucci, Christian Dior and Chanel, have opened stores in India in recent years. India is among the most brand-conscious countries in the world, with 35 per cent of Indian survey respondents re-porting that they buy designer goods.[6] Like China, rising affluence has increased brand awareness among Indian consumers, and consumer spending has increased dramati-cally over the past ten years. India is also attempting to establish an infrastructure that will promote industry growth through focused fashion and business education courses for emerging designers, whose graduates will slowly be able to infiltrate the growing market. In 2008, a group of domestically established designers founded the Fashion Foundation of India. Another industry association, the Fashion Design Council of India, launched its first fashion week in New Delhi in 2000 with the aim to assist designers and fashion manufactures in fostering the growth of the Indian fashion in-dustry at an international level. These fashion weeks have expanded to include Mum-bai, Bangalore, Jaipur, Hyderabad, Chennai, Kolkata and Bhopal. While globalization is undoubtedly making the world a smaller place and promoting a melting pot of cul-tures into a homogenous mass, India seems to be one of the few developing coun-tries clinging to its national costume as a mainstay in an ever-changing international fashion market.

Designers

This section highlights the designers who have presented their fashion in the major fashion centres of Paris, London or New York and have established long-term sustainability in the Indian fashion arena. Ritu Beri, who began her designing career in 1990 after graduating from the National Institute of Fashion Technology in Delhi, became the first Indian designer to present a collection in Paris, and then later in the United States and London. Others followed, including Tarun Tahiliani, Rohit Bal and J.J. Valaya. Tahiliani, one of the first Indians to graduate from the Fashion Institute of Technology (FIT) in New York, returned to India to open the first fashion boutique called Ensemble in 1987. He established the Tarun Tahiliani Design studio, and his designer label Ahilian sold in stores around the world. Considered one of the pioneers of India's fashion industry, his elegant work is characterized by its heavy borrowing from traditional garments, styles and embroidery (Plate 31).

The designer Bal was described by *Time* magazine in 1996 as 'India's master of fabric and fantasy' as he developed a very sophisticated method of draping sumptuous fabric (Arora, 2012). His work is sponsored by the Swatch Group and has been shown in New York, Paris and Singapore. Valaya is an alumnus of the National Institute of Fashion Technology (NIFT), an institute linked to FIT in New York, and he was the first Indian designer to win the Prix d'Incitation in 1990—a competition for young designers held in Paris. His work is elaborately detailed and embellished, and he is renowned for his Indian wedding dresses. These designers might be classified as traditionalists, just as has Ritu Kumar, who combines simplicity, delicate embroidery and rich colour to epitomize India's heritage and has established a unique reputation since 1994 for designing and dressing the Miss India contestants for international beauty pageants. Referencing Indian traditional craftsmanship has been the essence of their fashion industry for many years, and only a few designers have successfully combined Western and Eastern styling in their work.

However, since the start of the new millennium, a number of other Indian designers, such as Rina Dhaka, Anamika Khanna, Manish Arora (Plate 32) and Manish Malhotra, have quickly gained international recognition.[7] Manish Arora attracted an international audience when he represented India at the Hong Kong Fashion Week in 2000 and participated in the first India Fashion Week held in New Delhi. Following this success, his colourful label Fish Fry was stocked at Lord & Taylor in New York, and he has since expanded into a cosmetics range. During 2004, he was named the Best Women's Prêt Designer at the first Indian Fashion Awards held in Mumbai, and MC2 Diffusion Paris started representing the label for the export business. The following year, Arora participated in the Miami Fashion Week in May 2005, where he was presented with the designer's choice for Best Collection Award. He had a successful debut at the London Fashion Week in September 2005 and received an overwhelming response from the press as well as the buyers. Arora exhibited some of his work in an exhibition called 'Global Local' (in association with the British Council, India) and displayed his collection at the 'Fashion in Motion' exhibition held at London's Victoria and Albert Museum in September 2007. In early 2011, he was appointed creative director of the womenswear collection of the French fashion house Paco Rabanne.

Some designers, including Manish Malhotra, designed costumes for actors in Bollywood films. In general, these stage garments are exaggerated versions of the sari and Indian wedding dresses made in bright colours with heavily embellished decoration. Often designed to emphasize the silhouette, detailed embroidery is placed on the edges of the garments to create a dramatic, theatrical appearance. Malhotra has created a glamorous and unique identity for many of India's leading ladies and is credited as 'adding glitter to Bollywood' by the popular press. Having become synonymous with style in Hindi film, he started his own label in 2004 and has been showcasing his collections at India Fashion Week, and others, since 2006. Malhotra uses unusual

Figure 12.5   Manish Malhotra, two-piece lace ensemble with wrap, Lakme India Fashion Week, Mumbai, ready-to-wear Autumn/Winter, March 2006. Photo: STRDEL/AFP/Getty Images. In this photo, Bollywood star Priety Zinta models this elaborately detailed and glamorous garment, typical of the stage work that Tahiliani produces for Bollywood productions.

materials, such as net and chiffon, to make up his wedding gown collections and is one of the first of the designers to convert to using the softer, more pastel colours (favoured in the West) such as beige, lavender and pink in this work. He adds elegance through the use of sequin work, crystal embellishments and embroidery. He was invited to exclusively design clothes for Michael Jackson for his appearance during the Bollywood awards held in New York in 1999 and for Jackson's concert in Munich later in the same year.

Drawing interest away from Parisian, British and American designers has been difficult, and changing perceptions of India as a design centre will take time. So far, Indian designers have been displaying their collections abroad under the labels of foreign fashion houses or retail chains, but there is now a growing trend for Indian designers to showcase their collections under their own labels. In 2011, fashion designers Manish Arora, Anamika Khanna and Rajesh Pratap Singh made an impact at the Paris Fashion Week under their own labels—a sign of India's growing presence in the crowded international arena. Abigail Chisman, the editor-in-chief of Vogue.com, said: 'At last people are going to the source—for years key designers such as Donna Karan have drawn inspiration from Indian design, while others such as John Galliano and Jean Paul Gaultier have been using Bombay's embroidery houses to help produce their couture collections' (Hastings and Edwardes, 2011). While, on the one hand, apparel manufacturers continue to shift production to low-cost Asian countries such as India, on the other, the Indian fashion industry has gained international acclaim and recognition at several global forums. This has helped attract a large number of international clients to the country.

Arguably, India had been a colonial British outpost for almost a hundred years (1850–1947) and had not been excluded from appropriating fashion styling from the Western world. Yet change has occurred very slowly in terms of adopting global international trends, and this has occurred through choice rather than directive. China, on the other hand, has been offered a window of opportunity of only a few decades to meet the Western world of fashion and now must make up for lost time. It would seem that the objectives of the two nations are much more focussed and driven. Both countries share a rapid population growth, sustained economic development and a growing middle class, and are very well placed to establish a promising fashion industry within their emerging international markets.

Conclusion

A Cultural History of Fashion in the 20th and 21st Centuries asserts that haute couture, in its ideal state, was primarily a nineteenth-century phenomenon that reflected the ideals and values outlined by Thorstein Veblen's *The Theory of the Leisure Class* (1899) and therefore was subsequently doomed in the new modern industrialized world. In sociological terms, for Veblen, clothing was a means to identify social class differentiation, to advertise one's wealth and position in society and to reinforce the prestige of upper-class men in a patriarchal society. The early couturiers were seen as 'artist-geniuses', acquiescent to their upper-class clients, with their astuteness in business dealings remaining invisible. Some designers, such as Poiret, went to great lengths to promote this myth. As social class distinctions began to blur when monetary status outstripped class status, it became clear that the focus of fashion would undeniably shift. Yet even before the turn of the twentieth century, a number of the most prestigious British and European haute couture designers recognized the unlimited middle-class market of fashion consumers in America, as well as in Britain and Europe. In other words, the elitist notion of haute couture was challenged even before it could attempt to consolidate its position in modern twentieth-century society or become a pivotal force in an emerging lucrative industry.

Coupled with the advent of technological improvements in manufacture in the 1910s and 1920s, key fashion designers were able to respond to modern life in ways that defied convention. Standardization—a prerequisite of machine technology—equally applied to fashion design. Standardized sizes, colours and styles became the most cost-effective means of production. This explains why Chanel's standardized 'little black dress', for example, was initially compared to Henry Ford's 1925 Model T in American *Vogue* (October 1926) for its practicality, minimalist styling and sleek, modern lines. Both were products of the machine age aesthetic.

In artistic terms, Schiaparelli was perceived as the 'Duchamp of the fashion world', offering a paradoxical element in her design that questioned the nature of high fashion itself. While she collaborated with many of the Surrealist artists in the 1930s, including Salvador Dalí, this critique of elitist practice later became fundamental to post-modernist discourse, and from the 1960s onwards was underlined by the adoption of popular culture, in its many forms, into all of the visual arts. As fashion parodied art and art attempted to parody life, fashion became more closely tied to street style dress. Popular Hollywood films, music and media advertising bridged the gap between high and low art and fashion. In a world of 'high tech', changes or fashion fads proliferated, and the notion of disposability became part of dress. In these circumstances, haute couture quite literally priced itself out of the market. Lifestyle dressing appeared in the 1970s and 1980s, and the United States became the centre of sportswear production. Dressing down rather than dressing up became the new vogue, further contributing to a visual levelling of social class distinction.

This fashion text has argued that the democratization of fashion during the course of the twentieth century has been effected by a multiplicity of social, economic and technological factors. These events include the rise of a fashion industry that catered specifically for a middle-class clientele, the merging of fashion, commerce and culture—with a shift from high culture to popular culture, the breaking down of haute couture concepts and traditions—initiated by key designers, the influence of American lifestyle dressing and finally the focus on the youth market and the subsequent use of fashion as a mode of social and political protest. In cultural terms, the interdependency of these factors led to not only changing notions of fashion but the gradual demise of the traditions of haute couture. While these events can be individually analysed, like the threads in a beautiful piece of fabric, ultimately, they must be viewed collectively in order to fully appreciate the subtleties and the complexities that contributed to the final outcome.

The rise of street style fashion, dictated by the young, which was quickly adopted by the couturiers, first became apparent in post-war youth subcultures, and this niche marketing was to impact greatly on the fashion industry in terms of styling, marketing and manufacturing. Views held by a number of prominent writers argued that contemporary anti-fashion was crystallized in the lifestyle promoted by the American hippie movement, initially informed by American anti-establishment trends. However, in England, founded on aggressive and extremist political views, and on social alienation and isolation, economic recession and growing unemployment amongst the young, British punk fashion in 1978 created a nihilistic sentiment that was seen in dress, behaviour and attitudes unsurpassed since the hostility and violence generated by the 1920s Dadaists in Berlin. Fashion codes were smashed and fashion canons demolished. This 'deviance' of fashion often responded beyond local or national issues and extended to radical feminist ideologies, unconventional sexual mores and attitudes, racism and gender-related issues, political corruption, and environmental and global concerns. Fashion's response to these sociopolitical issues in the 1970s, 1980s and 1990s emphasized the effectiveness of fashion as a visual arts tool to communicate sociopolitical ideas and to incite revolution. Arguably, when Paris catwalk designer wear succumbed to the voice of street style, the final step in the process of democratization in fashion was realized.

Throughout the book, the term *anti-fashion* has been used to show that fashion and anti-fashion have always been one and the same thing. Change is an inherent part of the fashion system, and anti-fashion—in terms of reacting against the fashion norm—simply completes the fashion cycle. Interestingly, even the adoption of ethnic non-European dress in the 1960s and 1970s was seen as a form of anti-fashion because it questioned Western mainstream directions. This cross-cultural trend was reconfirmed in the early 1980s when the 'second wave' of Japanese designers stormed the Paris catwalks with their version of street style fashion. Using a divergent approach, Yohji Yamamoto and Rei Kawakubo totally deconstructed style, image, methodology, presentation and display in both their work and marketing strategies. The book has argued that the Japanese designers, more than any others, led the way towards invigorating a flagging European fashion industry that had become entangled in the web of appropriation and pastiche. Instead, their work has generously contributed to a more subjective, humanistic and retrospective response to societal mores. Meaning and memory—both of which have come to play an inherent part in their clothing design—have contributed to the broader idea that fashion has finally become something more than just a second skin. The chapter on 'Japanese Conceptual Fashion' has emphasized the magnitude that cross-cultural differences and aesthetic anomalies, which predominate in the work of the Japanese designers, have had on Western fashion sensibilities over the past thirty years.

The last five chapters of this new edition have dealt primarily with the ways that fashion has responded to last decade's difficult times. If global fashion means global manufacturing, global marketing and global distribution, then it has forced the individual to become a homogenized citizen of the world. The latter part of this book provides an overview of how fashion, as a commercial entity, has met many challenges in recent years. It has pointed out how political unrest and instability, a flagging economy and sophisticated technological advancements have impacted greatly upon fashion business practices globally. Specifically, it has provided a detailed account of how international marketing campaigns have relied heavily on the concept of brand loyalty, authenticity and quality to both lure new multicultural customers and to sustain their existing Western clientele; it has considered how advanced technology, in terms of the digital processing of information, has reached a very sophisticated level, forcing completely new methods of marketing and promotion upon designers, retailers and distributors so that they may stay abreast of fashion's changing consumer markets; it has shown that Web-based shopping allows consumers to dictate their methods of purchase, pricing and distribution as they are able to search the world 'for a better deal' or more environmentally sustainable clothing; and it has suggested that new technologies—based on virtual reality marketing—have led to new media methods of social networking, which have, in turn, impacted greatly on the demise of existing retail and social structures.

One might also consider the implications of new business frontiers developing rapidly in Asian and Indian economies that could eliminate the relevancy of Paris as the centre of the fashion world as we know it today. A global consciousness, over the past several years, has forced many to reconsider their priorities concerning the impact of technology and industrialization, wastage and pollution upon world communities. But what will happen if we are not able to secure an environmentally sustainable industry?

Whilst only meant to provide an inventory for the reader to review, *A Cultural History of Fashion in the 20th and 21st Centuries* provocatively asks the student of fashion to consider the issues confronting the future of the fashion industry. Arguably, this book implies that further consideration should be given to the direction that fashion will take during the twenty-first century.

Today's fashions are tomorrow's memories and yesterday's visions.

Bonnie English

Notes

CHAPTER 1 THE INTERPLAY OF COMMERCE AND CULTURE BEFORE THE FIRST WORLD WAR

1. More recent research by Beverley Lemire (1991) suggests that the ready-made clothing industry and consumerism were well under way in the eighteenth century in Britain. In particular, she discusses ready-made gowns that could be purchased for eight shillings by working-class women in 1777 (1991: 313), cheap, ready-made leather breeches sold at the Rag Fair in the late 1780s (1991: 315), fifteen types of plain cotton hose available by the 1770s (1991: 316), and ready-made cotton shirts for working men which appeared regularly in drapers' ledgers from 1791 (1991: 316). However, it must be noted that the eighteenth-century ready-made industry catered only to the working classes, as the garments were considered inappropriate for middle-class consumers.
2. Stanley Chapman and his colleagues (Chapman et al., 1993) argue that the British ready-made clothing industry 'was largely complete by 1860, a date at which the sewing machine was only beginning to come into widespread use'. He points out that the sewing machine was fifty times faster than the quickest seamstress, but because some parts of the garment were not accessible to the machine, there was a considerable resistance to its use. He maintains that the 'rapid development of ready-made [garments] in the 1840s and 1850s stimulated a demand for machinery rather than vice versa' (Chenoune, 1993: 22–3).
3. Evening gowns, wedding gowns and other dresses continued to be available to individual demand, cut to fit the client.
4. Letter from A. Bouçicault to his secretary M. Karchon, 16 September 1876, which calls for greater publicity concerning the store's ready-to-wear dresses.
5. Taken from the original text, *Présentation* (1927, n.p.).
6. See Rappaport, Erica (2000), *Shopping for Pleasure; Women in the Making of London's West End*, Princeton, NJ: Princeton University Press; and Reekie, Gail (1993), *Temptations: Sex, Selling and the Department Store*, St Leonard's, NSW: Allen & Unwin.
7. See also Abelson, E. (1989), *When Ladies Go A-Thieving: Middle-Class Shoplifters in the Victorian Department Store*, New York: Oxford University Press.

8. Gleveo's writings called for the introduction of more window displays in the form of dramatic tableaux.

9. In 1913, Bon Marché mailed out a fifty-page catalogue entitled 'Clothing and Goods for Travel and the Automobile, Bicycle and Assorted Accessories, Games for Open Air, Sports'.

10. Mail-order catalogue of 1844 from the Petit Saint-Thomas, a Parisian Left Bank firm; another in 1871 from the Bon Marché.

11. Full-page advertisements frequently announced enormous 'lots' of dresses for sale.

CHAPTER 2 THE DEMOCRATIZATION OF FASHION: MACHINE AGE AESTHETICS

1. Vionnet was one of the first haute couture designers to copyright her designs by photographing the garments from the front, back and side. These photographs were then lodged with the Chambre Syndicale in Paris.

2. Also, the word 'couture' was only used in the masculine form (Charles-Roux, 1981: 182).

3. After the Russian Revolution of 1917, members of the aristocracy fled Russia, leaving their properties and possessions behind.

4. In fashion, the kimono was introduced as a beach coat, yet more importantly was seen as a simple modular design, being made up of eight pieces, which became a canvas for asymmetrical decoration. Oriental art has consistently impacted upon Western artistic sensibilities since the nineteenth century, and particularly upon the decorative arts—including fashion. The Philadelphia World's Fair in 1876 provided an opportunity for American artists and craftspeople to view Eastern decorative art for the first time. In both technical and decorative terms, the impact of Japanese art, in particular, became evident in the use of motifs, colouring and surface rendering. By the turn of the century, it was a major influence on the art nouveau style in jewellery, furniture and architectural design. In the 1920s, Eastern art impacted upon art deco styling, where broad, flat areas of colour were defined and arranged in a two-dimensional pattern.

5. Undoubtedly, this reference refers to the most memorable of the nineteenth-century dandies, Beau Brummell, who won the respect and admiration of the Prince of Wales and the British court for his refined manner of dress, which was impeccable yet totally unadorned. It suggests that 'good' taste rather than expensive taste was the indicator which allowed for social mobility.

6. Costume jewellery was made from plastic products introduced in the 1920s as a result of war technology. It was the first time that imitation jewellery was worn with couture clothing.

CHAPTER 3 FRAMING FASHION: THE ARTISTS WHO MADE CLOTHES

1. Hugo Ball, reciting the sound poem, *Karawane*, at the Cabaret Voltaire on 23 June 1916, wore blue cardboard tubes on his legs, a huge cardboard collar and a blue and white striped witch doctor's hat (Goldberg, 1979: 40).

2. An evening at the Hotel Claridge was organized by the collector Laurent Monnier to raise money for the treasury of the Organization of Russian Pages, whose charitable concerns were directed towards an influx of Russian refugees into France from the Bolshevik regime. The evening included Russian folk dancers and an elaborate parade of fashions from the past, present and future (Buckberrough, 1980: 64).

3. An exhibition organized by the Union of Russian Artists in Paris, which included Delaunay, Goncharova, Larionov and Leger.

4. Schwitters used paper as his source material and often used newspaper clippings and fashion magazine materiality in his collaged works. O'Neill states: 'Paper is the best substance for the craft of fashioning; the cut of his scalpel blade into paper is identical to the cut of shears into cloth; the concept of fashion is defined by the activity of making' (O'Neill, 2005: 181).

5. This inferred voyeurism is reminiscent of the work of Duchamp and Atget (see Chapter 1).

6. Nationalism inspired the couturier M. Grès to base her 1940 collection on the French tricolour after the Germans occupied Paris.

7. Dalí's motivations were often criticized by other members of the Surrealist movement. When his art and his behaviour became overly sensationalist and publicity-seeking, they expelled him from the group.

8. Viktor & Rolf mimicked Gilbert and George's 'living sculptures' when they dressed in identical clothes and posed, like the earlier conceptual performance artists had in 1969, as a personification of art itself.

9. Excerpts from this section taken from English (2004).

10. Hussein worked with the London-based engineering and concept creation firm 2D3D to set up the computers needed to format the movements, as well as Moritz Waldemeyer, who is at the cutting edge of mechatronics and who worked with Ron Arad and Zaha Hadid, and Philips Design Probe for lighting effects.

CHAPTER 4 FASHIONING THE AMERICAN BODY

1. German and Central European immigrants arrived around the middle of the nineteenth century at the proto-industrial phase, and in the early twentieth century a largely Eastern European workforce (mainly Russian Jews) powered the garment trades.

2. The American clothing workers' unions initiated historic strikes in 1909 and 1910 when over ten thousand women walked off the job in New York. It became one of the most powerful unions in the country.

3. By the 1820s, an increasing number of ready-made garments of higher quality were being produced for a broader market.

4. Beginning in the 1860s, the machines were mass-produced by American firms, and were widely used both commercially and in the home (Crane, 2000: 75).

5. With the increasing sales of sewing machines (by 1875, one-third of skilled and unskilled families in Massachusetts owned machines—see Massachusetts Bureau of Statistics, 1875: 436), the production of paper patterns followed suit; these were marketed as a way to dress in the 'most fashionable styles' of the day, whereas in Europe the marketing strategy was aimed at 'making clothes cheaper'. One company alone sold six million patterns per year (to a US population just above 38.5 million). In 1926, a pattern was designed by the Women's Fashion Institute for a dress that could be made in one hour. The 'one-hour dress' was meant to encourage home sewing and became a successful marketing ploy.

6. For a comprehensive development of ready-to-wear in the United States, see Kidwell and Christian (1974).

7. One of the most famous and main sources of French fashion was the magazine *L'Art et la Mode* (1888–1967), which was used to copy couture styles.

8. Chanel produced costumes for three Hollywood films in the 1930s. The Hollywood actor Gloria Swanson encouraged the directors to use Chanel's talents. In 1931, the film *Now or Never* featured particularly glamorous garments.

9. The mafia exerted a powerful and debilitating influence over this industry by infiltrating the trade unions. In the early 1920s, mafia member Lepke Buchalter deployed 250 Jewish and Italian gangsters to 'persuade' garment company owners to join the union by threatening them and throwing acid on their merchandise. By the early 1930s, Buchalter had became a very powerful figure—particularly when he persuaded the Amalgamated Fabric Cutters' local branch to align with him, and used the strike force of these 1,900 workers, who cut the cloth and shipped the goods, to close down the industry at will. He offered protection from other mafia bosses, and coerced the garment companies into signing sweetheart deals with trucking firms that gave him financial kickbacks. Often mafia bosses would work both sides of a strike for mutual benefit. This type of graft and corruption became an inherent part of New York's garment industry. Buchalter died in the electric chair for the murder of a trucker, and his plea for clemency—based on naming corrupt top officials in the Roosevelt government—was turned down.

10. The knitting machine became extremely popular in the 1950s and 1960s, when body-hugging clothing became the new direction in fashion.

11. In Paris, only four new couture houses opened between 1970 and 1995.

12. The first known licence was created by Schiaparelli in 1940, but licences were more consistently created by Dior in the 1950s.
13. Carlo Gambino assumed mafia control of the garment district in 1957, and took over the Consolidated Carriers Corporation, the largest and most important trucking business in the area. As distribution costs soared, America's $2.5 billion fashion industry suffered. As a result of these corrupt practices, from 1955 to 1992 business shrank by 75 per cent, costing New York some 225,000 jobs.
14. Marshall McLuhan became famous for his books entitled *The Medium is the Message* (1967) and *Culture is Our Business* (1970).

CHAPTER 5 POSTMODERNISM AND FASHION

1. Rabanne used revolutionary new methods, including electronic welding to seal seams of plastic garments, in his Barbarella collection. The theme of engineered couture is evident in Rabanne's method of constructing chain mail garments by linking discs and squares using metal rings.
2. The fashion press in the United States was largely supported by chemical companies which promoted these new fabrics, such as Bri-nylon, Ban-lon and stretch fabrics such as Crimplene and Lurex (Bliekhorn, 2002: 68).
3. The boutique, owned by Barbara Hulanicki and her husband Stephen Fitz-Simon, successfully seduced customers away from the larger establishments and became synonymous with London's ready-to-wear fashion.
4. According to Glynn (1978), Marks and Spencer remained the classic of the genre, 'keeping up with its customers so adeptly that [they] could be anything from a duchess to a cleaner'. Between the wars, Marks and Spencer 'had a price limit (as did Woolworth's), which restricted its fashion sales: five shillings' (1978: 205).
5. There is some controversy regarding this claim. According to *Vogue*, the Munkasci photo of Lucille Brokaw was the first action photo made for fashion (see *Vogue*, 1 April 1947: 141 and 1 November 1954: 86; Radner 2001: 188). According to *Harper's Bazaar*, the first fashion photograph taken 'on the move and on the street' was taken by Jean Moral in 1932, but the most famous was Munkacsi's shot; both were taken for *Harper's Bazaar* (Harrison, 1991:11).
6. The Musée de La Mode, Paris staged the retrospective exhibition in summer 1986 and in Moscow in December 1986. It opened in the Hermitage Museum in Leningrad in February 1987.
7. The fashion fad faded for two reasons: it became ecologically unsound to use a natural material such as paper in such a wasteful way; and manufacturers came to realize that costs were not substantially lower than those of conventional dress construction.

CHAPTER 6 ANTI-FASHION

1. Interview with Richard Pankhurst, son of suffragette Emily Pankhurst, in *The Suffragettes: 100 Images of the Twentieth Century*, video, New York: CAPA Productions.
2. Laver (1982: 77–8), amongst numerous other authorities, explains how the elitist fashion of slashing in clothes resulted after a torn and tattered Swiss peasant army cut pieces of rich and sumptuous silks and satins and quite literally 'stuffed' them through the holes of their clothing for warmth after they had defeated the army of Charles the Bold, Duke of Burgundy in 1476 and plundered his storage tents. Ironically, this visual disarray—popular amongst the military—was quickly consumed and adopted by the upper classes as a sign of status by revealing the underlying expensive layers of clothing.
3. Holland was ruled by a prosperous bourgeoisie, a body of pious merchants and magistrates (Laver, 1982: 108), who reacted against pretentious sumptuousness by using their new-found wealth to establish a new aesthetic of dress which replaced silks, satins and velvet fabric with calfskin and wool. These swashbuckling musketeers, seen in many of Frans Hals's paintings, became the new heroes of a restructured society.
4. Growing disenchantment with the corrupted Bourbon court forced the dematerialization of colour and fabric in their garments, with skirts shrinking and jewellery disappearing. Ribeiro (1988) describes a young man of one of the first families in France 'attending the Theatre in boots, his hair cropt [sic] and his whole dress slovenly' (1988: 70). Clearly, it had become unhealthy to advertise one's elitist position in society. Again, the crinolines, bustles and corsets disappeared and rich fabrics were replaced with muslin, cambric or calico. At the same time, history also acknowledges the irrationality of dress worn by the Merveilleuses and the Incroyables during the 1790s Reign of Terror. A volatile mixture of youth rebellion and political dissent lent itself to the wearing of unkempt, crumpled clothing: men had long, straggly hair and wore exaggerated cravats and extremely high-waisted pantaloons with undersized vests; women wore oversized bows and bonnets, shapeless garments and had wild, untamed hair.
5. This anti-fashion was again visually acknowledged in Galliano's 1983 final-year student collection at St Martin's School of Art, in which he called his garments Les Incroyables.
6. Numerous authors, including Cronin (2004: 2) and Sabin (1999: 3), insist that punk originated in New York in 1973 because of the existence of early punk bands such as the Ramones, Television and the New York Dolls, and point out that New York punk had a distinctly different look, sound and attitude to that which emerged in London in 1976.

7. Statistics (Global Issues Primer, online) illustrate that, for example, the Gross Domestic Product (or GDP) of the poorest forty-eight nations (which make up one-quarter of the world's countries) is less than the wealth of the world's three richest people combined. Also, nearly 1 billion people entered the twenty-first century unable to read a book or sign their name; and less than 1 per cent of what the world spends every year on weapons was needed to put every child in school by the year 2000 —yet it didn't happen.
8. The British Equal Pay Act of 1970 was amended in 1983, the Equal Opportunities Commission established in 1985 and the Sex Discrimination Act 1975 was revised in 1986; the French Human Rights Act and Equal Opportunity Commission was established in 1986; the US Equal Employment Opportunity Act of 1972 led into the Affirmative Action Act for Women in 1992; and in Australia, the Equal Opportunity Act was signed in 1984.
9. Turn-of-the century women had adopted tailored jackets and ties from male riding dress for daytime office wear, as a number of women moved into secretarial and office work.

CHAPTER 7 JAPANESE CONCEPTUAL FASHION

1. The term *hifu* is an old one used in Noh theatre, indicating a form or style that is 'incorrect'.
2. Feminist artists such as Barbara Kruger, Cindy Sherman, Moriko Mori and the Guerilla Girls, among others.
3. Minagawa is a third-generation Kyoto kimono-maker who is esteemed for her exemplary expertise in the craft. She has been the leading researcher and designer of woven fabrics at MDS since 1971. She combines a rural craft tradition with cutting-edge technological fabric science. The tactile subtlety of her surfaces and the minimalist simplicity of her fabrics gained the 1990 Amiko Kujiraoki prize of Manichi Fashion.
4. Miyake says: 'These clothes are meant to be rolled for travelling and are inexpensive to own. It is like buying a loaf of bread' (Saiki, 1992: 34).
5. This culminated in the international publication of Aoki (2001).

CHAPTER 8 GLOBAL PRACTICES—1980S ONWARDS

1. In 1992, 75 per cent of the couturiers were over fifty, and four were over seventy (Crane, 2000: 143).

2. A diffusion line is a cheaper production line of apparel, which is marketed to a wider audience at lower prices.
3. In literature, as in the arts, writers criticized consumerism and media manipulation. John Kenneth Galbraith wrote *The Affluent Society* and Vance Packard wrote *The Hidden Persuaders*, *The Status Seekers* and *The Pyramid Climber*.

CHAPTER 9 POST-2000: GLOBAL RECESSION AND IDEOLOGICAL CONFLICT

1. Despite the fact that 'Nothing even remotely politically correct gets a look in at a Westwood show. Rather provocation—and often blatant media manipulation—continues to be the name of the game' (Frankel, 2001: 104).
2. Museum Boijmans Van Beuningen, Rotterdam exhibition, 1997.
3. Lagerfeld describes how, on London's streets (or on any other city's streets for that matter), people are indistinguishable by their clothing, and suggests that this clothing no longer has meaning and no longer individualizes the wearer. In winter, the weather and environment are bleak, and the clothing in public places is predominantly plain and dark and is characterized by 'the same mixture of unremarkable casual wear—almost regulation office wear' (Hill, 2005: 69).
4. Slimane left Dior in 2007 to concentrate on his photography but re-emerged in March 2012 as the creative director of YSL Womenswear.
5. In 2010, Patrick Grant, recipient of the British Menswear Designer of the Year Award, 'decried the declining dress standards of British men, branding them as "scruffy"' (Fox, 2010). The remark, 'Fashion is nothing more than the most marketable form of conformity', was posted on the same Web site (www.guardian.uk.com) by a blogger who did not appreciate Grant's comments.

CHAPTER 10 THE CHANGING FASHION MARKET IN THE LATE TWENTIETH AND TWENTY-FIRST CENTURIES

1. Digital IQ Index® (Galloway and Mullen, 2009). Professor Scott Galloway, of New York University's Stern School of Business, was the developer of the Digital IQ Index.
2. Marketing survey by Management Consultants Accenture UK (Simms, 2008),
3. This strategy resulted in dipping sales, so Lang rejoined the Paris catwalk the following year.
4. Quote by an anonymous official from the Italian Institute for Foreign Trade in Shanghai.

5. The issue of counterfeiting is discussed in a January 2009 special edition of *Harper's Bazaar* and on numerous Web sites, including www.counterfeitchic.com and www.fakesareneverinfashion.com.

6. 'Buyers of counterfeit goods in Italy are liable for a fine up to 10,000 Euros' (Bowman, 2008: 4).

7. 'In 1943, the first New York Fashion Week was held, with one main purpose: to distract attention from French fashion during the Second World War, when workers in the fashion industry were unable to travel to Paris' (Wikipedia, n.d.). This became a prime opportunity for American designers to exert their own autonomy in the international fashion industry.

8. Curated by Diana Vreeland, former editor of American *Vogue*.

9. Past momentous travelling exhibitions include: 'Giorgio Armani' at the Guggenheim, New York, in 2000, Bilboa in 2001 and the Nueu Nationalgallerie, Berlin, in 2003; 'Vivienne Westwood' at the Victoria and Albert Museum, London, ANG, Canberra, and De Young, San Francisco, 2004–2007; and Maison Martin Margiela '20' at the Modemuseum, Antwerp, 2008, Munich in 2009 and Somerset House, London, in 2010 (see Chapter 3).

10. One of the most influential is www.bryanboy.com, run by an entrepreneur from Manila.

11. www.facebook.com/press/info.php?statistics.

12. www.socialmediatoday.com.

CHAPTER 11 ECO-FASHION, SUSTAINABILITY AND ETHICS

1. 'I'd rather go naked than wear fur' (PETA, or People for the Ethical Treatment of Animals, anti-fur campaign, 1994).

2. Nielsen 2008 Global Online Survey on Internet shopping habits. Eco-aware designers who were referenced included Armani, de la Renta, McCartney, Betsey Johnson and Tom Oldman.

3. The Ethical Fashion Show in Paris (2004–2006) and the Anti-apathy re: Fashion event held during London Fashion Week (February 2005); Sao Paulo, Brazil's Fashion Week in 2007, which introduced recycled e-fabrics for elegant evening gowns.

4. Only one of thirty-seven UK institutions since 2007 to have signed up to the United Nations' principles for responsible management education.

5. While sustainability advocates focus on water and fossil fuel scarcity, cotton, which requires large amounts of both resources, has faced a global shortage in the past year (Kaye, 2011).

6. Liliana Pomazan (English and Pomazan, 2010) describes this process: through this innovative technique, at least two garments are simultaneously cut from one length of cloth, one from the positive pieces and one from the negative. Depending

on the design, the negative (anti) may be patched with other fabrics to complete the garment, or they may be left open and worn over the classic (positive) garment, almost as an accessory, or used as a diffusion line called 'waste collation' (2010: 220).

7. Halle Berry, December 2002; Liya Kebede, May 2005; Jennifer Hudson, March 2007; and Michelle Obama, March 2009.

CHAPTER 12 LOOKING AHEAD: THE EMERGENCE OF ASIAN AND INDIAN FASHION DESIGN INDUSTRIES

1. Franca Sozzani, 2011 *Vogue* Italy: Editor's Blog, 'What about China's Fashion Designers? And Fashion in China?', www.vogue.it/en/magazine/editor-s-blog/2011/03/march-30th.
2. The International Federation of Periodical Press estimates that in 2004 around 9,000 magazine titles were published in China, with the four titles that dominated the market being *Cosmopolitan, Elle, Rui-li* and *Esquire*.
3. Designer Laura Biagiotti was the first to showcase her collection in China in 1988, and Zegna did so three years later.
4. Fendi presented its collection on the Great Wall in 2007; Ferragamo celebrated the eightieth anniversary of the label in 2008 in Shanghai; Gucci created a Chinese collection to correspond with the Olympic games; Max Mara, to celebrate fifty-five years in business, set up an exhibition of coats at the National Art Museum in Beijing; Lagerfeld, using the theme 'Coco—from Paris to Shanghai', showed his pre-collection (before showing it in Paris), and Dior followed suit by showing its 2011 pre-collection in Shanghai; and Armani was the first to launch online shopping for its Emporio line in China (Sozzani, 2011).
5. According to the Nielsen Global Luxury Brands Study, consumer spending on fashion products has grown at 7.1 per cent annually between 2002 and 2007.
6. Between 2008 and 2012, the Indian fashion industry is expected to grow 178 per cent, and reach $189 billion by 2012 (Grail Research, 2009).
7. Rajesh Pratap Singh, Rina Dhaka and Ashish Soni all presented a more international look.

Bibliography

Allen, J.S. (1983), *The Romance of Commerce and Culture*, Chicago: University of Chicago Press.

Anscombe, I. (1984), *A Woman's Touch: Women in Design from 1860 to the Present Day*, London: Virago Press.

Anti-Counterfeiting Group (2005), ⟨www.a-cg.org⟩.

Aoki, S. (2001), *FRUiTS*, London: Phaidon Press.

Arnold, R. (2001), *Fashion, Desire, and Angst: Image and Morality in the 20th Century*, London: I.B. Taurus.

Arora, T. (2012), 'India's Fashion Bad Boy', *Bangkok Post* (Asia focus), 2 July, ⟨www.bangkokpost.com/print/300644/⟩.

Artley, A. (1976), *The Golden Age of Shop Design: European Shop Interiors 1880–1939*, London: Architectural Press.

Bailey, A. (1988), *Passion for Fashion*, London: Dragon's World.

Baillen, C. (1973), *Chanel Solitaire*, trans. B. Bray, London: Collins.

Banner, L. (1984), *American Beauty*, Chicago: University of Chicago Press.

Barker, E. (1999), *Contemporary Culture of Display*, London: Yale University Press.

Barnard, M. (2002), *Fashion as Communication*, London: Routledge.

Barwick, S. (1984), 'Century of Style', in *Harper's Bazaar* (Australia), September, pp. 121–24.

Basye, A. (2010), 'One Day in Fashion: Cinemode', 13 August, ⟨www.onthisdayinfashion.com⟩.

Batterberry, M. and Batterberry, A. (1982), *Fashion: The Mirror of History*, London: Columbus Books.

Battersby, M. (1988), *The Decorative Twenties*, Whitney Library of Design, New York: Watson-Guptill.

Baudot, F. (1999), *A Century of Fashion*, London: Thames & Hudson.

Bayer, P. (1988), *Art Deco Source Book: A Visual Reference to a Decorative Style*, Oxford: Phaidon.

Bayley, S. (ed.) (1989), *Commerce and Culture*, Design Museum Books, London: Fourth Estate.

Beard, N. D. (2008), 'The Branding of Ethical Fashion and the Consumer: A Luxury Niche Market or Mass-Market Reality?' *Fashion Theory*, Vol. 12, No. 4, pp. 447–68.

Beaton, C. (1954), *The Glass of Fashion*, London: Weidenfeld & Nicolson.

Bell, Q. (1992), *On Human Finery*, London: Allison & Busby.

Bellafante, G. (2004), 'The Frenchwoman, In All Her Moods', *New York Times*, 5 March.

Benaim, L. (1997), *Issey Miyake*, London: Thames & Hudson.

Benjamin, W. (1970 [1936]), 'The Work of Art in the Age of Mechanical Reproduction', in H. Arendt (ed.), *Illustrations*, pp. 219–53, London: Cape.

Berry, J. (2005), 'Re: Collections—Collection Motivations and Methodologies as Imagery, Metaphor and Process in Contemporary Art', unpublished DVA thesis, Griffith University, Brisbane.

Best, K. N. (2010), 'Fashion Journalism', in J.B. Eicher (ed.), *Berg Encyclopedia of World Dress and Fashion*, Vol. 8, London: Berg.

Betts, K. (2004), 'Rei Kawakubo: Comme des Garçons, Avatar of the Avant-Garde', *Time*, 16 February, p. 40.

Betts, K. (2009), 'Will Fashion's Biggest Names Kiss the Runway Goodbye', *Time*, 10 December.

Black, S. (2007), *Eco-Chic: The Fashion Paradox*, London: Black Dog Publishing.

Bliekhorn, S. (2002), *The Mini-Mod 60s Book*, San Francisco: Last Gasp Publications.

Boodro, M. (1990), 'Art and Fashion—A Fine Romance', *Art News*, September, pp. 120–27.

Borelli, L. (2002), *Net Mode: Web Fashion Now*, New York: Thames & Hudson.

Bouillon, J-P. (1991), 'The Shop Window', in J. Clair (ed.), *The 1920s: Age of Metropolis*, pp. 162–80, Montreal: Museum of Art Press.

Bouquet, M. (2004), 'Thinking and Doing Otherwise', in B.M. Carbonell (ed.), *Museum Studies: An Anthology of Contexts*, Oxford: Blackwell.

Bourdieu, P. (1984), *Distinction: A Social Critique of the Judgement of Taste*, London: Routledge and Kegan Paul.

Bowman, J. (2008), 'Culture Shock: Comparing Consumer Attitudes to Counterfeiting', in *WIPO 4th Global Conference*, Geneva: WIPO.

Bray, E. (2009), 'The New Link Between Music and Fashion', *The Independent*, 21 August.

Breward, C. (2003), '21st Century Dandy', exhibition catalogue, in *Art Architecture & Design*, London: British Council.

Breward, C. and Evans, C. (eds) (2005), *Fashion and Modernity*, Oxford: Berg.

Broinowski, A. (1999), 'Japanese Taste: Askew by a Fraction', in B. English (ed.), *Tokyo Vogue: Japanese/Australian Fashion*, exhibition catalogue, Brisbane: Griffith University.

Brown, S. (2010), *Eco Fashion*, London: Laurence King.

Business of Fashion (n.d.), ⟨www.businessoffashion.com/tag/qui-hao⟩.

Buckberrough, S.A. (1980), *Sonia Delaunay: A Retrospective*, Buffalo: Albright Knox Gallery.

Carbonell, B. M. (ed.) (2004), *Museum Studies: An Anthology of Contexts*, Oxford: Blackwell.

Carnegy, V. (1990), *Fashions of the Decades: The Eighties*, London: Batsford.

Carter, E. (1980), *Magic Names of Fashion*, London: Weidenfeld & Nicolson.

Casadio, M. (1997), *Moschino*, London: Thames & Hudson.

Chadwick, W. (1990), *Women, Art and Society*, London: Thames & Hudson.

Chapman, C., Lloyd, M. and Gott, T. (1993), *Surrealism: Revolution by Night*, exhibition catalogue, Melbourne: National Gallery of Victoria.

Chapman, J. and Gant, N. (eds) (2007), *Designers, Visionaries and Other Stories*, London: Earthscan.

Charles-Roux, E. (1981), *Chanel and Her World*, London: Weidenfeld & Nicolson.

Chenoune F. (1993), *A History of Men's Fashion*, Paris: Flammarion Press.

Chipp, H. B. (1973), *The Theories of Modern Art*, Los Angeles: University of California Press.

Christodoulides, G. (2009), 'Branding in the Post-Internet Journal', *Marketing Theory*, Vol. 9, pp. 141–4.

Cicolini, A. (2005), *The New English Dandy*, London: Victoria & Albert Press.

Clair, J. (ed.) (1991), *The 1920s: Age of Metropolis*, Montreal: Museum of Art Press.

Cohen, A.A. (ed.) (1978), *The New Art of Colour: The Writings of Robert and Sonia Delaunay, The Documents of 20th-Century Art*, trans. D. Shapiro and A. Cohen, New York: Viking Press.

Colchester, C. (1991), *The New Textiles: Trends and Traditions*, London: Thames & Hudson.

Copping, N. (2009), 'Style Bloggers Take Centre Stage', *Financial Times*, 13 November.

Craik, J. (1994), *The Face of Fashion*, New York: Routledge.

Crane, D. (2000), *Fashion and Its Social Agenda*, Chicago: University of Chicago Press.

Cunningham, B. (2010), *Bill Cunningham New York*, video by Richard Press/Philip Gefter (producer).

Daily, J. (2011), 'China's Emerging Fashion Designers', 23 March, ⟨www.signature9.com/fashion/chinas-emerging-fashion-designers-powerhouses⟩.

Damase, J. (1972), *Sonia Delaunay: Rhythms and Colours*, London: Thames & Hudson.

D'Avenel, G. (1989 [1898]), 'The Bon Marché', in S. Bayley (ed.), *Commerce and Culture*, pp. 57–59, London: Fourth Estate.

De Grazia, V. (1991), 'The American Challenge to the European Arts of Advertising', in J. Clair (ed.), *The 1920s: Age of Metropolis*, pp. 236–47, Montreal: Museum of Art Press.

Delaunay, S. (1978), *Nous Irons Jusqu' au Soleil*, Paris: Editions Laffont.

DeLong, M. (2009), 'Innovations and Sustainability at Nike, *Fashion Practice: The Journal of Design, Creative Process & the Fashion Industry*, Vol. 1, No. 1, pp. 109–14.

Di Grappa, C. (ed.) (1980), *Fashion Theory*, New York: Lustrum Press.

Dormer, P. (1993), *Design After 1945*, London: Thames & Hudson.

English, B. (ed.) (1999), *Tokyo Vogue: Japanese/Australian Fashion*, exhibition catalogue, Brisbane: Griffith University.

English, B. (2004), 'Japanese Fashion as a Re-considered Form', in The Space Between: Textiles–Art–Design–Fashion Conference CD, Vol. 2, Perth: Curtin University of Technology.

English, B. (2005), 'Fashion and Art: Postmodernist Japanese Fashion', in L. Mitchell (ed.), *The Cutting Edge: Fashion From Japan*, Sydney: Powerhouse Museum Publications.

English, B. (2011a), Interview with Zang Yingchun, Director of International Fashion and Textile Design Education, Tsinghua University, Beijing, 18 October.

English, B. (2011b), *Japanese Fashion Designers: The Work and Influence of Issey Miyake, Yohji Yamamoto and Rei Kawakubo*, Oxford: Berg.

English, B. and Pomazan, L. (eds) (2010), *Australian Fashion Unstitched: The Last 60 Years*, Melbourne: Cambridge University Press.

Evans, C. (1998), 'The Golden Dustman: A Critical Evaluation of the Work of Martin Margiela and a Review of Martin Margiela: Exhibition (9/4/1615)', *Fashion Theory*, 2/1: 73–93.

Evans, C. (2003), "Yesterday's Emblems and Tomorrow's Commodities', in S. Bruzzi and P. Church-Gibson (eds), *Fashion Cultures*, London: Routledge.

Evans, C. (2003), *Fashion at the Edge: Spectacle, Modernity and Deathliness*, New Haven: Yale University Press.

Evans, C. and Thornton, M. (1991), 'Fashion, Representation, Femininity', *Feminist Review*, Vol. 38, pp. 56–66.

Ewen, S. (1976), *Captains of Consciousness: Advertising and the Social Roots of the Consumer Culture*, New York: McGraw-Hill.

Ewing, E. (1981), *Dress and Undress: A History of Women's Underwear*, London: Bibliophile.

Ewing, E. (1986), *History of 20th-Century Fashion*, London: Batsford.

Farrar, L. (2011), 'Will Chinese Designers Get Left Behind in China's Fashion Boom?' *CNN*, ⟨www.edition.cnn.com/2011/09-1/living/china-fashion-designers/index.html⟩.

Featherstone, M. (1982), 'The Body in Consumer Culture', *Theory, Culture and Society*, Vol. 1, No. 2, pp. 18–33.

Featherstone, M. (1984), 'Lifestyle and Consumer Culture', *Theory, Culture and Society*, Vol. 4, No. 1, pp. 55–70.

Financial Times (2003), 'The Rise of Asia Gathers Speed', 29 December.

Finkelstein, J. (1996), *After a Fashion*, Melbourne: Melbourne University Press.

Finnane, A. (2007), *Changing Clothes in China: Fashion, History, Nation*, London: Hurst & Co. Publishers.

Fletcher, K. (2007), 'Clothes That Connect', in J. Chapman and N. Gant (eds), *Designers, Visionaries and Other Stories*, London: Earthscan.

Fox, I. (2010), 'British Men Are Too Scruffy, Says Menswear Designer of the Year/Life and Style', *The Guardian* (UK), 10 December.

Frankel, S. (2001), *Visionaries*, London: Victoria and Albert Museum Publications.

Frankel, S. (2006), 'French Fashion Draws a Veil Over Our Faces', *The London Independent*, 9 March.

Freud, S. (1965), *The Interpretation of Dreams*, trans. and ed. J. Strachey, London: George Allen & Unwin.

Frith, S. (2000), 'Fashion as a Culture Industry', in S. Bruzzi and P. Church-Gibson (eds), *Fashion Cultures*, London: Routledge.

Gale, C. and Kaur, J. (2004), *Fashion & Textiles: An Overview*, Oxford & New York: Berg.

Galante, P. (1973), *Mademoiselle Chanel*, Chicago: Henry Regnery Co.

Galloway, S. and Mullen, M. (2009), 'The Biggest Opportunity for Luxury Brands in a Generation', *The European Business Review*, ⟨www.europeanbusinessreview.com/?p=2391⟩.

Garland, M. (1970), *Changing Form of Fashion*, New York: Praeger.

Gill, A. (1998), 'Deconstruction Fashion: The Making of the Unfinished, Decomposing and Re-assembled Clothes', *Fashion Theory*, Vol. 2, No. 1, pp. 25–49.

Gill, A. (2006), 'In Trainers: The World's at Our Feet and the Multiple Investments in High Performance Shoe Technology', conference paper, Cultural Studies Association of Australia's UNAUSTRALIAN conference, University of Canberra, December.

Gilligan, S. (2000), 'Gwyneth Paltrow', in S. Bruzzi and P. Church-Gibson (eds), *Fashion Cultures: Theories, Exploration, and Analysis*, New York: Routledge.

Glasscock, J. (2003), 'Bridging the Art/Commerce Divide: Cindy Sherman and Rei Kawakubo of Comme des Garçons', ⟨www.nyu.edu/greyart/exhibits⟩.

Glynn, P. (1978), *In Fashion: Dress in the Twentieth Century*, New York: Oxford University Press.

Golden, A. (1997), *The Memoirs of a Geisha*, New York: Alfred A. Knopf.

Goldberg, R. L. (1979), *Performance Live Art—1909 to the Present*, New York: Abrams.

Goldberg, R. L. (2001), *Performance Art: From Futurism to the Present*, London: Thames & Hudson.

Grail Research (2009), 'Nielsen Global Luxury Brands Study', Fashion Industry Analysis, September, ⟨www.grailresearch.com/pdf/ContenPodsPdf/Global_Fashion_Industry_Growth_in_Emerging_Markets.pdf⟩.

Gronemeyer, A. (1999), *Film: A Concise History*, London: Lawrence King.

Hartley, J. and Montgomery, L. (2009), 'Fashion as Consumer Entrepreneurship: Emergent Risk Culture, Social Network Markets, and the Launch of *Vogue* in China', *Chinese Journal of Communication*, Vol. 2, No. 1, pp. 61–76.

Hastings, C. and Edwardes, C. (2011), 'Film Stars Shun Paris Fashion for Indian Designers', *The Telegraph*, 3 December.

Hauffe, T. (1998), *Design: A Concise History*, London: Lawrence King.

Healy, R. (1996), *Couture to Chaos*, Melbourne: National Gallery of Victoria.

Hebdige, R. (1987), interview in video *Digging for Britain: Postmodern Popular Culture and National ID*, Hobart: Tasmania School of Art.

Hebdige, R. (1997), 'Posing . . . Threats, Striking . . . Poses: Youth Surveillance and Display', in K. Gelder and S. Thornton (eds), *The Subcultures Reader*, pp. 393–405, London: Routledge.

Heinze, A. R. (1990), *Adapting to Abundance*, New York: Columbia University Press.

Heller, N. (1987), *Women Artists*, New York: Abbeville Press.

Herd, J. (1991), 'Death Knell of Haute Couture', reprinted in *Courier-Mail*, Brisbane, 10 August.

Hill, A. (2005), 'People Dress So Badly Nowadays', in C. Breward and C. Evans, *Fashion in Modernity*, Oxford: Berg.

Holborn, M. (1988), 'Image of a Second Skin', *Artforum*, Vol. 27, November, pp. 118–21.

Hollander, A. (1983), 'The Great Emancipator—Chanel', *Connoisseur*, February, pp. 82–91.

Hollander, A. (1984), 'The Little Black Dress', *Connoisseur*, December, pp. 80–89.

Hollander, A. (1988), *Seeing Through Clothes*, Berkeley: University of California Press.

Horyn, C. (2000a), 'On the Road to Fall, Paris at Last', *New York Times*, 1 March.

Horyn, C. (2000b), 'Galliano Plays His Hand Smartly', *New York Times*, 21 May.

Horyn C. (2004), 'A Store Made for You Right Now: You Shop Until It's Dropped', *New York Times*, 17 February.

Horyn, C. (2006), 'Balenciaga, Weightless and Floating Free', *New York Times*, 4 October.

The Independent (2010), 'Top Menswear Designers Mix Cheeky with Elegant', 28 June.

International Centre of Photography (1990), *Man Ray: In Fashion*, exhibition catalogue, New York: International Centre of Photography.

Jackson, T. and Shaw, D. (2008), *Mastering Fashion Marketing*, London: Palgrave Macmillan.

Kapferer, J. N. and Bastien, V. (2009), *The Luxury Strategy: Break the Rules of Marketing to Build Luxury Brands*, London: KoganPage.

Kaplinger, M. (2008), 'Combatting Counterfeiting and Piracy: A Global Challenge', in *WIPO 4th Global Conference*, Geneva: WIPO.

Katz, I. (1996), 'Hollywood's Smash Its', *The Guardian*, G2, 14 August.

Kawamura, Y. (2004), 'The Japanese Revolution in Paris', *Through the Surface*, ⟨www.throughthesurface.com/synopsium/kawamura⟩.

Kaye, L. (2011), 'Textile Recycling Innovation Challenges Clothing Industry', *The Guardian*, 23 June.

Kidd, W. (2002), *Culture and Identity*, New York: Palgrave.

Kidwell, C.B. and Christian, M.C. (1974), *Suiting Everyone: The Democratization of Clothing in America*, Washington, DC: Smithsonian Institute Press.

Kinsella, S. (1995), 'Cities in Japan', in L. Skov and B. Moeran (eds), *Women, Media and Consumption in Japan*, Honolulu: University of Hawaii Press.

Knafo, R. (1988), 'The New Japanese Standard: Issey Miyake', *Connoisseur*, March, pp. 100–109.

Laurentiev, A. (ed.) (1988), *Varavara Stepanova: A Constructivist Life*, trans. W. Salmond, London: Thames & Hudson.

Laver, J. (1967), 'Fashion, Art and Beauty', *Metropolitan Museum of Art Bulletin*, Vol. 26, No. 3, pp. 130–39.

Laver, J. (1969), *A Concise History of Costume*, New York: Abrams.

Laver, J. (1995), *Costume and Fashion: A Concise History*, London: Thames & Hudson.

Lehnert, G. (1998), *Fashion: A Concise History*, London: Lawrence King.

Lemire, B. (1991), *Fashion's Favourite: The Cotton Trade and the Consumer in Britain 1660–1800*, Oxford: Oxford University Press.

Leong, R. (2003), 'The Zen and the Zany: Contemporary Japanese Fashion', *Visasia*, 23 March, ⟨www.visasia.com.au⟩.

Leymarie, J. (1987), *Chanel*, New York: Skira/Rizzoli.

Lipke, D. (2008), 'Is Green Fashion an Oxymoron? *Women's Wear Daily*, 31 March.

Lipovetsky (1994), *The Empire of Fashion: Dress in Modern Democracy*, trans. Catherine Porter, Princeton: Princeton University Press.

Lloyd, M. (1991), 'From Studio to Stage', *Craft Arts*, Vol. 22, pp. 32–35.

Lodder, C. (1983), *Russian Constructivism*, London: Yale University Press.

Loschek, Ingrid (2009), *When Clothes Become Fashion*, Charlotte: Baker & Taylor.

Lowthorpe, R. (2000), 'Watanabe Opens Paris with Technology Lesson', *The London Independent*, 9 October.

Lynam, R. (ed.) (1972), *Paris Fashion*, London: Michael Joseph.

Lynton, N. (1980), *The Story of Modern Art*, Oxford: Phaidon.

Mackerell, A. (1992), *Coco Chanel*, London: Batsford.

Madsen, A. (1989), *Sonia Delaunay: Artist of the Lost Generation*, New York: McGraw-Hill.

Mah, A. (2006), 'Fakes Still Have Their Niche in China', *International Herald Tribune*, 5 March.

Martin, R. (1998), *Cubism and Fashion*, New York: Metropolitan Museum of Art.

Martin, R. and Koda, H. (1993), *Infra-Apparel*, Metropolitan Museum of Art, New York: Harry Abrams.

Marly, D. de (1980), *The History of Haute Couture 1850–1950*, New York: Holmes & Meier.

Massachusetts Bureau of Statistics (1875), in D. Crane (2000), *Fashion and Its Social Agenda*, p. 75, Chicago: Chicago University Press.

Massenet, N. (2005), 'www.Couture.com', in *The Australian Wish*, December, p. 50.

McDermott, C. (2000), 'A Wearable Fashion', in *Vivienne Westwood; A London Fashion*, London: Philip Wilson.

McDowell, C. (1987), *McDowell's Directory of Twentieth-Century Fashion*, New York: Prentice-Hall.

McDowell, C. (1997), *The Man of Fashion: Peacock Males and Perfect Gentlemen*, London: Thames & Hudson.

McDowell, C. (2000), 'Fantasy and Role Play', in *Fashion Today*, pp. 460–92, London: Phaidon.

McFadden, D. R. (1989), *L'Art de Vivre: Decorative Arts and Design in France 1789–1989*, Smithsonian Institute, New York: Vendome Press.

McMahon, K. and Morley, J. (2011), 'Innovation, Interaction, and Inclusion: Heritage Luxury Brands in Collusion with the Consumer', in *Fashion and Luxury: Between Heritage and Innovation*, Paris: Institut Francais de la Mode.

McRobbie, A. (2000), 'Fashion as a Cultural Industry', in S. Bruzzi and P. Church-Gibson (eds), *Fashion Cultures*, London: Routledge.

Mendes, V. and de la Haye, A. (1999), *20th Century Fashion*, London: Thames & Hudson.

Menkes, S. (2000), 'Fashion with Bells on It: Haute Couture or Caricature?', *International Herald Tribune*, 13 July.

Menkes, S. (2005), 'Hussein Chalayan: Cultural Dialogues, New Feature', *International Herald Tribune*, 19 April.

Menkes, S. (2006), 'What Is Hidden, Secret and Interior Will Become the New Erotica', *International Herald Tribune*, 2 March.

Menkes, S. (2010), 'Celine's Chic Severity', *New York Times*, 7 March.

Metropolitan Museum of Art (1977), *Arts Décoratifs et Industriels Modernes, Paris Exhibition, 1925*, pp. 42–44, New York: Garland.

Miller, M. B. (1981), *The Bon Marché: Bourgeois Culture and The Department Store 1869–1920*, Princeton, NJ: Princeton University Press.

Milbank, C. R. (1985), *Couture: The Great Designers*, New York: Stewart, Tabori & Chang.

Mitchell, L. (1999), 'Issey Miyake', in B. English (ed.), *Tokyo Vogue: Japanese/Australian Fashion*, exhibition catalogue, Brisbane: Griffith University.

Mitchell, L. (ed.) (2005), *The Cutting Edge: Fashion from Japan*, Sydney: Powerhouse Museum.

Miyake, I. (1978), *East Meets West*, Tokyo: Heibon-Sha Ltd.

Moore, B. (2009), 'The Fashion Industry's Old Business Model Is Out of Style', *Los Angeles Times*, 13 September.

Moore, B. (2005), 'Tone in Chic', *Los Angeles Times*, 27 August.

Morgan, A. (2011), 'New Business Degree Makes Sustainability Its Starting Point', *The Guardian*, 14 April, ⟨www.guardian.co.uk/sustainable-business/blog/one-planet-mba-university-exeter.com⟩.

Morris, B. (1978), *The Fashion Makers*, New York: Random House.

Mower, S. (2006), 'Paris Fashion Weekend; Special Report', *The Guardian*, 28 February.

Mulvagh, J. (1992), *Vogue History of 20th Century Fashion*, London: Bloomsbury.

Musée de la Mode et du Costume (1984), *Exposition—Hommage à Elsa Schiaparelli*, Paris: Palais Galleria.

The Nation (2008), 'DHL Partners with eBay to Enhance Shipping Solutions for eBay Sellers', 9 December, ⟨www.nationmultimedia.com/⟩.

Neret, G. (1986), *The Arts of the Twenties*, New York: Rizzoli.

New Policy Institute and Joseph Rowntree Foundation (1993), 'Monotony, Poverty and Social Exclusion', ⟨www.poverty.org.uk⟩.

Newman, A. and Patel, D. (2004), 'The Marketing Directions of Two Fashion Retailers', *European Journal of Marketing*, Vol. 38, No. 7, pp. 770–89.

Niwa, M. (2002), 'The Importance of Clothing Science and Prospects for the Future', *International Journal of Clothing Science and Technology*, Vol. 14, Nos. 3–4, p. 238.

Okonkwo, U. (2010), *Luxury Online*, London: Palgrave Macmillan.

Olds, A. (1992), 'Archives: All Dressed Up in Paper', *ID*, Vol. 39, No. 3, p. 17.

O'Neill, A. (2005), 'Cuttings and Pastings', in C. Breward and C. Evans (eds), *Fashion and Modernity*, Oxford: Berg.

Palmer, A. (2001), *Couture and Commerce: The Transatlantic Fashion Trade in the 1950s*, British Columbia: UBC Press.

Palmer, A., and Clark, H. (eds) (2005), *Old Clothes, New Looks: Second Hand Fashion*, London: Berg.

Palmer White, J. (1986), *Elsa Schiaparelli: Empress of Fashion*, London: Aurum Press.

Palmer White, J. (1988), *Haute Couture Embroidery: The Art of Lesage*, New York: Vendome Press.

Palmer White, J. (1991), 'Paper Clothes: Not Just a Fad', in P. Cunningham and S. Voso Lab (eds), *Dress and Popular Culture*, Ohio: Bowling Green State University Popular Press.

Pankhurst, R. (1999), interview with Richard Pankhurst, son of suffragette Emily Pankurst, in *The Suffragettes: 100 Images of the Twentieth Century*, video, New York: CAPA Productions.

Penn, I. (1988), *Issey Miyake: Photographs by Irving Penn*, ed. N. Calloway, A New York Graphic Society Book, Boston: Little, Brown & Co.

Poiret, P. (1915), 'From the Trenches', *Harper's Bazaar*, Vol. 50, No. 2.

Poiret, P. (1931), '*En Habillant L'Époque*', n.p.

Polhemus, T. (1994), *Street Style: From Sidewalk to Catwalk*, London: Thames & Hudson.

Polhemus, T. (1996), *The Customised Body*, London: Serpent's Tail.

Polhemus, T. and Proctor, L. (1978), *Fashion and Anti-Fashion: Anthropology of Clothing and Adornment*, London: Thames & Hudson.

Power, D. and Hauge, A. (2006), 'No Man's Brand—Brands, Institutions, Fashion and the Economy', research paper, Centre for Research on Innovation and Industrial Dynamics, Uppsala Universitet, Uppsala, Sweden.

Radner, H. (2001), 'Embodying the Single Girl in the 60s', in E. Wilson and J. Entwhistle (eds), *Body Dressing*, pp. 183–97, Oxford: Berg.

Red Luxury (2010a), 'The China Opportunity: Younger and Richer', 16 July, ⟨www.red-luxury.com/2010/07/16/the-china-opportunity-younger-and-richer⟩.

Red Luxury (2010b), 'China's 8 Most Popular Luxury Brands', 10 November, ⟨www.red-luxury.com/2010/11/10/chinas-8-most-popular-luxury-brands/⟩.

Red Luxury (2010c), 'Women in Chinese Cities Love to Shop', 27 Aug, ⟨www.red-luxury.com/2010/08/27/women-in-chinese-cities-love-to-shop/⟩.

Red Luxury (2011), 'Made in China Chic Is Making Chinese Proud', 24 August, ⟨www.red-luxury.com/2011/08/24/made-in-china-chic-is-making-chinese-proud/⟩.

Reinach, S. S. (2005), 'China and Italy: Fast Fashion versus Prêt a Porter. Towards a New Culture of Fashion', *Fashion Theory*, Vol. 9, No. 1, pp. 43–56.

Ribeiro, A. (1988), *Fashion in the French Revolution*, London: Batsford.

Richter, H. (1965), *Dada—Art and Anti-Art*, New York: Abrams.

Rissanen, T. (2005), 'From 15%–0: Investigating the Creation of Fashion without the Creation of Fabric Waste', presented at the conference Creativity: Designer Meets Technology, Europe 27–29 September, Copenhagen, Denmark, KrIDT, and Philadelphia University (US), ⟨www.kridt.dk/conference/speakers/Timo_Rissanen.pdf⟩.

Rovine, V. L. (2005), 'Working the Edge: XULY.Bët's Recycled Clothing', in A. Palmer and H. Clark (eds), *Old Clothes, New Looks: Second Hand Fashion*, London: Berg.

Sabin, R. (ed.) (1999), *Punk Rock: So What? The Cultural Legacy of Punk*, New York: Routledge.

Saiki, M. K. (1992), 'Issey Miyake—Photographs by Irving Penn', *Graphis*, July/August, Vol. 48, No. 280.

Saisselin, R. G. (ed.) (1984), *The Bourgeois and the Bibelot*, New York: Rutgers University Press.

Sarabianov, D. and Adaskina, N. (1990), *Liubov Popova*, New York: Abrams.

Scaturro, S. (2008), 'Eco-tech Fashion: Rationalizing Technology in Sustainable Fashion, *Fashion Theory*, Vol. 12, No. 4, pp. 469–89.

Schiaparelli, E. (1984 [1954]), *Shocking Life*, London: J. M. Dent & Sons Ltd.

Schwartz, B. (2009), 'Style-Fashion in Dark Times', *The Atlantic*, June.

Scottish Arts Council (1975), 'Fashion 1900–1939', exhibition catalogue, Edinburgh: Scottish Arts Council.

Seebohn, C. (1982), *The Man Who Was Vogue: The Life and Times of Condé Nast*, New York: Viking.

Shonfield, S. (1982), 'The Great Mr Worth', *Journal of the Costume Society*, No. 16, pp. 57–58.

Simms, J. (2008), "E-male Order: Buying Clothes on the Net Is No Longer Just for Girls', *The Independent*, 28 April.

Simon, J. (1999), 'Miyake Modern', New York: Little, Brown & Co.

Somervillo, K. (2011), 'Rebels & Rulebreakers', in *Manstyle*, Melbourne: NGV.

Sozanni, F. (2011), 'What About Chinese Fashion Designers? And Fashion in China?' ⟨www.vogue.it/en/magazine/editor-s-blog/2011/04/april-1st⟩.

Standen, D. (2011), 'John Varvatos style.com, *Runway Review*, 18 June.

Staniszewski, M-A. (1998), *The Power of Display*, Cambridge, MA: MIT Press.

Steele, V. (1988), *Paris Fashion*, Oxford: Oxford University Press.

Steele, V. (1991), *Women of Fashion: Twentieth-Century Designers*, New York: Rizzoli.

Steele, V. (1998), *Paris Fashion: A Cultural History*, Oxford: Berg.

Steele, V. (2000), *Fifty Years of Fashion: New Look to Now*, New Haven, CT: Yale University Press.

Steele, V. (2011), 'Fashion and Art', lecture, November, Queensland University of Technology, Brisbane, Australia.

Stern, R. (2004), *Against Fashion: Clothing as Art 1850–1930*, Cambridge, MA: MIT Press.

Storey, H. and Ryan, T. (2011), 'Catalytic Clothing', Dezeen Blog Archive, 15 June, ⟨www.dezeen.com/2011/06/15/catalytic-clothing-by-helen-storey-and-tony-ryan/⟩

The Story of Fashion: The Age of Dissent (1985), video, London: RM Arts Production.

Taylor, L. (1999), 'Wool Cloth and Gender: The Use of Woollen Cloth in Britain 1865–1885', in E. Wilson and A. de la Haye (eds), *Defining Dress: Dress as Object, Meaning and Identity*, Manchester: Manchester University Press.

Taylor, L. (2002), *The Study of Dress History*, Manchester: Manchester University Press.

Thomas, D. (2005), 'If You Buy One of These Fake Bags . . . ', *Harper's Bazaar*, April, pp. 75–76.

Thomas, S. (2008), 'From "Green Blur" to Ecofashion: Fashioning an Eco-lexicon', *Fashion Theory*, Vol. 12, No. 4, pp. 525–40.

Tomlinson, A. (ed.) (1990), *Consumption, Identity and Style*, London: Routledge.

Townsend, C. (2002), *Rapture: Arts Seduction by Fashion*, London: Thames & Hudson.

Trebay, G. (2001), 'Boys Don't Cry: Fashion Falls for a Tough Look', *New York Times*, 3 April.

Trebay, G. (2004), 'Fashion Diary: Making a Surreal Trip onto a Nightclub Runway', *New York Times*, 4 March.

Trebay, G. (2006), 'Woman Masked, Bagged and, Naturally, Feared', *New York Times*, 1 March.

Troy, N. (2003), *Couture Culture*, Cambridge, MA: MIT Press.

Tsui, C. (2009), *China Fashion: Conversations with Designers*, London: Berg.

Tyabji, L. (2010), 'Fashion in Post-Independence India', in J. B. Eicher (ed.), *Berg Encyclopedia of World Dress and Fashion*, Vol. 4, London: Berg.

Undressed: Fashion in the Twentieth Century (2001), video, Little Bird/Tatlin Production, London: Beckmann Visual Publications.

Varnedoe, K. and Goprik, A. (1990), *High and Low, Modern Art and Popular Culture*, Museum of Modern Art, New York, New York: Harry Abrams Press.

Veblen, T. (1965 [1899]), *The Theory of the Leisure Class (The Writings of Thornstein Veblen)*, New York: Macmillan.

Von Hahn, K. (2006), 'Noticed Sad Chic', *Globe & Mail*, Toronto, 18 March.

Walsh, M. (1979), 'The Democratization of Fashion', *Journal of American History*, Vol. 66, No. 2, pp. 299–313.

Watson, L. (2003), *Twentieth-Century Fashion*, London: Carlton Books.

Whitely, N. (1989), 'Interior Design in the 1960s: Arena for Performance', *Art History*, Vol. 10, No. 1, pp. 79–90.

Wikipedia (n.d.), 'Fashion Weeks', ⟨en.wikipedia.org/wiki/Fashion_week⟩.

Wilcox, C. and Mendes, V. (eds) (1998), *Modern Fashion in Detail*, London: Victoria and Albert Museum.

Wilson, E. (1985), *Adorned in Dreams*, London: Virago.

Wilson, E. and de la Haye, A. (1999), *Defining Dress: Dress as Object, Meaning and Identity*, Manchester: Manchester University Press.

Winge, T. M. (2008), 'Green Is the New Black: Celebrity Chic and the "Green" Commodity Fetish', *Fashion Theory*, Vol. 12, No. 4, pp. 511–24.

Worth, F. C. (1895), *Some Memories of Paris*, trans. F. Adolphus, New York: Henry Holt.

Wu, J. (2009a). *Chinese Fashion: From Mao to Now*, Oxford: Berg.

Wu, J. (2009b), 'Internationalizing and Industrializing Fashion: Shanghai International Fashion Culture Festival (SIFCF) Review', *Fashion Practice: The Journal of Design, Creative Process & the Fashion Industry*, Vol. 1, No. 2, pp. 259–66.

Wynhausen, E. (2008), 'Following the Thread', *The Weekend Australian*, 6–7 September.

Yamamoto, Y. (2002), *Talking to Myself*, Milan: Carla Sozzani.

Yan, H. (2011), 'Lower Tariffs Might Boost Luxury Buys', *China Daily Business News*, 16 June ⟨www.chinadaily.com.cn/bizchina/2011-06/16/content_12714105.htm⟩.

Yee, B. and Qin, J. (2006), 'China's Designers Become Fashion Force', *Wall Street Journal*, China, 29 September.

Yves Saint Laurent Retrospective (1987), exhibition catalogue, Sydney: Art Gallery of New South Wales.

Zola, E. (1989 [1883]), 'Au Bonheur des Dames' in S. Bayley (ed.), *Commerce and Culture*, pp. 53–56, London: Fourth Estate.

Index